THESE RUSSIANS

THESE RUSSIANS

BY
WILLIAM C. WHITE

CHARLES SCRIBNER'S SONS
NEW YORK · LONDON
1931

TO THE MEMORY OF
FREDERIC COURTLAND PENFIELD
WHO MADE IT POSSIBLE FOR ME
TO MEET THESE RUSSIANS

PREFACE

THE Soviet Union has been variously described as "The Workers' and Peasants' Government," "The Great Experiment," "The Great Menace," "The Land of Paradoxes." These descriptions have one common characteristic: they treat the hundred and sixty million people of Soviet Russia as an entity, never considering them as individuals. The guiding philosophy of the Soviet State, with its emphasis on Class, likewise ignores the individual.

A revolution has whirled across the lives of the hundred and sixty million; and it affected them as individuals. To some it has brought tragedy, darkness, to others it has meant the dawn of a fairer day; —but on no two individuals have its effects been the same.

The complete story of the effects of the revolution on the Russian people will be written, but not in our time; when it is written it will not emphasize data on credits, factory production, or raw materials. The truth about changes in human lives, beliefs, and aspirations does not lie at the bottom of a sea of statistics.

Here, without statistics or any attempts to generalize about classes or groups, are accounts of the effects of the revolution that is to abolish Individualism on a few of the hundred and sixty million individuals, as they told them to me.

WILLIAM C. WHITE.

CONTENTS

IN MOSCOW

IN THE PROVINCES

The author wishes to thank *The Forum, Asia,* and *The Philadelphia Forum Magazine* for permission to reprint those chapters which first appeared in their pages.

IN MOSCOW

I

MARFOUSHA: THE HOUSEWIFE

LIKE every American who would settle in Moscow for any length of time, I learned how difficult it is to find living quarters. I finally shared one small room in the city's largest apartment building with a young bank clerk. "You'll have to eat in restaurants," he said, "but Marfousha, from next door, will do the cleaning. She's just an old village woman."

She came the following morning—a woman looking, as they say, "thirty with a little tail on," meaning forty. Every day, I found, she wore the same costume, a flannel waist, a drab skirt, sideworn slippers. After the revolution made Moscow the Centre, she and her husband had come to the city from a village a hundred miles away. Here things were doing, here there was none of the unchanging sameness of the provincial town; here there was no need "to sit by the sea and wait for weather." Besides, food rations were higher in Moscow than elsewhere and jobs more plentiful.

They found a room in a damp basement. When her father died, her mother sold the house, the horse, the cow, and came to town to join them, bringing a smaller daughter and her most cherished possession, an old American sewing machine. With the money the whole family exchanged their basement for a room in this apartment, which before the revolution had been one of the finest in the city, built for rich and satisfied mer-

1

chants and wealthy professional men. Then in its hundred flats, each with seven or eight rooms, were housed wives and daughters gowned from Paris. Each apartment had its own kitchen with a stove large enough to prepare a ten course dinner for twenty guests; each apartment must have cost five or six thousand rubles a year. On the six floors there lived probably five hundred people, including servants.

Now its courtyards are dirty, some of the plaster bas-reliefs on the walls have fallen, there are a few bullet scars up near the eaves, the roof is a mass of tangled aerials, and over one door, inside the court, is a sign, "House Committee." At one corner of the dirty yellow brick pile is another sign, "Communal Restaurant on the second floor." And on each of the elevators is a placard, fly-specked and dirty, "Elevator not running." In the elevator itself are stored bed frames, mattresses, baby carriages.

"Do you live like this in America?" Marfousha asked, describing the neighbors in detail. "In this apartment there are six families besides your roommate. In my room are six people, counting the two children. The Bogolubovs—husband, wife, and mother —have the best room and new furniture. He earns a lot of money. Next to you are the Krassovs. He had a wife, but he chased her out four months ago. He's a former 'White' officer—the scamp! Then the Blitzmans—he's a Jew. There's always a Jew in every apartment. And their dirty children! But he's rich. His wife always fights in the kitchen—says we take her kerosene or her soap or her hot water. Next to them are Adamov and his wife—he's a railroad conductor, often away for a long time. And what his wife does when he's away is a shame! He belongs to the Party and works hard. Then beyond the kitchen are the Laptevs—factory workers. They have four children and the worst room—it stinks."

"That's about twenty-five people in this seven-room apartment?" I asked.

"Yes, and then there are servants. Three of these families each have one—my sister helps me. You must have a servant if you have a family—to look out for the children, to stand in line at the stores. They are pretty lucky—get fifteen rubles a month and their trade union says they must have a month's holiday each year with pay. And they take it—try and stop them and they drag you off to court. They sleep out in the corridor here. Of course, it's against the orders of the house committee, but my husband is the representative in this apartment and he only says, 'They must sleep somewhere—better there than with their masters.'"

All this because the impoverished government could not build fast enough to offset the rush to the Centre. A city with less than a million people grew to two millions when it became the political and economic capital of the land. Some buildings had been destroyed in 1917 and, in addition, many Moscow homes had to become government offices, embassies, shelters for state institutions. One fine set of apartments became the Foreign Office; one splendid home, a Secret Police prison. Suburbs, with poor communication and few conveniences, are not popular except in summer, so the two million must live in the Centre itself, while the Government tries to divert to other cities this "on to Moscow" movement.

"Is your husband a Party member?"

"No, he's too lazy. He works in an office and earns only a hundred rubles a month. He's a good husband, but he drinks too much. He came home, beat me once, and I divorced him. My mother said it was foolish, that husbands always beat their wives. 'Beat a coat to make it softer, beat a wife to make her dearer,' she says. He had nowhere else to go, so he came back. I was glad he did. I've been married six years. . . ."

She finished cleaning and left with a warning, "Keep your room locked. With all these strangers around. . . ."

So lives most of Moscow—a family to a room; two thousand people finding shelter in a house which formerly held five hundred; each of the seven hundred rooms of this warren harboring one family. Occasionally there is an apartment whose former owner has a room to himself. There are those fortunate persons who have two rooms or more, but they are not twenty per cent of the population. "What is your conception of an ideal home?" was a theme an English teacher assigned to a class in Moscow. One answer said: "A room through which strangers do not have to pass to get to their room."

One room houses husband, wife, children, and any

relatives who have nowhere else to go. In one room are the sick and perhaps some member of the family who may be mildly insane, for even the asylums are overcrowded. Side by side, within the same four walls, live professors, policemen, clerks, conductors, actors, accountants. They may be, and usually are, strangers to one another, but their lives are intimately bound together. At four in the afternoon seven housewives or their servants crowd in each kitchen, preparing seven kinds of soup with seven conflicting odors, while fourteen small children—or so it seems—clutter up the free space. On the stove, itself unheated, seven little "primus" kerosene stoves roar in flaming discord. Seven families in one apartment—seven families who should fight over their turn at the bath.

These people are neighbors, but they are not particularly friendly with each other. When they want friends they find them in other parts of town. There are other peculiarities of life in a Moscow apartment. Each room has two sets of windows—inner and outer: with October comes the ceremony of puttying up the outer frame, leaving a little pane that can be (but seldom is) opened for ventilation. The appearance of putty is the first sign of the coming winter. Heating in an apartment with central heat is regulated by law. No matter how cold it may be, the heat does not begin until October 15th, and goes off promptly April 15th. There are many such little things— the milk delivery, for example, delivered in suspiciously gray cans by peasant women from nearby villages. One look at the woman and you boil the milk not once but twice. Moscow water, however, does not need boiling. Then there is one surrender to old custom. The rooms have hardwood floors; so every month a merry soul comes with a pail of beeswax to polish the floor. His method is simple. The floor is soaked with the mixture and dries. Then, barefooted, he skates over the floor on brushes and the polish shines. Finally there is the corridor, cluttered up with trunks, baskets, mattresses, bags—and the endless noise, all day, of doors shutting, children romping, and women in the kitchen, often quarreling.

"Did you hear all that scandal last night?" Marfousha asked one morning. "It was that Jewess, Blitzman. Her relatives have come from Gomel and she borrowed some mattresses somewhere. The way the Jews come to Moscow! They say one went to the Communist leader, Kalenin, one day with a big key. 'I want to give you this,' he explained. 'I'm from Berditchev. I'm the last one to come to Moscow, so I locked up the place.' Well, at night Blitzman's relatives sleep on the mattresses on the floor and in the daytime she puts the mattresses out in the corridor. One fell down and nearly killed little Masha Lapteva. So we made Blitzman put them in her room. If only she'd move away! But there is always trouble around here. Adamov comes home late and likes a cup of tea about eleven. His wife puts a kettle on the primus. Three nights last week she came back after twenty minutes and found the water was still cold. So she watched and saw one of the Blitzman brats come, quietly fill *their* teapot with *her* hot water, and put the kettle back on the

stove refilled. A big scandal. . . . And there is always
trouble about cleaning the corridor and the bathroom.
Each family is supposed to take turns. Those families
without maids say, 'Let the maids take turns and we
will pay.' The maids fight about it—they had a hairpulling a month ago. . . .

"And the telephone—everybody wanted it put in
and each was to pay his share. Now three of them
refuse. They say, 'We don't use it.' Their friends call
them up and *still* they won't pay. 'It isn't our fault if
our friends call on this phone,' they claim. The house
committee has been planning to settle this at its
meeting this month—it always plans things but never
does them. . . . And fights about the electric bill.
One meter for the whole apartment, and each room
had the same number of lights. That didn't work.
The Bogolubovs have money and they bought an
electric hot water heater and an iron. Clever, they
were. We didn't know it for a long time and won-
dered why the bills were so high. Then their old
woman forgot to turn the iron off and there was a fire.
Now anybody who wants to use such things must put
a separate meter in—that costs thirty rubles. But I
think somebody in this apartment still has a water
heater—the Blitzmans perhaps. There's a fine if
they're caught.

"Then bugs . . . in an old house like this. We had
them cleaned out but they come back again. From the
Laptevs, most likely—they live so dirtily and we can't
make them clean up. You'll have to get some powder.
Of course, in the village it is much worse, but here

we are used to them. We used to believe that to rid a
house of roaches you had to put as many roaches in a
bast sandal as there were members in your family and
drag it across the threshold and over the road to the
other side. Here we use powder or kerosene!"

Moscow usually buys its food at the corner stores,
now operated by the government, which never have
sufficient supplies. Before 1929 there was no rationing system; the result was summed up in the remark,
"Prior to the revolution the plural of the word 'man'
was 'men.' Now, after the revolution, the plural is
'queue.' " With poor distribution, stores received limited
amounts—and lines formed. Now, with ration cards,
lines though continuing have been somewhat shortened,
but rations seem severe—three quarters of a pound of
bread per person per day, one quarter of a pound of
meat per person several times a week, a pound and a
half of sugar a month per person, twenty-five grams of
tea per month—and so on down a discouragingly long
list of products. The factory-working class receives
double these rations. Vegetables are bought from
street stands or in stores and are not on ration cards.
On a recent anniversary of the revolution, November 7th, the government sold every citizen two
pounds of *white* flour—a most special dispensation,
for, to this time, flour was very scarce and white bread
grew murkier and murkier. Within the limits of the
rations the prices are low. A few private stores exist
where one can buy to any amount, but their prices
are high and the average Muscovite cannot pay them.

In such stores government taxes and private profit make butter three dollars a pound; in government stores the month's ration, about three quarters of a pound, costs a ruble, fifty cents.

"Can you lend me three rubles?" Marfousha asked one morning. Her wages were five rubles a month. "To-day is only the 14th, you know." I didn't know the significance. "Oh, everybody in Moscow is paid on the 16th and 30th, so the days just preceding are hard. On those nights everybody eats well. Where do you eat now?"

"In restaurants—anywhere I happen to be."

"Eating is the worst part about living here. The kitchen is so crowded—and cooking on that primus . . . in the village that was better. There we had a big brick stove with lots of room. In winter we slept on top of it."

"But what about these communal apartment kitchens?"

"We have one here, but no one goes—the food is poor and it costs too much. But it would be a good idea—and a communal laundry too. Things would be easier."

"What do you cook here?"

"The same as in the village. Breakfast of tea and black bread. You don't have our black bread in America? I couldn't live without it. We did have jam, too, but now it is hard to get sugar. Then, about four o'clock, when work is over, we have soup, cabbages, potatoes, carrots. And tea in the evening."

"And meat?"

"We have it sometimes, but it is expensive and there is little of it at the stores—we use it in the soup. So much is scarce now—macaroni, buckwheat. We do not have much money—clothes are so expensive and my husband only earns a hundred rubles. The scoundrel, he'd drink it all if I didn't watch him. He had two rubles yesterday to buy some socks with, but he drank it up. . . .

"The worst thing is standing in line. I don't know why, but there never seems to be enough food to go round, even with ration cards. Yesterday I stood two hours for sugar and when it was my turn the clerk said, 'Sold out.' In summer it's not so bad—there are all the neighbors . . . and the gossip and what they say about the government. . . . But now it's so cold to stand on a corner for an hour or two. Sometimes I and my sister and my husband are standing at three different stores at the same time. And the same thing for manufactured goods—always queues!"

To prove the paradox, Marfousha's little daughter came in one evening to invite me to a party. It was in honor of her mother's name day. A dozen guests, none of them from the apartment, were gathered in her room. The room was large but seemed crowded with gaudy second-hand furniture. There was a narrow iron bed on one side and a cot on the other. "One of the most remarkable results of the revolution," a friend said to me, "is to make two people sleep in a bed that scarcely held one in Tsarist days." In one corner, curtained off, were two bunks for the children; in an opposite corner a mattress stood ready. In the centre was a large table, covered with food. On a cheaply ornate sideboard was an old, American, portable sewing machine, pre-revolution, and, on the window sill, a crystal radio set. There were a great many hooks, hung with clothes, and under each bed were boxes and bags. In one corner hung an ikon with a little red oil lamp burning before it. On the wall were cheap lithographs of Lenin and Kalenin, the President of the U. S. S. R.

From somewhere, on a hundred ruble salary, a ham, a goose, cold sturgeon with carrots, red caviar, bologna, and seemingly endless vodka had appeared. Marfousha's husband, Andrei, was already well ahead on the vodka.

When most of the food was eaten and the vodka running low some one brought out a guitar. One village song followed another until the neighbors next door began pounding on the wall. "Those Bogolubovs!" said Marfousha. "Can't they let us have a party? When they had their party last month did I pound on the wall?" The pounding eventually stopped, discouraged, for the singing continued louder, if anything, and even more out of tune. One of the men stood up for a moment and sat down with a bang—the chair collapsed under him.

"Thank God it's our chair!" said Marfousha. "I had to borrow some from the neighbors."

I asked my roommate next morning how they did it on their salary.

"They're 'dark people,' illiterate—Andrei can scarcely read and write, but they always manage to have a couple of parties a year, on name days and

Easter. God knows how. The ham and the goose came from the village, and they save up to buy the rest. Now they will eat potatoes and cabbage for six months and look forward to the next feast."

For one thing, rents are low. The house is managed by a committee made up of one member from each apartment. In addition there are two or three salaried members who devote all their time to finances, to arranging for repairs, to registering passports and personal papers. They set the rents, which depend on the amount of space occupied, the number in the family, and the salary and profession of the tenant. There is nothing to bar you from all the space you want if you can pay the increased rent—and if you can find the space. A factory worker with a large family will have a big room for a few rubles a month; a doctor will pay more; and a private merchant, if he is allowed to have a room at all, will pay even ten times as much as the factory hand. If the tenant is unemployed and in good standing, the rent is almost nothing. The committee collects the money and apportions it for repairs; for major repairs they can borrow money from the government.

Andrei came in one evening to collect the rent. He is a messenger boy in a government office, a most important job in a city where it often takes three days to deliver local mail. In addition he is the member of the house committee from the apartment.

"This committee work keeps me busy, as if six hours each day in my office wasn't enough. Each week there is something. Meetings, meetings, nothing but meetings everywhere—in offices, in clubs. Give us one grand meeting to end all meetings! And the house committee must campaign for government bonds, for the Red Cross; it conducts a day nursery for children while their mothers go to work, and a school to 'liquidate illiteracy' in the evenings. The devil take it, we are always in trouble! They blame the committee members for everything, just as if we were paid for our services. On the tenth anniversary of the revolution, we decided to have a cinema for the small children in the morning. How were we to know that the two pictures Sovkino promised us for the event would be 'The Evils of Prostitution' and 'Abortion'? The parents went out of their minds. And then, in winter, when the janitors get drunk and the fire goes out. . . . Thank God, it hasn't happened for a long while."

"What happens when it does?"

"Oh, we have complaints and hold a special meeting of the committee." He changed the subject abruptly, "Is it true you have prohibition in America? Life must be awfully lonesome there without vodka."

"We have homebrew."

"That's good—here we have it, too. It's much better than vodka—vodka is only forty per cent. They talk about prohibition here—more meetings. Last year they had a big anti-alcohol festival. They buried a bottle of vodka in the cemetery. The same night a lot of people went out to dig it up—a bottle of vodka free! No, when they tried prohibition here the peasants made homebrew and the government didn't get any money out of it. Now they get a big tax. The best way to end with vodka is for us to drink it all up."

One morning Marfousha's fifteen year old sister, Tamara, came to tidy up. "Marfousha isn't well," she said. Marfousha came the next morning, looking a few years older.

"You men have the best of everything," she said after a minute. "How old do I look—thirty-five?"

My embarrassed silence was a positive answer.

"I am twenty-six, but I have had nine abortions." She spoke as if discussing dentist dates. "Andrei won't do anything about it. He spends his money for vodka and besides . . . it's wrong, or so he says. I don't know. I do know that the doctor said two days ago that I must never have another one. But I can't have any more children, on a hundred rubles a month. I've had four—two have died. Abortions are free. You go to the hospital and they do them without asking any questions, but they give you nothing to stop the pain. Often the clinic is crowded. I went down at two in the morning and had to stand in line until nine. There are private clinics that charge thirty rubles and it's not painful there, I've heard."

The Government has instituted free abortions, for ignorance, superstition and religion act as barriers to the spread of birth control information.

"You can get medical attention free, can't you?" I asked.

"Yes, if you belong to the trade union. And everybody does, except the 'former people.' But the free clinics are awfully crowded. My little Tania has worms and I took her to a clinic last week. They gave me an appointment three weeks from now. The clinics where you pay are much better. The hospitals are crowded, too. But it is much better than in the village. We had no hospital in our village before the revolution; everybody used *znakarki* (old women 'hex doctors'.) In the village the husband always wants many children—the more he has the more shares of land he gets."

"But it must be hard for children in an apartment like this."

"Yes, but they go to the nursery every day and play, or your servant takes them out to play in the Square."

"What about marriage and divorce, Marfousha?"

"Marriage is just as it always was. You must be married in church. . . ."

"The law doesn't say so. It says civil marriage is what counts—church marriage is optional."

"I don't know, but I don't believe marriage is good unless you do go to church. The government is trying to close churches, but that isn't right. You must have churches for marriage, for baptisms, for funerals. I always go to church on Easter and on some holidays, too. We have an ikon in our room and I always wear a cross. So does Andrei, although he says religion is bourgeois—opium for the people. He read that somewhere—I don't know what he means. In the village we went every Sunday, but here in Moscow . . ."

"And what about divorce?"

"I don't know. Without children it's all right, although some of the young people divorce too often. I know one girl, nineteen, who has had nine husbands in the last two years. The law is good—it makes a man pay when he gets a girl in trouble. I don't know about Tamara—I worry about her. She goes out every night —down to Alexandrovsky Gardens where the soldiers are walking. Before the revolution if a girl got in trouble it was only shame for the whole family. Now, if she has a baby, she can get alimony taken right out of the soldier's pay—she need only prove the father and tell the Commandant. We have another good law too. If a man throws his wife out in the village, she can have half the property they have acquired while they were married. Before the revolution a single peasant often took a woman in the spring and kicked her out with nothing in autumn, after she had worked hard in his fields all summer. But one thing I don't like— a lot of old men have thrown out their wives and taken new ones. That's not right. What can a woman fifty years old do if she has no children to go to? Everything is too easy for men."

To ease the rooming congestion the government encourages the formation of cooperative building and loan societies; a number of employees in one institution get together and pay so much a month. At the end of several years the government advances the money and a new apartment house is built, each apartment having three rooms and all conveniences. The members continue to pay until the debt is repaid— usually about eighty rubles each per month. I lived later in one such house. All the employees of one theatre—leading lady, orchestra, cast, chorus, and stage hands—dwelt in adjoining apartments, one family to an apartment. But such houses are few, and not all families can afford the monthly payment.

"The Blitzmans are moving," said Marfousha enviously one morning. "I am glad. But they are going to their own apartment. That's all Blitzman has been talking about in the kitchen for the last six months. Imagine it, a three-room apartment—three rooms! Gas in the kitchen and in the bath. They'll use their bath —here no one ever does. We use ours here for laundry, and bathe at the public baths. The Blitzmans belong to a cooperative at the Foreign Office, where he works—it's hard to join them and they cost a lot. But these Jews have everything. The Blitzmans have relatives abroad and they receive money. . . ."

For those housewives who do not work—although many Moscow wives do—the affairs of a few strangers, neighbors by chance, are the important things in life, just as in the village, where every one knows everything about every one else. Births and deaths are matters of course. The Moscow housewife usually goes to a free "Birth Home," operated by the government, when her time comes; if she herself works, she gets two months' vacation before and after, with pay. There are government burying establishments also, but the private shops get most of the trade. Little is needed for funerals. If it is a baby, the husband buys a casket at the store, and he and the wife drive in a cab to the cemetery, the little white box bouncing on their knees. If an adult, the few relatives and friends follow the

hearse on foot to the cemetery. If the deceased is a
Party member, the casket and decorations are red; if
non-Party, white—and for swank a priest goes ahead
of the procession with an ikon. But this is rare now.
The Government is trying a campaign to popularize its
new crematorium, but few non-Party people use it.
The revolution comes with its propaganda, with its
new ways, in death as well as in life. Cemeteries are
bourgeois—"they help strengthen the traditional hold
of the priest on the people."

I was going abroad for a change. The apartment
knew of it. "I have a big request," said Marfousha,
timidly. "Can you bring me some stockings for the
children and some material for their dresses? Here
those things are so scarce—everything on rations and
of such poor quality. . . . And one other thing. Can
you bring me a pair of silk sockings?"—speaking very
quickly—"everybody wears them abroad, don't they?"
I agreed—and I asked a question. We foreigners
look on the Soviet Union from the vantage point of
another background; with our passports we can leave
at will and Soviet Russia is only a temporary dwelling
place. There are so many things to confuse our judg-
ments about the results of the revolution on the people. "Marfousha," I asked, "I have never heard you
use the word 'revolution' once or talk about it. With
all these things you want and can't have, with the
food shortage, what do you think—is it better now or
worse?"
She looked at me in surprise. "Why, of course it's

better. Look at us—Andrei is a worker, not a peasant. That's better. And we have a room in Moscow. . . ."

"But with the food shortage and overcrowding. . . ."

"It's hard, yes, but it's better to be in the city than in the village."

"Yet I don't understand why the city is better after the revolution than the village before."

"I can't explain. If you were a Russian. . . . Well, Moscow is the Centre. Life is more interesting." A long pause. "And you won't forget the silk stockings?"

II

VLADIMIR ALEXEITCH: THE PROFESSOR

"HE is in charge of a large laboratory and teaches physics at the University," said a friend in Paris. "He likes foreigners and he helped me very much when I was there."

"Anti-Soviet?"

"I don't think so. His work absorbs him and he doesn't care much for politics. He was wealthy before the revolution and a socialist. But when I saw him last, in 1925, he said nothing that would label him. But his wife. . . . By the way, will you carry some coffee to him? That will be better than a letter of introduction. He writes that he can't get it there."

I went to his apartment on my first afternoon in Moscow. It was July, 1927. A woman across the hall told me that the professor and his family were at their *datcha*—their summer cottage—ten miles from the city.

Eventually I found it, standing amid pine woods, near the Moskva River. A group of women sat on the porch, around a steaming samovar. One of them greeted me, in English.

"We expected you. You have the coffee? Thank you. Will you please go now? Vladimir Alexeitch has been 'sitting' (in jail) for two months and only came out yesterday. He will notify you when he can see you."

Two months later he wrote inviting me to his lectures. "I should have come to your house before, but it was not wise," he said. "My family is opposed to my seeing you. The government is very suspicious about our contacts with foreigners; when the Communists broke with England, I 'sat' two months a little while ago, just because I knew an Englishman connected with their legation." He invited me to come Sunday to tea.

His apartment had four rooms, each one crowded with furniture; even in the dining room there was a bed. His study was lined with books. There were more books and boxes, trunks and mattresses in the dark narrow corridor. He apologized. "In America your professors do not live like this? I have been very lucky to keep half of my former apartment. Chiefly because of my books—the Government Library wants them, but has no place as yet to put them. Of course, we are a bit crowded. We have most of the furniture for an eight-room apartment in these four rooms. My wife is here; also her sister and a cousin of mine and his wife. And friends sometimes stay with us when they have nowhere else to go."

Tea was very formal, even a trifle stilted, as if the relatives considered this new foreigner only a potential source of danger for Vladimir Alexeitch. It was I who was questioned. They asked a great deal about America—how high was the "Voolvort" Building, how many cars did Ford make a day? (His autobiography was then selling by thousands in Russia.) How much do things cost in America—rooms, silk stockings, Coty's Rachel powder, and finally, "How do you like Russia by this time?"

"I think it is very interesting," I answered carelessly. A painful halt in conversation followed my answer.

As I was leaving, Vladimir Alexeitch took me into his study. "Everything here is very confused. I should like to see you frequently—I must have contacts abroad. But you should be very careful. No—not for yourself; the government is too eager to keep a good reputation in America and it will harm none of you. But you must be careful whom you see, for *their* sake. Communists, workers, and peasants you can see as much as you like. Among the intelligentsia, however, there is great fear of the consequences of contact with all foreigners, even those like the Englishman who came here shortly after the revolution. He works around town and says he is in full sympathy with the proletariat. He seems to believe that by smoking cheap tobacco, by refusing to wash or to clean his nails, he can more closely approximate the class he loves. It is too bad, but it is so. We are not against the proletariat, but because we are not of it the Communists regard us always as potential enemies. So, seeing foreigners too often gets some of us in jail, especially if the foreigner becomes *persona non grata* later." He smiled bitterly. "The Government is suspicious of all close contacts except those for business —and the GPU, the secret police, is everywhere. Yet I must keep in touch with more than merely the scientific developments in the world outside. Have you any magazines or new books you can bring me?"

The revolution came early to the universities; some of the professors went abroad. Those who remained were divided into two classes: the group whose subjects could have no possible political bearing and that group whose subjects—history, politics, economics—had to be taught on the basis of the new philosophy of class. The first group continued to teach; the most famous of the second group were pensioned, the others dismissed, and a new set, the "Red professors," arose. These were chiefly younger men, members of the Party or in sympathy with its philosophy.

At the same time "class consciousness" was applied in admitting students. Entrance examinations were continued, but equally important was the examination into the student's social origin—was he the son of proletarian or peasant parents, or from the bourgeoisie? For the latter there were and are no places in the higher schools. Some creep in through various subterfuges, but there is an annual "cleanout" to detect those with bourgeois background parading under the proletarian banner. Further, Communist Party committees (or, more usually in the universities, Young Communist League committees) were given as large a part in the management of the University as the faculty.

"Every year," said Vladimir Alexeitch, "our work becomes more difficult." He had been asking me about my impressions of the First Moscow University.

"Every year the Communist Party reaches out for greater control; there was a time when the professors who help determine entrance could make mental attainment the basis for admittance to the University; now a Communist Party committee meets with the professors and has more power in granting or refusing entrance than we have; of course, a good Communist—'his father from the plow, his mother from the loom'—even if dumb as a cork, is to be preferred to the bright son of bourgeois stock. Class . . . class . . . the bourgeoisie all are evil, the proletariat are the Children about to be shown the Light. Have you seen *Faust* here? They even get their class philosophy into that. In the third act, Faust sings an aria about the power of evil in this world. The libretto at the Moscow Opera reads, 'Now Faust sings—of the power of Capitalism in this world.' "

He questioned me about the professors I had met. Most of them, teaching politics and law, were, of course, Red professors.

"Loudspeakers for the Communists, that's their profession. They have no claim to scholarship—their idea is to cull anthologies from Lenin and Marx, to rewrite each others' books and theories, to issue needless potboilers. It all pays pretty well—books like 'The Peasant on the Way to Socialism,' 'Results of the Fourteenth Party Congress,' 'Lenin on Disarmament,' 'Lenin on Community Kitchens,' Lenin on practically everything. They say some medical student wanted to offer a thesis—'Lenin on Appendicitis.'

"The title 'professor' used to mean here what it still

means in Germany; it does yet, to some extent, in science and medicine. But in other fields—! Those of us who aren't 'Red' are watched closely for any 'counter-revolutionary' manifestations. They haven't troubled me much; I have my teaching and the government is helping me build a laboratory With its limited means the government does its best for science. Besides, it is difficult to be counter-revolutionary in physics. Yet one colleague got in trouble not long ago when he said that history shows that everything is transient, and that it is impossible to say that one form of social structure or one set of institutions is any better than any other. 'What of the dictatorship of the proletariat?' a student asked. 'Pff,' was the answer that got him in hot water. Even in art you can offend the powers that be. A year ago, a professor was invited to contribute to a memorial volume in honor of one of our great artists, planned and published by some Russian emigrés in Berlin. He sent an article. When it appeared, with articles by the emigrés too, the Soviet papers nearly demanded his trial for this 'contact with the enemy.' He almost lost his position and had to promise never to do it again."

"But do such instances occur frequently?" I asked.

"No, not frequently—but they always can occur. We must always be careful. Your professors in America live differently, don't they? Yet some of my colleagues have done great research—all the greater if you consider the atmosphere we work in. And we work loyally—those of us whom they allow to work. After all, we believe Communism is a passing phase. Russia will find herself. They need us here—we are few. We have our work. Thankful for having that, we ask no more. Oh, yes—we must work; it is the one firm rock left for us. I sometimes put in fifteen hours a day at the new laboratory which the government is building for us. It would be easier if we had more money, but we are very poor. I receive two hundred and twenty-five rubles a month. By writing I can earn three hundred more."

"Yes, and what happens to a lot of it?" asked Natalya Ivanovna, his wife, as she brought in the tea. "You must contribute to state funds for homeless children, for class war prisoners. And bonds. . . ."

"Your American universities don't make their professors buy state bonds each year, do they? Here the state issues a new loan. Every institution has a drive, conducted by the Communists in that institution. Names are posted of those who have not subscribed, so you subscribe 'voluntarily.' The goal is to have every one subscribe one month's income."

"But can't you sell the bonds back?"

"Oh, yes, but a new loan is being announced now in which we can't. Selling bonds at will is called a 'bourgeois custom.'

"The biggest difficulty is to get *valuta* (foreign currency). The bank used to let me exchange fifty rubles each month for dollars and send them to my sister in Geneva. A lot of us have to support relatives abroad. Now they are short of foreign money and refuse to exchange any whatever, except ten rubles a month for books and magazines. Of course, my laboratory has an account and we get many foreign scientific periodicals. But what books and newspapers can I buy for five dollars a month? Do you receive any foreign newspapers? Here we see only foreign Communist papers. And the Moscow papers. . . ."

"I haven't read a Russian paper since 1918," said Natalya Ivanovna. "They were right who said, 'In *The News* there is no truth and in *The Truth* there is no news.'" She changed the subject abruptly—"You can go to church in America as you wish, can't you?"

"My wife is very religious," Vladimir Alexeitch explained, without expression.

"What else is there to hold to? If you like church music, you should go to the church at Nikitsky Gate. The choir is composed of artists from the opera. No Chaliapin, of course. He's getting rich in America, isn't he? The government tries to break up the choir, but artists here are unusually privileged."

"Tell about last Easter, Nalya."

"Oh, yes, the Communists tried their usual anti-Easter campaign. To keep the opera choir from getting to the midnight service on Saturday, they scheduled *Boris Goudinov,* which plays from seven-thirty till half past twelve. There would be no choir at the Nikitsky Church that night. Yet, when the service began, the choir was in its place. The artists had taken the opera at presto tempo, cut all the intermissions, and finished at eleven sharp. The Communists cannot destroy the church, no matter what foolish things they do, any more than they can destroy Russia. The Russian soul is religious."

"You are wrong, Nalya. There is no such thing as 'the Russian soul.' That is the invention of foreigners who created it to explain what they could not understand in Russia."

"*Hospodi*, Lord, with all this propaganda against the church? Who opposes the church? Who runs the Atheists' Society? Jews, Jews, Jews! Always Jews. . . ."

"Is there anti-Semitism in America, too? Here they tell the story of two Jews who met. One asked the other, 'Abram, who are the members of the Soviet in your village?' 'Well, there is Goldman, Cohen, Levy, Bernstein, and Ivanov.' 'Ivanov? A Russian?' 'Yes, a Russian.' 'Oi,' said the second, 'God knows how these Russians crawl in everywhere.' "

Natalya Ivanovna did not laugh. Rather it seemed as if she shuddered. "To think that Russia should be fought for between a Jew (Trotsky) and a Georgian (Stalin)! *Svolochi,* scoundrels!"

"Right there you have a result of the revolution," he smiled. "Before the revolution you wouldn't have used that word in company, Nalya. But you know what they say—'One Jew is a Nepman.* Two Jews are a trust. Three Jews are an opposition. One Georgian is a bootblack.† Two Georgians are a Caucasian Restaurant.‡ Three Georgians are a Politburo.' "§

"And one Russian?"

"Oh, one Russian is one fool. Two Russians are two fools. And three Russians are three fools. . . ."

*A private merchant.
†As are most of Moscow's bootblacks.
‡With which Moscow abounds.
§Controlling body of the Party.

"They are all fools. Will you have more tea? Fools. . . ."

"But what would you have us do, milaya?"

"We have waited too long to do anything positive. But Russia still stands and Christianity remains. Wait, wait. There will be a pogrom. . . ."

"Do you dream of it, Nalya?"

"When this damned system breaks there will be a pogrom. You will be able to row on Jewish blood from Arbat Gate to Red Square."

"Before the revolution there were very few Jews in Moscow and those only on permission," Vladimir Alexeitch explained to me. "They were a terribly persecuted people. There was a special district for them and there they had to remain. Many times we helped them—Jewish students, intelligentsia you know. We pitied them."

"And what have we got for it? Now they are everywhere, running everything. It is all Jewish."

"Comrade Stalin isn't, my dear."

"What difference is there between a Georgian and a Jew? Wait, *amerikanyetz,* until trouble begins. The first thing will be a pogrom, and the worst in history. Before the revolution the Jews lived in one section. Now they are everywhere, a family in each apartment. And each apartment will have its own little pogrom."

"My dear, the great Russian fault has always been not blaming things on defects in our own character but on the Jew. They are our great national excuse. . . ."

"But now everything is the fault of the Communists and they are all Jews."

"My dear, not ten per cent are Jews."

"But the Jews control the whole system," she said triumphantly.

"*Golubchik*, my dear, you remind me of the sign in the kosher butcher shop. It was the anniversary of Lenin's death and the butcher, patriotically, hung the official banner in his window. It read, 'Lenin Is Dead But His Work Goes On.' It fell down and partly covered another sign already there. From the street, the sign in the window of that kosher store read, 'Lenin Is Dead But His Work Goes On . . . Under The Supervision of Rabbi Cohen.' Dear, please get us some more tea." Natalya Ivanovna nodded approval and left the room.

"It must be hard for you foreigners to understand us," he continued. "We have each suffered differently from the revolution. And you must evaluate the whole mass of Russians to find out what is present-day Russia. Even then, many of them would lie. My wife feels the social effects of the revolution. She belongs to the *bivshii lyudi*, the 'former people,' or, in the new popular phrase, 'the decomposing elements.' Her father was a nobleman—bankrupt, of course, but a nobleman. She was educated as a nobleman's daughter: in music, foreign languages—she speaks good English, doesn't she? —and the social graces. Our marriage was looked upon as a step down for her, for my family had produced only scholars for four generations. All that is gone.

Her friends are scattered and dead and the Communist evaluation of the social graces is less than zero.

"The one thing that was left was the church, and she clung to that. Many of her friends did not. Those of us who had little faith have lost that; those who had much have become fanatic. We have prayed long for deliverance—and what is the use? But for my wife it is everything."

"It is hard to make her views on pogroms coincide with her religion," I said.

"But why not? She would not take personal part in the slaughter. Did missionaries ever protest when the soldiers came to punish natives who had become too aggressive around their settlement? She is foolish to blame everything on the Jews, she is too typically Russian, but I think she is right about the pogrom. It will come to herald the passing of this system. Go into the villages—there you will hear anti-Semitic remarks far more fiercely expressed than here. I spent a month in Ukraine some time ago. 'Are there many Jews in Moscow?' one peasant asked. 'Well,' he then replied, 'why don't you kill them when you've got them so neatly collected where they can't run?' What is your delightful American phrase—'bury the hatchet'? In Russia, it is only hidden in the closet. The Communists know it—they are not always foolish. Why do they put up posters—'Anti-Semitism Is a Bourgeois Prejudice. Anti-Semitism Is Counter-Revolutionary'? That is why a man who cried, '*Bay zhidov!*' ('beat the Jews') in a street would be shot by morning, even if he were drunk. For a pogrom is the first form that a violent demonstration against the Communists will assume.

"Yet, while the education of my wife may have been insufficient from the Communist point of view, there is one thing magnificent about it. Never once has she wanted to emigrate—not even in the worst days of 1919 and 1921. In those days the cities were starving, but there was food in the villages. With a sack and some trinkets, a watch, some petty jewelry, I would go perhaps five hundred miles from Moscow, trying to find a peasant who would take the watch in exchange for potatoes. Money, of course, was valueless. Sometimes I would be gone two weeks. Then, if I did find a sack full, I had to get a place on a train —on the roof, in the corridors, anywhere—and sit up to guard that bag. Trains went on intuition and not on system. It took me four days to get from Ryazan to Moscow (one hundred and twenty miles) one time. Another time I managed to buy a side of hog. While riding to Moscow on the roof of a carriage, a pair of lads smelled the pork. When no one was looking they rolled me off the roof and stole the meat. Thank God the train was moving slowly. But the loss of that pork meant more to me than a broken arm and a cut face. Some of your liberal professors would welcome a revolution, wouldn't they? Let them travel five hundred miles for potatoes. . . . Yet, through it all, Natalya Ivanovna never murmured about going abroad. Most of her friends had gone to Paris or Prague. We could have sneaked out somehow. Yet when I asked her she said 'No, anywhere else we would be strangers, foreigners. We shall stay here.' "

"And you?"

"Why should I leave? My work is here, and during those days we were thankful for our work. We worked harder than ever. It was our one surety. Here is my laboratory. I am terribly busy directing it. What could I do abroad? Without my work I should go out of my mind. I have not sold myself—I am not working for the Communists; I work for science. Communism is a phase which will pass. Science continues. All those Russians abroad are terribly homesick. They would give much just to hear once more the crackling voice of a Russian peasant. For a long time I thought Natalya Ivanovna despised the emigrés more than the Jews. 'Generals and Russian nobles—' she would say, 'foreigners must think that pre-revolutionary Russia was peopled only with generals, princes, grand dukes, and Jewish fur merchants. Let them stay in Russia that bore them to suffer the pain that comes to nobles and generals—just as, before the revolution, they enjoyed the privileges.' But who should criticize a man for saving his life? The revolution taught us very early that it was every man for himself. We chose to stay." He sighed very deeply. "Have you heard of the two men who met for the first time since 1917? 'Hello,' said one, 'how are you? By the way, how old are you now?' 'I'm thirty,' said the friend. 'Thirty? Why you were thirty when the revolution began.' 'I know,' the friend said bitterly, 'but you don't count the ten years since the revolution as life, do you?' "

"But, Vladimir Alexeitch, wouldn't you like to go abroad for a visit?"

"I should—very much. I was abroad each year till 1914. The Government sends some of us each summer. It is difficult, for there is little money and foreign travel requires foreign currency. There is work being done in other lands that I should like to see. But now, now I am afraid to go. The effect of the contact, you know—your peaceful life. . . . No, it is better for me to stay here. I have my work. I must not think of travel. A friend of mine went abroad last year and stayed only a week. The difference between life there—! No, here is my work."

I called one evening, unexpectedly. Vladimir Alexeitch was not home. His wife was entertaining three women. "Vladimir Alexeitch is very busy these days," she said. "He may be home at any minute." I was well known by now, so they continued their conversation, speaking in French. "So servants won't understand," she explained, "one can never tell who are spies."

". . . So they dumped all the furniture out into the courtyard and where was she to go with her daughter?" one friend concluded.

"We are talking about *lishentsi* (the deprived)," said Natalya Ivanovna. "A school friend of ours has been deprived of her right to vote because her father owned an estate; you know, that means that she is therefore branded as belonging to the 'undesirable element'— she has her food card taken from her, she loses her job, and her rent goes up to a figure she can't pay. She lived in the smallest room of her former apartment, but the House Committee ordered her out—and also her daughter. Her daughter had an abortion three years ago and is out of her head. Now the House Committee has chased them out and dumped all their furniture in the courtyard."

"But what will she do?"

"Her friends. . . . She will live here for a while and her daughter will go to other friends. Places in hospitals are crowded and workers, peasants, and members of trade unions come first. It is hard. . . ."

"How long can this absurdity last? It is already twelve years," sighed one of the women.

"They say that Stalin is very sick with the 'Lenin disease.' . . ."

"They say the GPU has arrested seven hundred this week. . . ."

"They say the Communists have taken down the Chudov monastery in the Kremlin to give more room for their army. . . ."

"I heard they wanted the space so that they could land an airplane inside the Kremlin in case they had to flee. . . ."

"They say the bread ration will be decreased next month. . . ."

"I stood in line three hours yesterday for three meters of cotton cloth, and such trash! 'Is it any good?' I asked the clerk. 'Well, it's Soviet,' he said."

"They say. . . ."

"They say. . . ."

Vladimir Alexeitch came in. He spoke to his wife aside for several minutes. One of the friends asked,

"How does it stand, Volodya?" "I shan't know until the next Party meeting," he answered, and excused himself. The women left soon after.

"Vladimir Alexeitch is much worried—you can see it, can't you?" said Natalya Ivanovna. "He is not a typical professor. He works loyally, as they all do, but when things displease him he says what he thinks. If he were world famous he could do that—he would be too valuable to touch. But there are other professors of physics. I am always afraid for him, for what he says, for the contacts he makes. *Akh,* this life of ours. . . . 'What does the coming day prepare for us?' How I envy you in America where all is quiet and peaceful. Tell me, how does it seem to you—will there be an end to this?"

I was noncommittal.

"But surely you've been here long enough to see that it isn't 'interesting,' as you described it the first time you came. Vivisection may interest the doctor, but not the dog. Their Five Year Plan, their world revolution —all bluff to hide their cruelty. Who lives happily in Russia? No one, not even the Communists. They are afraid themselves, else why do they use terror, terror, the GPU . . . Praise God that I have no children to live under it. Especially no daughter—to marry and raise little atheistic brats."

Vladimir Alexeitch called me into his study. He seemed depressed and very nervous. "Did my wife tell you? They are trying to throw me out of my laboratory. They want to put a Communist in my place and let me be assistant. They say I am getting too old.

They mean it is too important a position for one as reactionary as myself—perhaps I have expressed myself too freely, with the GPU everywhere. Science should be apart from politics; yet when I object to some of the things that are done, the kind of students that are admitted, some little jealous Jew 'Red professor' goes to the Party committee in the University and reports. I can lecture but no longer direct my laboratory. They wish to pass Moscow University over to Party committees—once it belonged to scholars! Now scholarship must be of a certain color."

I met him some time later on the street. He asked me to call.

"I am finished," he said. "I have been 'cleaned out' from my laboratory, but I may continue to lecture. That's it. I may continue to lecture, for they have no one else. They are trying to train their own teachers and professors, but until then they must use us. Science belongs to the workers—have you seen that sign over the University? Am I to blame if God gave brains to other classes as well? Social origin, social origin—that determines everything. It determines whether you have the right to vote, and therefore all other rights, even to the education of your children. Only last week one of my nephews, the nine-year-old son of one 'deprived,' was dismissed from school and came home crying, 'They said that places in schools were for peasants' and workers' children first and that there was no room for me. Papa, why aren't you a worker?'—this to his father, one of the most brilliant judges in Russia before the revolution and now seeking a job for the last four years. One thought always haunts me—if anything happens to me, what of my wife? She can earn nothing. None of us has any insurance as in your country. I have nothing saved.

"This system—espionage, GPU, executions, midnight arrests, in short, Communism! What place is left for us? Before the revolution I was a radical, as were many in the University. Radicalism appeals to the intellectual; it is essentially individualistic—so is he. Who would not have opposed the stupidity, the brutality, the selfishness of the Tsar? Now we have gone back to the same things, but we have a million Tsars where before there was but one. I was a socialist—there were many features of capitalism I abhorred. But Communism? I am competent to pass on that. No, it was not our revolution. And the intellectuals are left without a place; they cannot stomach Communism. Look at those who are now in exile—some who worked just as hard against the Tsar as ever Stalin did. Where are the intellectuals who were once in the Communist Party? There is no middle ground for us. We cannot revolt—we are simply to be used until that rare species, the Communist Intelligentsia, ripens.

"I am amazed at some of your professors who come over here. They are shown some small change for the better, perhaps a few schools of a new type, and they thereupon approve the whole system. But they have foreign passports and can leave. Most of them can't even speak Russian—what right have they to judge? Little they know. Yet why are they so blind? Would they like a similar proletarian dictatorship in their own country? That might bring them the few new schools about which they were so wildly enthusiastic here. But at what a cost! Can't they see that they too would lose their middle ground and their illusions—and that their individualism would get them in trouble with the American GPU? For no dictatorship can stand without secret police. I heard that some American here this summer said 'America owes a debt of gratitude to Russia for trying this tremendous experiment.' Bah!" With his hand he brushed the world aside. "Let me speak—as one of those who has been experimented upon.

"The revolution has put our faith in everything to the test and we have all failed. There is nothing left in which we can believe. We are the Great Disillusioned —and many of the Communists are too, I think. So we live and the GPU is always ready if we speak too loudly about it. They have had me once. They will have me whenever they think I need a reminder that the proletariat is still dictating. I am afraid of them only for my wife. For myself—we have even lost the illusion of danger."

He reached for a book. "Russia is best summed up as an Englishman, Powys, once summed up Africa—another savage and uncivilized country. 'Africa, like one of her black-maned lions, laps up the life blood of all the delicate illusions which have too long danced before the eyes of men and made them happy. Truth alone is left alive. What was suspected in Europe is made pain here—'*at the bottom of the well of life there is no hope.'* That the revolution has taught me. You will never know it in America, for you have too much sense to run to revolution.

"Well, good night. Come and see me at my *datcha* some time."

Late Spring turned into summer. One August Sunday afternoon I went out to the *datcha* where, more than two years before, I had gone with the coffee. I found only a servant. She said the family had returned unexpectedly to town.

I went to their apartment. I found three or four women in the dining room, sitting around Natalya Ivanovna. Her crying added to the funereal air of the place.

She spoke bluntly: "Vladimir Alexeitch has been arrested by the GPU. You know how he stays in town in the week and only comes out to the *datcha* on Saturdays. Wednesday night, at midnight, two GPU agents came to the apartment. They searched his room for three hours. Look!" Through the open door I could see his study in great disorder. "And they took him off. He left this note." I read a scribbling, "I have been arrested by the GPU." "We didn't know it until he failed to come to the datcha last night."

"But why?"

"*Chort znayet,* the Devil knows! He has done nothing. But the loss of his laboratory made him bitter. He may have said something, or have seen someone. *Akh, svolotchi!* They must come at midnight, they must be dramatic. . . ." She broke into tears.

Two months later I met a friend and asked about Vladimir Alexeitch.

"He was in Butirka prison for a while, but now he has been moved elsewhere. Perhaps to another prison in Moscow. Two years ago, when he was arrested, he walked home one morning, freed, without any previous notice. Perhaps this time he will get 'minus three' or 'minus six'—that is, he cannot live in the three or six largest cities in Russia. Or it may be exile to the prison camps at Solovetski or Narim—he has a bad heart and life up there, in the far north, would kill him."

"How will you know?"

"If he doesn't walk home one day, then sometime his wife will get a post-card from him saying, 'Here I am—in Narim or Beryeozev—please send me some warm clothes.'"

III

ADAMOVA: THE STUDENT

THE professor stepped to the front of the platform in the large lecture hall of the First Moscow University. Behind him, in fresco on the rear wall, was a huge head of Lenin. The babel from the crowded benches ceased. "Comrades, to-day we take up the subject . . ." he began. He got no further.

A girl in a black leather coat, a red bandanna tied round her head, a bulging briefcase under her arm, rushed from the outside corridor to the platform. "Excuse me, comrade," she nodded to the professor, "comrades," turning to the students and in a shrill voice, "this lecture cannot be held to-day. The meeting of the *Comsomoltsi* scheduled for this evening has been moved to this hour." There was scattered applause and the class broke up.

"That was Adamova," said my friend Voronov, another student. "She's a peasant, the secretary of the *Comsomoltsi*—the Young Communist's League. They have as much power in this university as the professors. Even more. Another meeting, the Devil, always meetings. I don't see how she keeps it up—she's in everything. This is her last year. Why is it that it is always the unattractive women who go into politics? Is it the same in America? The size of her hands and feet! Now that little *blondinka* down there"—pointing to a student below—"she's non-Party. But she's

42

just as busy as Adamova . . . with other things," and he winked.

The First Moscow University specializes in politics, economics, law, languages, and literature; the Second University teaches the sciences. The First University has two thousand students. Side by side sit boys and girls of eighteen, just in from provincial cities, with policemen, detailed by their superiors for college education; factory workers of forty on leave of absence for a few years; the brighter pupils from Moscow's secondary schools. Russians and swarthy Uzbek from Turkestan, Jew and Georgian, brooding Mongol and laughing Ukrainian are students together beneath the slogan "Science belongs to the workers." They are lucky to be there—ten times their number have been refused admission.

Admission depends on the entrance examination grade and on very close scrutiny into the applicant's "social origin." The last is the ultimate test; with limited facilities there is no room for the children of the "former people," nor for the children of priests, private merchants, or other classes potentially hostile. The number of places granted to children of the intelligentsia is small. "Science belongs to the workers"— and the children of the factory worker or of the peasant have come to claim their right. No wonder one embarrassed applicant filled in the answer to the question "What is your social origin?" with "Father,—two workmen; Mother,—one peasant."

Each student receives a "stipend"—twenty-seven rubles a month, thirteen dollars and fifty cents. This is the sole income for most of them. Those who can find space in the inexpensive dormitories live there. Others room wherever they can. It is not easy. The students eat at restaurants run for them and share in perquisites, a few theatre tickets now and then, medical attention, cheap transportation home. But twenty-seven rubles a month presents problems even to the most economical.

One wing of the main building is the students' club. In the main club room, formerly the university chapel, there are still a few frescoed angels high up in the corners which have not yet been painted out. On the floor beneath are lounge rooms, chess boards, a ping-pong table, and a crowd of students in the evenings. And always an argument.

I sat with Voronov one evening. Adamova was the centre of a little group near by.

". . . It is hard," her voice topped the others, "but she should have known that marriage is impossible. . . ."

"They are talking about Pyatnitskaya," Voronov interpolated. "She married another student last year. They tried to live on their stipend . . . there was a baby. Why they had it God knows! She couldn't keep on at the University but she needed the stipend so she had to continue somehow. Then her husband divorced her and left Moscow . . . and she killed the child and committed suicide too last week."

"But what could she do?" asked one student.

"Do? What do the rest of you do—marry? No, all

student marriages turn out badly and interfere with our work."

Someone mentioned the need for higher stipends.

"Comrades, what are you saying? Is our government a millionaire to give big salaries to the students? We must make sacrifices too. No marriage . . . it is unnecessary."

Another student spoke of a secretary of a Young Communist League group who had been officially disgraced and dismissed for using his position to force favors from the girls in his unit.

"And rightly so," said Adamova. "We must have standards and high standards. No swine such as that one, using his official position in such a way, has any right to be in it. Wasting his time when he should have been doing his work, soiling our Party's reputation, giving our enemies material to use against us. If that gets abroad the capitalist press will say, 'See, that's what all Communists do.' *Svoloch,* he should be shot. . . ."

The others were inclined to agree.

"From women such as Adamova, deliver us, oh God," Voronov whispered to me. "She's like the woman in the play. Two chemists discover a new brand of soap. What shall they call it? One suggests a catchy name, 'Karl Marx's first kiss.' The other vetoes that and they agree to name it 'Soviet Woman.' But then, how shall they advertise it? They draw a big picture of a fat cow, with a red bandana tied around its head. And underneath they write—'Soviet Woman.' " He asked, "Coming home, Adamova? We live in the same dormitory," he explained. She rose, strapped tight her briefcase. *"Nu, poka* (so long)," and she came with us.

"I heard there was an American student here," she said when we were on our way. "Tell me, why did such a cultured country as America kill Sacco and Vanzetti?" She continued without a pause, "I know, it is because the class war in America gets keener every day, isn't it so? And why does civilized America treat the negroes as inferiors? Don't you realize that all race hatreds are fostered by the capitalists; they direct the discontent of the oppressed workers against the negro peoples. It is the same as the Tsarist autocracy did here with the Jews. Your workers must not be led astray by the enemies of their class. . . ."

"But, Adamova," said Voronov, "labor unions in America will not admit negroes. . . ."

"Of course not, but that is because the American Federation of Labor is controlled by the capitalists. If it is not so, why don't the American trade unions demand that America recognize us and strike until recognition is granted? Trade unions? They are farces. But our Communist unions are growing in America." She quoted statistics. "Look at us in the University, Karelian, Russian, Chuvash, Jew—all together. Under socialism there is no race hatred." Her interest in America was most alive—but principally in wages, labor conditions, social legislation, immigration. "You see we know more of America here in Soviet Russia than you in America know of us. We want to learn—we are a backward country and you can teach us much. But in America you think 'Pff, what can we learn from Russia?' and when you do think of it you think of beards and of revolutionaries throwing bombs. I know America—I have read Upton Sinclair, Jack London. We shall learn all we can from you, catch up to you—and overtake you. We are a young people. We are building. . . ."

The dormitory was a former wealthy merchant's house. We went through a dark courtyard, past the broken front door, and up to the second floor. "Come in and see where I live," she said.

In a room twenty feet square there were ten beds. By each bed stood a little table and under the beds there were boxes and bags. In the centre of the room, beneath a powerful electric light, was a long wooden table. In one corner some one's laundry was hanging on a cord stretched to the window. At the table a few girls, with tea and black bread before them, were reading and making notes; they paid no attention to us. "When you are through in the ladies' department, come down the hall where the men live," said Voronov, leaving.

"It is crowded and studying here is so difficult—noise and people coming in and out. Have you any extra tea?" she asked. One girl gestured "Help yourself." "I've only one glass—wait, I'll borrow Sacha's," and she took a glass from an opposite table. "I'm sorry I haven't any bread or *kolbasa* (bologna). You know, they call *kolbasa* the student's standby."

"And awful stuff it is getting to be," said one of the

girls at the table. "Did you hear of the woman who was standing in line at the meat counter in a store and suddenly fainted? The clerk put a piece of *kolbasa* under her nose and revived her immediately."

Adamova nodded but did not laugh. "You think this is a bad way to live? Crowded—of course, but we are used to that in our villages. There were eleven in our family and we lived in a two-roomed hut. The old folks slept on the stove and we kids slept on the floor. But living like this costs us only a ruble a month— and we do most of our studying in the library. . . .

"The worst thing here is our health—we are all in poor condition. We are trying to introduce frequent compulsory medical examination for all students. Tuberculosis . . . and in winter everybody gets tonsilitis. But look at how many want to get in the University. Here education is free, for everybody. . . ."

"But supposing your social origin is unfavorable?"

"Oh, of course, for those . . . but we have no room to educate our enemies. Your American universities keep out certain classes, and so do we; only here education is for the majority, not for the pampered minority. I know how education is in America. I have read about it. We in Russia have made education for the masses. Look at me, before the revolution should I have come into Moscow University? I grew up in a village in Karelia (far north of Leningrad), a hundred miles from a railroad. There were eleven in our family and my father had three acres of land; that was all. I know what hunger is and famine, too.

"The revolution came, but I was too young to

know what it meant. When I was thirteen I ran away
—there was no food in our village. There was little
more in Leningrad. I joined the *Comsomoltsi.* I did
agitation work among the soldiers at the front. Then,
at sixteen, I married a soldier. He died. I married
another. All girls had to make that choice; in those
days marriage might mean food. In Moscow it meant
a room. Later he divorced me. Then I continued agitation work in a factory in Leningrad and went to
school at nights. And here I am, in the university in
Moscow. But what about women in your universities? Are they interested in labor problems, in factory production? Do they take an interest in politics, in helping to run your country? Here we are so
busy. . . ."

One of the girls at the table interrupted. "Adamova,
did you see the cartoon in *Chudak?* An old man sat on
a bench and saw a small boy resting. 'Ah,' murmured
the man, 'how I envy the lad—carefree, happy, no responsibilities, all day to play.' 'Hey, old man,' said the
boy, 'can't I rest a minute without being moralized
about? I had a meeting of the Pioneers at eleven, another one comes this evening, and in the meantime, six
committee meetings in our school.' "

"Yes," said Adamova, "here even the children are
learning that in Russia they are part of one united
people working for a definite end. I have work in the
Comsomoltsi, I am one of the representatives from
our University in the Moscow Soviet, I teach a group
in a factory to read and write three evenings a
week. . . ."

"But what about studying?"

"I do that of course. But our universities are not only for studying. All our social work is part of our education."

"And examinations?"

"They are usually oral. The professor asks us a question or two on his lectures and that is all. . . ."

Voronov came in. It was after eleven. "Come down to our quarters. Some comrade is trying to learn your frightful English language and wants to know how to pronounce 'th'!"

Across the lobby in the main university building three months later there hung a red banner with the wording: "Any student who knows reasons why another student should be deprived of his right to vote is obligated to report to the Students' Committee." On a bulletin board was tacked a paper, "The following are barred from the right to vote for the reason appended," and there followed a list of a dozen names, and after each name "daughter of a priest," "son of a factory owner," "daughter of a landlord." This was the *chistka* (cleanout) before the annual elections; the right to vote, too, depends on social origin, so the *chistka* is an opportunity to discover which members of the disenfranchised classes were in the University under false colors.

I found Adamova in the little cafeteria, a crowd around her. They were talking about the *chistka*.

"How those students slip in, I don't know."

"Oh, they falsify their identity cards."

"They come from far away and think we shan't find out. . . ."

"There is no room in the university"—Adamova was speaking—"for these 'former people.' There are too many workers trying to get in."

The group broke up and Adamova said, "How are you getting on? Come down to the rest hall. I have ten minutes. I am so busy with this *chistka*—committee meetings every day. You can't understand how we feel about it, can you? You fail to see how deep our revolution goes. Did you hear that one of the girls whom we 'cleaned out' yesterday committed suicide last night? You feel sorry, but you don't understand. She had no business here. If she chooses to come and is found out—well, she must pay the penalty.

"The 'former people' had their chance to run Russia; we have abolished them and there is no longer a Russia. It is our Soviet republic . . . *ours*. Did these 'former people' protest when Lenin was exiled to Siberia, when the Tsar's gendarmerie shot two hundred and seventy workers in the Lena fields in 1912? Who felt sorry then? They thought their power was invincible. We, the masses, would never be able to destroy them. Well, we have. And now, building the Soviet Union and Communism all the world over has become our life.

"Do you know many 'former people' here?" She turned the question suddenly. "You don't take your opinion of Soviet Russia from them, I hope. What do they know? Their desire that somehow we shall fail keeps them from trying to find out how we are succeeding. We have some of them here in the University—professors whom for the moment we must use. Can we build in ten years a whole set of intelligentsia? They work, but only half loyally, and we know it. We watch them and in the meantime we are training our own intelligentsia; peasant boys, instead of following the wooden plow round their narrow fields, will be doctors, engineers, professors. And peasant girls too. Women can do anything men can do provided they have the necessary knowledge.

"Never forget for a minute that the revolution is continuing. We have enemies both external and internal. Against those who would creep into our institutions unwanted, we have the *chistka;* against those in our institutions who misuse the trust we put in them we have the GPU. That is our army on our internal front. Did you see in the paper last week that three former mine owners who were working as engineers were shot by the GPU? Of course they were guilty—former mine owners! There was no need to publish details about the diabolical tricks they were doing. Their background is conviction enough. . . .

"You do not understand. We must rule here by force. We know that many here in Moscow hope and wish and even pray for the crash of Soviet government. We must be on guard against them for some of them are mad enough to try their petty trickeries in the hope of bringing about that crash. So we need the GPU. Do you realize that every major conspiracy against the government since the Kronstadt revolt of 1921—and there have been many—has been discovered in time? The GPU is alive, it is a loyal and necessary organ of our Dictatorship. Look at the number of conspiracies it discovers and shoots out; that proves the necessity for the secret police. . . .

"So don't look for sentimentality. We must be severe. What if a thousand, what if a million perish (as your lying press in the West frequently reports) if we shall be able to build socialism in our country for the remainder? We make mistakes—of course. We must constantly find new roads, retreat, detour. We are not afraid to criticize ourselves unflinchingly when we are wrong. But it is better that a hundred innocent perish than that one guilty conspirator against our class escape."

Many of the university courses use the precept method: after the lecture the large group is divided into small discussion classes for an additonal hour. I went with Voronov and Adamova to their precept in the course on "Political Grammar," the history and theory of Communism—a course compulsory for every student in every school in Moscow, whether it be the ballet school, the nursing schools, the universities, or the conservatory.

The assignment that day concerned the World War. "What is imperialism?" "Can imperialism develop peacefully?" "What were the principal groupings of the European Socialists before and during the war?" "Must European workers refuse to take arms when a war breaks out?" These were among the questions asked. To the last question one student replied "Yes." The whole class roared "No!"—and half a dozen were on their feet to explain that the workers *must* take arms, not for use against the workers in opposing armies, but for use against their own capitalists. "Why is a general strike insufficient Communist activity during a war?" "What differences are there between the war of 1914 and the coming imperialist war against the USSR?" Each question brought a ready answer.

"The questions are printed at the end of the text," whispered Voronov. "All you have to do is memorize the book."

Yet the serious air of the group was impressive as the professor explained and summarized the day's assignment. "Remember, comrades, the slogan of our Lenin—'The imperialist war must be turned into a civil war' "—and the class was dismissed.

"Adamova, are you going to the skating rink this evening?" Voronov asked. "There's going to be an orchestra to-night." Then to me—"Students get in free—you come too."

"Comrade," Adamova replied angrily, "with courses in *politgrammar,* the history of the labor movement in Europe, civil law, criminal law, local government, the history of the Paris Commune, plus that damned German language, what chance have I to go skating?"

She had a chance later, when Christmas vacation brought two weeks' rest. Voronov was going off skiing and had managed to get a free place in one of the sanatoria near Moscow. "Adamova," he said, "is leading a party out through the villages in the Vladimir district to raise enthusiasm there for the new gov-

ernment loan. I can think of better things to do than
that during vacation. Go home? I live in Siberia—
wouldn't my old man be surprised to see me?—first
time in six years. Phew," he shook his head, "what
a headache I've got. Some of us were at a beer hall
last night, drinking beer and vodka mixed."

"Where did you get the money?"

"We got our dole yesterday. And I shall live free
for the next two weeks at the rest home."

It was about this time that the *Comsomoltsi* (about
sixty per cent of the students) broke out in uniforms.
They wore khaki shirts and khaki trousers or skirts and
everyone boasted a new "Sam Browne" belt. Newspapers were prophesying with increased vigor an im-
pending attack on Soviet Russia by some alliance of
European powers. There were endless series of mass
meetings. At one of them I heard Adamova speak.
She talked for an hour.

". . . We must always be ready, comrades. The capitalist West grows more jealous every day as they see
our Soviet power growing. The capitalists, led by the
English and the French, see that their own pockets are
menaced by a successful workers' democracy in which
private profit has been eliminated. With them are
allied their tools, the governing officials and the priests.
They are always allied. It was so in Russia before the
revolution, was it not, comrades?" She stopped and
coughed raspingly.

"We can understand why the western capitalists
hate us. Here there is peace and all our energies are

devoted to building our future. We are a menace—a menace to their blood sucking system. Here the working class moves forward to achieve itself. On the other side of the barrier there are class contradictions, continuous friction, strikes, unemployment—all the inevitable accompaniments of the exploitation of man by man. We declare that such a system is wrong. We are proving that on the basis of socialism we can build a new world and we find allies daily among the workers of other lands. . . ."

Voronov was sitting next to me. "She's a good speaker, isn't she?" he whispered. "But she sounds just like the newspapers. Did you hear the story about Kalenin ('president' of the USSR) making a speech in the village? He said 'I want to tell you today, comrades, about the new harbor we have just opened. Fifty steamships a day come in to discharge their cargoes and fifty boats heavily laden leave there daily.' A young man in the crowd said, 'Michael Ivanovich, that isn't true. I work in that harbor. Not one steamship comes in and not one steamship goes out.' '*Akh*,' Kalenin replied, 'what do you know? You ought to read the newspapers.' "

Adamova was nearing the end. ". . . But this time the capitalists will find the Red Army united and strong. Four million of us, proletarian youth, are ready to meet the attack. And behind their own lines their own workmen will rebel and refuse to serve in any army that marches against us. The international proletariat know that nationalism is a tool to force workers into wars of aggression in which the capitalist makes his profit and the workers meet their death. The international proletariat know that the workers have no fatherland except our own Soviet Union which is the proletarian fatherland for the workers of the world. Be ready to defend it."

I saw her several days later. She was in uniform. "Are you going to wear this all the time?" I asked.

"Of course—we must. We never know when the war against us will break out and we must be ready. And then, *amerikanyetz,* will you be on this side of the barricade—or on that side?"

There was a gala anti-religious evening in the speakers' club on Easter Eve. The hall was crowded. A leader of the Atheists' Society spoke for an hour and Adamova followed, speaking for half an hour on religion as a tool of capitalism. Her hacking cough interfered. "The church has always stood with the capitalist class against the workers. 'Come unto me, all ye who are weary and are heavy laden,' say the priests, and their paymasters, the capitalists, take those weary and heavy laden and raise their hours from eight to ten. 'Because of competition,' they lower their wages ten kopecks an hour at the same time. Then the priests chant in chorus, '. . . And I will give you rest.' "

Following their speeches there was an American comedy film. About eleven of the chairs were cleared from the middle of the hall and a little brass band mounted the platform. As a very rare privilege there was to be a dance continuing until two A. M. to hold any students who might backslide and go to midnight mass. The dances were the old waltz and a whole series of Russian dances—the men dancing alone, then the women, then a wild whirling waltz with couples separating, turning, rejoining. The brass band blew louder, the dance swirled faster, the room grew hotter. The tuba player, his horn pointed at the two little frescoed angels up in the corner which had survived the revolution, was a trifle off key.

Adamova was sitting in a corner. "I don't dance," she explained. "And I am so tired. Spring usually makes me feel fresh . . . but not this year," and she coughed unpleasantly. We moved into the buffet.

"I do not approve of all this—it is bourgeois," she said, gesturing at the dance. "Your American dancing, the *foukstrot*—is worse and we cannot allow it. Yet even an evening like this strengthens whatever bourgeois leanings there may be in the student body. We have many such here—careerists. Your friend Voronov has already been six years at the university. You know the proverb, 'God's bird knows neither care nor toil.' He is God's bird. Every year he has managed somehow to wangle a stipend when he should have been out working long ago. We expelled him yesterday from the *Comsomoltsi* when he said he was coming back to the University for another year. Some of our students are spoilt here. After four years of city life they no longer want to return to their villages. They say the villages are lonesome, there is no life there. Oh, to be in Moscow! Last year a newspaper discovered lots of young doctors, engineers, and teachers working in Moscow at any kind of a job rather than practise their profession in the village, where they are needed. But we shall force them out into the provinces. Our students must understand that we do not educate them for themselves."

The sounds of the band and particularly the tuba reached us in the hall. "I don't know much about music, I have had little time. I went to 'Prince Igor' last month. Such rot. What has it to do with our present day experiences? Fancy opera! All art, music, and literature here must grow out of our present life. Of course we have produced little as yet, it is only twelve years since the revolution. We are like children. How can we express ourselves when we are still busy learning the alphabet?

"The artistic world, too, is not with us. Many of the old actors and actresses are left and they cannot grasp our revolutionary psychology. There are too many careerists among them. They put on potboilers which, because the hero is a workman, they think portray the class struggle. The actresses too, with their Paris gowns . . . going abroad to have their faces lifted, as the chief ballerina at the opera does each year, at government expense. There is too much failure to realize that life for us is a fight against ignorance, superstition, in a country which fifty years ago was mediæval.

"There is too much plotting, this trying to arrange things to make it easy for friends, for relatives, for one's self. Even among high officials! We call it in Russian 'looking out for one's God child.' One 'important bird' wrote a play 'Rags and Velvet' for his wife, Rozanelle, the actress. On the night of its first presentation he found a little note pinned on the door of his box." She stopped and coughed. "The note was a little poem addressed to him—

> 'You've written a play, "Rags and Velvet,"
> We hope that it goes well,
> We in the cast—we get the rags
> But the velvet's for Rozanelle.'

"Many of us here cannot understand, so how can you foreigners comprehend our revolution? revolution usually means a new political group coming into power by force; that is what it has always meant in your experience. But here it is a revolution in which the political overturn is only one side. To guarantee the continuance of our political policy we must change every feature of our people's life. This is a poor country, with half the population illiterate. Now can you understand why we are so busy, so serious, and why everything—art, literature, music, recreation—must combine to help us remodel our people?"

I saw her in June, at the central railroad office, standing in line for a ticket to the Persian border.

"Going on vacation?" I asked.

"No, I am leaving to-night for a position in Turkestan," she replied. She got her ticket and we went to a tearoom in the same building.

"I didn't know what to do when my work at the university was finished. There is plenty of Party work for me to do in Moscow but here there are many willing and eager to stay in the Centre. Then I got a letter telling me about the need for a women's organizer down near Askabad, a very backward region: the women still wear veils. The best chance for work I could possibly find. The same chap who wrote me about the job said he had a big room and asked me to come down and share it with him. . . ."

"What wages do you get?"

"Seventy or eighty rubles, enough to buy food and clothes. What more do I need?" She stopped and coughed; it was worse than when I last heard it. "The climate may help this cough of mine, I don't know. Perhaps I shan't live long. But while I live there is work for me to do. And when I am gone there are four million like myself to carry on the task of building up our Union. You know, the revolution has put meaning into life for us, just as it will for millions around the world who now see no meaning in their eight-hour labor in someone else's factory, at monotonous toil at someone else's machines. Remember, our example will spread through Europe. It shall reach the Atlantic. . . ."

"And beyond?"

"And beyond. . . ."

IV

ABRAM MOSEVITCH: THE MERCHANT

THE second hand shoe dealers clutter up one section of Smolensk market, in Moscow. I passed by their wares, spread out on the cobbles, and came to the long row of stalls owned by private traders where there are stocks of meat, butter, flour,—those goods which are scarce in the government stores. "Speculators," *chastniki,* "the private ones," are the slurring epithets officially applied to these petty merchants. There are almost no privately owned stores in the city; any who wish to continue the unpopular profession of merchant for their own profit must trade from these rickety stands in the market places or at street corners. And almost all these "private ones" are Jews.

As I passed one stand, piled high with butter and eggs, the proprietor, a Jew, middle aged, with a long forked beard, called me, "Hey, *amerikanyetz,* come over here." I could not remember ever having seen him before. He explained that we lived in the same apartment house and that he had recognized me.

He stood behind mounds of fresh butter, salt butter, jars of boiled butter, and baskets of eggs. Over his stand was the sign "A. M. Silverson—Butter." The sign needed repainting. The "s" in *maslo* (butter) had faded so the sign read *malo* (little). I found that he was fond of pointing to that sign and saying that it described both his business and his profits. On one side was Samuels, a butcher, and, on the other side, Goldman, selling nuts, rice, and buckwheat.

Smolensk market is a village scene moved to a metropolis. Peasants come from villages near Moscow and in summer there are enough cabbages, beets, and potatoes here to make the daily pot of soup for all the city. The ribbed peasant wagons cluster together in one corner of the square and the peasants, in their bark sandals and ragged leggings, wait for the Moscow housewives. The noise of bargaining, argument, and recrimination rises and falls amid the clatter of the passing trolleys, the rumble of the busses, and the rattle of the heavy drays on the cobbled streets. A Chinese juggler, a dancing bear, a few gipsy dancing girls, attract crowds who leave just before the collection is taken. There are barbers whose chair is the soap box they carry, and itinerant cobblers with their lasts under their arms. To Smolensk market, on Sundays, once came the "former people," to sell what few pitiful valuables they still possessed and thus gain bread for one more week. Foreigners always came here hoping to find rare jewels or precious ikons; they usually found only old postcards and mismatched and broken china. This feature of the market has now been abolished. But every day business goes on and it is one of the last standbys of the *chastniki*.

"We want you to tell us something," said Abram Mosevitch. "Maxim Maximovitch," pointing to the butcher, "has a son in America, in New York. He writes that the tax on an income of ten thousand rubles ($5,000) in your America is less than a hundred rubles. Is that so?"

"That's approximately right, I think."

"There," he pointed jubilantly at Goldman, "just what I said. That is why America is such a wealthy country—because her taxes are low. Now here . . . *akh!*"

While he was talking I looked at the price list; the best butter was six rubles a pound; eggs were two rubles and a half for ten. On Goldman's stand prices were equally amazing—forty cents a pound for rice, thirty cents for a pound of buckwheat, and a little jar of white flour was marked fifty cents a pound.

"My son is in the fur business in New York," said Goldman who continued to look at me rather sceptically. Then, as if to test finally my veracity, he said, "He writes that he earns two hundred dollars a month but that living in New York is so expensive that he can only send me fifteen dollars monthly? Is it really as expensive as that? That would be four hundred rubles and on that one could live nicely here. Perhaps he could send us more. . . ."

"How can this American tell what your son spends?" demanded Abram Mosevitch. "You are lucky to get fifteen dollars a month. Of course, if the bank would pay it to you in dollar bills. . . ."

". . . but they always pay it in rubles," said Goldman, a trifle sadly, "and take a tax on it in addition."

"Taxes!" and Abram Mosevitch sighed.

He came to my apartment one evening with a request. Foreign currency is difficult to secure in Russia. Banks will not exchange rubles for it except under extraordinary circumstances. The government needs all the foreign currency it can get to buy goods abroad, for the paper ruble does not circulate outside the boundaries of the Soviet Union. There is a highly illegal trade in foreign currency on the "Black Bourse," conducted in secret by various citizens, and sold at a large premium; a dollar commands two rubles at the bank but it can be exchanged for eight on the "Black Bourse."

"This *valuta,* foreign currency, shortage," he began. "I have a son in Tel Aviv, in Palestine, and I used to have permission to send him thirty dollars a month. Now the government refuses to exchange any money whatsoever. If I pay you sixty rubles here, which is what you would get at the bank, can you arrange abroad to have him sent thirty dollars? He needs it. I don't know what else to do."

I explained that it was the fourth request I had had that month to arrange something similar.

"I understand. Only from foreigners can we get *valuta.* Even if you buy *valuta* on the 'Black Bourse' you cannot mail it out. They are suspicious if we merely keep it. Oh, yes, some one in the market to-day told a story about a man who went to the secret police. 'I have a wonderful dog,' he said, 'that is trained to smell out *valuta.*' The police were sceptical but agreed to try him. When they led him down the street he seized a man by his pants. The man was searched and his pockets were found full of dollars. So they tried him a second time. This time he stopped another man and barred his way. When his pockets were searched they were found filled with marks. So they tried him a third time. This time he passed a man and suddenly lay down, sick, in the gutter. . . ."

"Well?"

"Oh, his pockets were full of Soviet rubles! Yet before the revolution I had a bank account in Germany. I am not from Moscow. I lived in a village in Lithuania. My father had a large business which I inherited, catching crayfish and exporting them to Berlin and to Moscow; you know, they are considered a great delicacy. Twenty people worked for me. After the war the Lithuanian government began dispossessing the Jews. At the same time there was much talk about the new rights and liberties in Soviet Russia. We had our choice given us—and I moved to Moscow. I believed these Russians. When could anyone believe a Russian? . . . My younger son stayed behind and later went to Palestine."

"You have no other children?"

"Yes," he snapped each word, "I have a son—here in Russia. I chose to come to Russia. I think sometimes I must have been insane. I have been here nine years —nine years of nightmare. I had a little capital and I have been a trader all my life. I am too old to change. Here I am 'deprived'—my profession is branded 'bourgeois'—and we suffer. Six years ago they took away my right to vote; because I had a store and a few employees I was branded an exploiter of labor. Do you know what it means to be 'deprived'? No trade union card, therefore no bread card—yet everything is sold by rations. My room costs me five times what a factory hand would pay, and no guarantee that one day we will not be swept out like old rubbish, when some loyal worker needs the room. Thank God I have no small children for they would be barred from school. And why? Why? When was being a merchant a dishonest and shameful occupation? When I came to Moscow I was without any experience for office work—that is the kind of work to have in this city with its government bureaus; I had no professional training. Of course, I opened a store. It was so heavily taxed that I had to close it. Then I opened this booth in Smolensk market; taxes may make me close that. Then what shall I do? I am old, I have my wife. *Akh,* life is impossible."

He came often to my room, late in the evening for he was at his stand from dawn till dark.

"The government is content to let us private merchants exist because they need us," he began. "We do bring certain supplies onto the market which perhaps would not reach there otherwise; so we may continue. Yet to-day I saw clearly their policy. They permit us to exist but tax us almost—but not quite—to that point at which we must close up shop. The *fin-inspector* (the tax commissioner) came to-day to my stand. 'How much was your income during the past six months?' he asked. I told him, 'About eighteen hundred rubles.' 'Well, we'll check that to see if it's true. If it is, your tax will be eight hundred rubles.' Just like that—setting it arbitrarily. And mind you, being 'deprived' means I have to pay more for everything. Where can I find eight hundred rubles? Borrow it? Interest rates here among private individuals are as high as fifty per cent. . . .

"Then the *fin-inspector* went to the neighbors in my apartment. He asked them 'Has Silverson's wife had a new coat? New clothes? Have they gotten new furniture? Are they talking about going away on a vacation? To where? For how long?' That's the way this Russian financial ministry stoops to check up on incomes—petty spying! If only I could find something else to do I should give up my stand, but, as one 'deprived,' I am barred forever from any government work. So they force us to continue private trading by closing everything else to us—and then try to stop us by preposterous taxes. The government is all-powerful. Tell me, what other government can fix prices, control supplies, determine incomes? Trade was possible for a few years after the new economic policy, in 1922, but now it is getting worse and worse and they can close us up when they wish. And the 'deprived' mark stays for life. What can I do? Life is impossible!"

"I don't see how you do any business at all with the prices you charge," I said.

"They call it speculating here," he replied bitterly. "I have two helpers. They go out to the villages and buy butter and eggs. The peasants would rather sell to us, for we pay higher prices than the government. We bring the goods to Moscow. Our taxes, our higher costs, and the pettiness of our operations necessitates our asking almost three times as much as the government stores. And our profits are small. But we have one advantage. The government sells everything by rations; just now it's three quarters of a pound of butter a month for each person. Whereas we can sell as much as the purchaser wishes. The government collects its butter and eggs in the villages. Then it figures out a minimum ration—and exports the 'surplus' to Europe to secure precious *valuta*. . . .

"Government power? What other government can determine how much butter its population shall eat per month? That is why food is scarce. I hear people saying, 'Food is scarce because the peasant keeps it and eats it himself—the peasant is eating too much.' What rot! I have been in villages last winter where the horses were killed for food. But I always reply 'That explains the firewood shortage also, I suppose. The peasants are eating too much of that, too?' Food is scarce because the government chooses to keep it scarce, and to export needed supplies abroad to get machinery that it doesn't know how to use.

"We *chastniki* do get supplies out of the village and bring them on the market. For those people who can pay there is all the butter they want—you foreigners use our private stands all the time, don't you? How else could you live here—on the official rations?"

He paused, then added, "You think me completely absorbed in this business of making a living? I think of nothing else just now . . . to keep myself from thinking of other things. How rapidly life changes! Twenty years ago in our little village there was quiet. I was just taking over my father's business. As a boy, I

remember how, on a winter's night in the big polished kitchen, our servant would tell us stories such as
you have never heard. Almost all the people in our
village were Jewish; we never mixed with the few
Russians. I never saw any oppressive anti-semitism for
we lived in a remote region. Every year the soldiers
would come to get out the conscripts and then there
might be trouble. My eldest son was going to be a
rabbi. . . . I feel more anti-semitism after this great
revolution, than I ever felt before. Particularly when
I travel in the villages.

"The peasants blame the revolution on the Jew.
Stupid, stupid Russians. Would there have been a
successful Communist party without the support of the
peasantry? They were the fools who brought it to pass.
Now the Communists say that peoples must mix, that
Jew and Russian must intermarry,"—he paused—
"they must not. We Jews are not like these lazy, vod-
ka-swilling, Tatar-blooded Russians. In every other
northern land the people are active, alert: laziness is
part of the tropics. Yet here in Russia . . . 'His children are far from safety and they are crushed in the
gate, neither is there any to deliver them!' "

He called me one evening about six. "To-day I
have not been in market—it is a religious holiday for
us. I am going to the synagogue now but I shall be
back about nine. Can you come to my room about
ten? My son will be there and I want him to meet
you. He is very much interested in America."

His room was on the sixth floor. "The many flights

of stairs are hard on my wife's heart," he said, greeting me, "but at least we have a room and a ceiling over it." His wife spoke little Russian and with a nasal accent. The son had not yet come. "He does not live in Moscow," Abram Mosevitch explained. "I am 'deprived' and since children suffer the same results therefrom as their parents, he works in Turkestan, he is an important Communist down there—he's in Moscow now for some conference. So he avoids any of the disadvantages of his father's deprivation—as it were, disowns me. That is the revolution!"

The son came late, about eleven, an overstuffed brief-case under his arm. "I am glad to meet an American," he said. "Tell me, do you know anything about cotton growing in your country?"

I confessed that I did not.

"You see, that is my work. We buy eighteen million dollars worth of cotton each year from America; now we are trying to raise our own in Turkestan and make ourselves independent of the West. We shall save that much *valuta* for other things. It is a fascinating problem; there in Turkestan we work with people who ten years ago were in the middle ages, living as though Tamburlaine had died only the day before. And now we are tugging and pulling them into the twentieth century; that is what the revolution means for them. Of course, we have a lot of backward customs to fight, conservatism and ignorance as well, but we are confident of winning. Don't you find life here exhilarating? We are moving so rapidly that everything in Europe must seem staid, flat?"

"You are moving but none of you know in which direction," said Abram Mosevitch. "Like the Jew who was caught riding on a train without a ticket, 'a rabbit' as they say in Russian. The conductor kicked him off. He climbed back and was booted off a second time. Again he climbed back. This time the conductor asked him 'Where are you going?' 'I don't know,' said the Jew, 'somewhere, wherever the train goes, if the seat of my pants holds out.' "

"You haven't changed much since I saw you last," said the son.

"How can I change? I am still 'deprived,' still a private merchant, overtaxed and kicked about . . . thanks to your Communist government."

"I have never known which you can least forgive— my being a Communist, or the fact that I married a *goy.*" (A none too polite word for "non-Jew.")

"Yes, that—but I can least forgive myself for choosing to come to Soviet Russia in 1919. I had lived all my life in Tsarist Russia, but when Lithuania was freed I should have stayed there. It is worse being *chastnik* in the Soviet Union than being a Jew in Ukraine before the revolution. Pogroms! Then death came quickly toward you; that is better than now, seeing life go slowly from you."

The son shrugged his shoulders. "What attracted you here? The rise of anti-semitism in Lithuania. The idea of equality of all nationalities, the fact that the value of the Jew would be recognized. No longer would the Jew be crowded into ghettos, barred from the big cities, put outside the Pale. No longer would careers in the army, in education, in government be closed to the Jew. Well, and so it is. Look at me—I have four thousand men under me, including Russians and a dozen other nationalities. I am playing a part in building our Soviet Union."

"And what part am I playing?"

The son had no ready answer—"Well, at least the government is equally severe with all private traders, whether they be Russian, Kalmuck, or Jew. . . ."

"But why should they be severe with anyone trying to earn an honest living?" Abram Mosevitch demanded.

"Because the principle of trading for private profit is wrong, because one must work for the State, for the common good."

"I should be willing to but being 'deprived' I can find no other work——"

"—And because the psychology of the petty trader, the petty bourgeoisie is a barrier to the achievement of socialism. Were you a socialist before the revolution? *Papasha*, there is a movement to get the Jewish traders out of the city and back on the land. A society organized by American Jews gives help to people in a predicament such as yours and once you work on the land the 'deprived' brand is removed."

"But I am too old to go to farming. And on what will your mother live while I wait for harvests? Antisemitism is strongest in the villages, among the peasants."

"*Papasha*," he reached in his briefcase for a newspaper, "did you see the report of these two trials? One concerned a father who, convinced that his paralytic baby was useless, gave him arsenic. He was held for trial. The other case was of a former White officer who annoyed a Jew living in the same apartment and made life so miserable for him that the Jew finally committed suicide. A case of the gross effects of anti-semitism! The officer came to trial also. To the man who killed his child the court gave three years and then, because he had committed no similar offense earlier, put him merely on parole. The officer was given," he read from the newspaper, " 'the highest measure of social defense,' that is, death by shooting. An example must be made of such a frightful case of anti-semitism. We punish these manifestations among the older generation and in the meantime we raise a younger generation that will never know anti-semitism. Young Jew and Russian now intermarry all the time, as I did. Thus, *papasha,* the Soviet Union keeps its word that classes will be treated unequally but that all nationalities here will be equal."

"Nationalities should be equal, but they need not mix. I am an orthodox Jew and you . . . I was raised to believe that the father heads his family and that his wishes should be obeyed."

"We have discussed that before. By the way, my wife is well and sends her greetings. . . ."

The old man was silent.

"Papasha, my wife sends her greetings, I said. . . . And we have another baby, Abram, we called him. I should have brought my wife but I knew you would not see her."

"You were wise, my son. I once told you, 'My son, keep thy father's commandments, and forsake not the law of thy mother. . . .' "

The son promised to call again before leaving Moscow and went away. Abram Mosevitch said to me, "I asked you to come to-night—it was so personal—for if there had not been an outsider here my son and I should have quarrelled."

A long time passed before I saw him again. He no longer lived in the same apartment house and, passing through Smolensk market I noticed that his stand was not there.

He came to my room one night with a burlap bag on his shoulder. "Do you want to buy any oriental rugs?" he asked. "If you don't, perhaps you can give me the addresses of other foreigners. I am doing this now, but even this is illegal. Rug selling has been made a State monopoly and I dare not carry them openly on the street. Hence the bag and at night."

"What happened to the butter business?" I asked.

"I had to stop—the government has been getting more severe and now taxes us out of business. It wants to control all the food supply. *Akh,* villains, they said my taxes were eight hundred rubles. I paid that. They returned and said there was a mistake—I must pay eight hundred more. If I had known it, I should have closed up before paying them that eight hundred. I had to close up anyway and I couldn't get the eight hundred back. There is no appeal. And I lost my room in this house. The house committee decided to expel all the 'deprived' from their rooms. I could do nothing. I was expelled."

"And where did you go?"

"I found a basement room with another family on Maroseyka. There is a Tatar rug merchant living there. I told him I knew some foreigners so he let me work with him. Here I am—do you want any rugs? And worst of all, they are planning to close our synagogue and turn it into a workers' club . . . *akh,* life is impossible. . . .

"What are we *chastniki* to do? There are various ways to get a living—dishonestly. Samuels, the butcher, you remember him? He is in jail for five years and when he comes out he will be barred from Moscow for five more years. Because there is never any accuracy in this country, when they gave out ration cards lots of extra ones fell into various hands. These ration cards were sold like meat or butter—eighteen rubles each. Samuels bought a lot of them. Then he had his relatives go to the stores on the days when they sold the ration of cotton cloth—you know, they are very short of it. With forty ration cards he managed to get about a hundred and twenty yards of cloth a week. He kept this in his apartment, and later peddled it out in the villages for five times what he paid for it. When he was caught, they found two thousand yards of cloth in his room—he had it hidden everywhere. And now he sits. . . .

"Other *chastniki* speculate in *valuta* on the 'Black Bourse,' or deal in contraband. Did you read of the trial last week? Some Jews in Riga opened an office and advertised 'Money forwarded to Russia.' To callers they explained that while the bank would only pay two rubles for each dollar sent, this company would pay three . . . so a lot of people gave them money to send. With these dollars they bought rubles in Riga —six for a dollar. They bribed a diplomatic courier to carry the rubles safely to Moscow. There was a whole system organized here. Three of each six rubles they forwarded as promised. With the balance, their profit, they bought diamonds and sent them back to Riga by the same diplomatic courier. Each month that pile of diamonds was their profit.

"The government caught one end of the network and pulled the whole system into court. Did you see the sentences? Three of the twenty caught were shot, the rest exiled or jailed, and the one woman mixed up in it was sentenced for three years. She had a child, whom the court ordered put in an orphanage, and she was declared 'deprived' of her maternal rights forever. She can never see the child again. They all were committing a crime against the State—but what else could they do? 'Deprived,' they are barred from the Labor exchange, they are not peasants able to go back to the land, yet their wives and children must not starve. Not these speculators but the government that makes such transactions necessary should go on trial. And now I am brought to this 'illegal' profession—peddling a few oriental rugs around when the government says that buying and selling such rugs is a State monopoly. . . .

"It is impossible to go abroad. Passports cost two hundred rubles, which must be paid when application is made. If the application is refused the money is forfeit. And very few people not going out on State business get passports—for that class passports cost nothing, of course. *Akh*, life is impossible. . . ."

He came again in November, on one of those autumn days when the heavy gray clouds come down to the pavements and the city walks benumbed and chilled through dripping fog. He seemed more worried than I had ever seen him.

"I had to stop the carpet business—I could sell nothing. Now that I am penniless I have heard of an opportunity! They have begun to sell machines here to weave stockings. Anybody can use them at home. The government counts such work 'honest labor' and perhaps I can have the 'deprived' mark taken off. Then my wife could go to the State hospital—she is sick.

"Earlier, when I had money, we didn't need such free aid—we could go to private doctors. But now! If I had two of those machines my wife and I could operate them at home and earn some kind of a living. Trading is impossible. But those machines cost a hundred and fifty rubles each—they are expensive for they come from abroad. Yet where can I find three hundred rubles? I cannot borrow it as I have no security. And how could I repay it? Yet here is a chance, perhaps, to make life bearable."

"Could you not write to your son?" I asked.

"Never—I have never asked him for help. If I

wrote, his wife would tell him to send the money . . . and I could not stand that."

Then, with the appearance of a man grasping at a last hope, he asked, "Can you lend me three hundred rubles?"

V

ANDREI GEORGIEVITCH: THE ENGINEER

HE is an architect, but by the Russian custom which classes all who work with plans and machines as engineers he is entitled to the green cap of their order. He wears it proudly. It is significant that most of the visible marks of the professions are gone, the student's cap, the professor's gown, the uniforms of the civil service; there remain only the badges of the soldiers and of the engineers.

It was Petr Petrovitch, formerly a lawyer, now, at nearly fifty, "a man about town," who first spoke to me about him. Petr called frequently, airing his virulent anti-Soviet opinions, seeking to know what I thought, especially interested in receiving clothes from abroad. He was always well dressed and his little moustache was neatly waxed.

This time he said: "You know, I found another room recently,—in the apartment of an engineer, Andrei Georgievitch. He expects soon to go to America. He has heard me speak of you and would like to meet you. Come with me now if you are free."

As we walked down Prechistinka, he explained, "Andrei Georgievitch is a very important man, and so busy. Scarcely home once a week. But he makes a lot of money, perhaps five hundred rubles a month. Engineers are better off than any other class in Russia—they are needed so much and there are so few. If only

I were one of them! They all get big salaries unless they are Communists. No, he is non-party. And what a charming apartment he has! And a lovely wife, Nadyezhda Ivanovna,—she was an actress in the Art Theatre. Happy man—and now he goes to America. Ah, how nice it would be if I could go to America! By the way, you don't know any foreigner coming from Berlin, soon, do you? I should so much like to have him bring me a pair of shoes, the latest sport style, an overcoat, and some cloth for a suit." As we turned into the courtyard of a new apartment house, he said, "What worries me most is moustache wax. I got a box from abroad a few years ago but it is almost gone. What shall I do then?"

Andrei Georgievitch, who seemed about forty, was most cordial. "Although I am very busy I have been studying English," he said. "But some of your technical descriptions puzzle me. If you could come once in a while and explain, I should be much obliged. Perhaps I can help you with Russian in return. That certainly is an easier language to learn than English."

He showed me his apartment. "We live very comfortably—everything we want." There were two bedrooms, a small living room, bath and kitchen. The maid's bed stood by the gas stove. There was electricity throughout. The furniture was new, ugly in its massiveness. A grand piano took up most of the space in the living room and forced the dinner table into one corner. "Our apartment house was built by a co-operative building society. We must pay so much monthly. The house has a tennis court and a court for *gorodki* (skittles). Of course we are very fortunate. It is very expensive, but we engineers are well paid. Some day, all of Moscow will live in houses like this." I noticed that the parquetry work was beginning to come unglued and that there was an inch of space between the baseboard and the floor. He understood my glance. "Oh, yes, poorly constructed, of course. These workmen of ours—no responsibility."

Nadyezhda Ivanovna, his wife, entered. She was well dressed, even to silk stockings. A blonde, heavily rouged, thirty years old perhaps, pretty but looking tired, as if running on the treadmill that would lead her back to twenty. Her first question was whether I had any foreign magazines showing what women abroad were wearing.

Andrei Georgievitch laughed. "My wife is interested only in clothes, music and, I hope, her husband." He smiled at her. "Of course, I shall have to leave her behind when I go to America, but it will be for only six months."

"I'll begin now getting ready the list of things I want you to bring me from Paris, Androusha," she answered.

There was tea, in glasses with silver holders, one of those expensive heavily iced cakes, and chocolates (at six rubles a pound). Petr Petrovitch joined us.

"When is the next lottery?" Andrei asked him, then to me: "Petr Petrovitch spends his time 'walking,' as we Russians put it; that is, he is unemployed."

"There is no place for a lawyer who knew Tsarist law in this lawless land," Petr growled.

"So with money he saved, he speculates in government bonds. Every bond has lotteries attached to it—some with prizes as high as fifty thousand rubles. He buys bonds of one series just before the drawings are held and sells them afterwards if he has not won a prize."

"I haven't won a prize for more than a year and then only a thousand rubles."

"I don't see how you keep on living, Petr. . . ."

"Everything gets worse and worse. Did you see about the sentence in the trial of Khalamov? He was an engineer. . . ."

Andrei nodded but said nothing.

"I heard to-day that, when his wife was taken to see him, just before he was shot, she wasn't allowed to go nearer than thirty feet. His last words were: 'Tell my friends not to think evil of me. I made no confession incriminating them.' The secret police guards began to drag him away but he shouted, 'The secret police tortured me until I signed a blank piece of paper.'"

Andrei replied, "I heard that story, too."

Nadyezhda Ivanovna interrupted, "You are always talking politics, Petr Petrovitch—forget it. I'll play the piano. I got a new American fox trot to-day—It's called 'Hallelujah.' Our Soviet music stores take a lot of your jazz music and add Russian words. Who says we aren't modern? Listen—this is called 'Tahiti' here. What was it called in America?"

"'Tea for two,'" I replied.

I saw him frequently, for his departure was chronically postponed. During the first months he spoke freely about his problems, describing his difficulties, but never complaining. The Russian language has had to go abroad for a word for "loyal"; he was *loyalnii* to the Soviet régime in everything he said. His father had been an engineer, killed in the war. Andrei Georgievitch had gone direct from technical school to the front in 1914; then he had served two years in the Red Army. His professional career only began in 1921 but he had risen to an important position as inspector of construction work. "Russia is a country for young men; I have gone up rapidly," he explained. "We need engineers so badly."

Petr Petrovitch was listening. "Wait till you get to America. There you will see a country really doing things," he remarked sarcastically.

"I am eager to go. But, I wonder, shall I find any real conception of what we are doing here? Our country covers a sixth of the globe, and we are trying to give it the factories, the roads, the power plants, that it has always lacked. Supposing all those things were destroyed in America to-morrow and you had to build them up immediately—that is what we are attempting, but without the experience of ever having had them, and with an illiterate population, with limited technical skill, and with little money. Have you studied the Five Year Plan?" he asked.

"The Five Year Plan is a joke," Petr Petrovitch interrupted. "All the figures in it were taken out of the blue sky; but now that the plan is part of the Communist creed, the blue sky has been made a sacred place! Change Russia to an industrial country in five years? Bah!"

"There are some here who joke about it," replied Andrei Georgievitch. 'What's the funniest story you know, in three words?' they ask. 'Five Year Plan.' At least it's unique. We have arranged a scheme for the unified development of all aspects of economic and cultural life of our country. It sets levels we must reach in industry, in everything, by 1933."

"Will it work?" I asked. Petr Petrovitch laughed.

"The first year looks good," Andrei Georgievitch explained, "although the cost of some of our achievements must be paid for by later generations. We go short on food now to build up some meager surplus for export and thus get foreign capital to buy the machinery we need."

"Yes," Petr Petrovitch interrupted, "as some peasant said, 'How fine it will be when each of us has an aeroplane. We can travel that much farther to try to find a dozen eggs.' Imagine having cloth, needles, rubber overshoes on ration cards as they now are. Where are there any signs of industrializing Russia, except for your statistics? There are fewer goods on the market. And no decent shirts, no decent woollen cloth, no good shoes. . . ."

"There are things more needed here than shirts, cloth and shoes. Not material things, either; but you wouldn't understand, Petr. As for material things we are putting what little money we have into electric stations, mines, foundries, cement works—primary undertakings that will provide the material to build your shirt and shoe factories. In the meantime consumable manufactured goods are scarce. If you cared to look, you would see that our pig iron production has increased tremendously in the past few months. But you don't use pig iron, Petr: therefore you say all the Plan is a failure."

"Well, if you say so—" Petr said sceptically. "But who can tell what is true when the Communists talk? With them it is always like the proverb, 'the dogs bark and the wind blows.' By the way," he asked, turning to me, "you don't know any foreigner soon coming from abroad? There is a *good* hair tonic in Berlin."

"I am glad you have nothing more to worry you than hair tonic," Andrei Georgievitch said. "But one of the problems in all Russia is with the poor quality of the labor. How can we build speedily? When we construct a building here, it takes us three months to erect the scaffold up which bricks and stone are carried. Hand labor is cheap here—and slow. If only we had your steel construction! That's what I shall study in America. Our workmen are inaccurate and careless. . . .

"How can we raise the quality of their labor? The revolution has not removed money as the chief incentive for working," he continued. "There is piece work in the factories and wages are still the sole end of labor. I once thought it might be otherwise; in those days we forgot that we were in Russia, on this planet, and not on some better world. A few months ago a factory near here won a money prize for having the best annual record. Did the workmen use the money to buy technical books or to start night courses? They went on a three days' spree which closed the mill."

"The workmen line up in front of every vodka store on Saturday," said Petr Petrovitch. "It takes more than a revolution to change a Russian."

"You might think," said Andrei, "that, in our Socialist state, you could tell them, 'Men, take pride in your work, these things are yours.' To the Communists and skilled workers that does mean something. The others only answer, 'How about raising our wages?'"

Nadyezhda Ivanovna entered. "Can't you men ever take an interest in anything in life except politics and economics?" she asked. "Come and talk to me. Tea is almost ready."

"In a minute, *milaya,* darling," Andrei Georgievitch answered.

"I know your minutes! Well, Petr Petrovitch, you come sing and I will play for you." They went out.

"There is always trouble with our superiors as well," continued Andrei Georgievitch. "In a private firm you are responsible to one head. Here you take orders from a half dozen government bureaus. One issues an order, then another, then a third contradicts both. And questionnaires! A department issued one last month with fourteen hundred questions and sub-divisions. If Soviet Russia ever goes under it will be from the weight of the orders, decrees, and resolutions of its bureaucracy! . . .

"Not far from Moscow a factory building was just being completed as the revolution began. It stood idle until some department decided it would be a place suitable for refining the rarer metals. Another department got the machinery, it was too large to go in the doorway, so the front of the building was removed. After the mill was rebuilt another department found that the machines were too heavy for the foundations; the plant stood on swampy land and the whole thing was in danger of sinking. The front was again torn down and the machinery taken out. It lay there to rust. Another department decided to use the plant to clean wool. Then it was found to be too far from the source of supply; so the mill stands idle to-day, the result of bureaucracy and red tape."

"But what about the Workers and Peasants' Inspection Commissariat?"

"Yes, that is an organ to investigate what they call looseness, sometimes counter-revolution, on the economic front. It is the busiest of all government departments for mistakes happen continually. A hydro-electric plant was begun in the Caucasus. It was discovered, after a million and a half rubles had been spent on it, that the river to operate it is dry nine months in the year. Again, another trust decided to concentrate all stores of horsehair at Kursk. Car loads from all over the Union moved on that city—but the department forgot to issue the order to provide storage space. And the cars still stand on the sidings."

"But in a country this size such things *would* happen occasionally," I said.

"Here these things happen continually and they cost us dear. Jail sentences follow in some instances; sometimes there are signs of sabotage. The Inspection Commissariat sometimes finds graft as well as red tape. You can't change the Russian civil service in eleven years. But we have eliminated most of the bribery and corruption. No, our difficulties are not from political rottenness."

He paused and opened an English grammar. "I am very much interested in what I shall see in America. Red tape in your government, yes, and perhaps corruption, yes, but in your business, ah, what is that word? Efficiency! We have neither the word nor the idea in Russian."

The door opened quietly and Petr Petrovitch came in. "What are you two babbling about?" he asked.

"Chiefly the English language," Andrei replied.

"Well, tea is ready," said Petr.

Through the open door Nadyezhda Ivanovna was singing,

> "A gypsy maiden I was born,
> Neath the wagon, near our fire.
> All my life have I been torn
> With passion's unrestrained desire."

"Andrei Georgievitch is not a member of the Party," his wife explained to me one evening while we waited for him to return from another journey of inspection. "He says, 'I am an architect and there is much for me to do. Let the Communists attend to politics.' Yet he is so busy, and recently so nervous. I wish he would go abroad: I see him little enough now. I gave up acting when we married but I am often tempted to re-

turn. Ah, the revolution—it has changed you all from
men into economic and political mechanisms!"

Her husband returned, tired. The authorities were
straining to increase production and headlines announced the rise or fall of output in factories and in
mines; there were gloomy editorials. People were be-
coming "production conscious," for the government
that owns both the factories and the newspapers was
intent on having its people realize that nothing mat-
tered more to the nation than what was being done in
those factories.

"The newspapers are saying that the figures of the
Five Year Plan are going to be hard to reach," said
Andrei Georgievitch after tea. "Goods, goods, and
more goods—material things to save the Soviet Union.
So the Five Year Plan says! Yet I see on every trip of
mine that we need more than goods. We need a new
attitude in our work."

"But what goods they make," said Nadyezhda Ivanovna. "I bought some silk chiffon to-day—eighteen
rubles a yard, and you can stick your finger through it."

"Yes. Remember what I told you earlier about government bureaus? Well, at the head of every industry
there is a trust which determines how much each of
its factories shall produce and how they shall operate.
Nothing is more important here than costs of production. Although our industries are government owned,
no individual stockholders, no fretting over dividends, no
banks to worry them—yet it is always a fight to bring
down our production costs. We are not efficient, we are
not skilled, and our costs stay high—in many lines

higher than in your capitalist world. The trust tells a mill, 'Your production costs must be cut twelve per cent.' And what results? If the director of the factory doesn't succeed, he and his staff will be replaced. So the easiest way to cut costs is to reduce quality."

"If you don't believe it, try these caramels," said Nadyezhda Ivanovna. "They taste of kerosene."

"To cut the costs the candy factory stopped using paraffin paper for wrapping and substituted something dipped in kerosene," Andrei Georgievitch explained. "From every side there are protests. One director admitted that fifty per cent of the satin he produced came back as worthless. A shirt factory had sixty-seven per cent of its output returned. . . ."

"The maid bought a can of sauerkraut and sausage this morning," said Nadyezhda Ivanovna disgustedly. "It used to cost seventy-six kopecks a can. Now it costs sixty-three—but there is only one little sausage in it instead of four as there used to be."

"Look at this in to-day's *Pravda*," replied Andrei. He read aloud: " 'The Tomsky laboratory found cans of fish that contained a mixture of sand, fish scales, entrails, even eyes. Twenty thousand cans from the Troisk factory marked "Lamb with Buckwheat" were filled chiefly with buckwheat—and bits of bone and hair!' The article concludes 'We demand immediate investigation by the courts.' "

"But how do such things cut costs?" I asked.

"They don't, of course. But a factory is ordered to produce so much and it does. Hurry! The Five Year Plan demands it. Director, Communist leaders, foremen—all combine, for they want to make a good showing. Just so they can say, 'We have produced more yet our costs are lower.' How to decrease costs, increase quantity yet still maintain quality is the problem which must be solved before the Plan can be realized. If we can't produce cheaper than the capitalist world, then what is the use of Socialism?"

"Do you think you can?"

"Sometimes I doubt it. I am afraid that the bureaucratic red tape, inefficiency, and the fetish of statistics will prevent us. A workman's wages are worth only as much as he can get for them in exchange: if he gets more in your capitalist West, if we can't produce more cheaply than you can, why continue this system? In that case the advantage of owning the means of production is only an empty and expensive honor. But I can never decide whether it is Socialism or Russia that causes the faults in our system."

"Andrei," his wife interrupted. "You waste your energy worrying. Why not do as other engineers? They take their salary, do their work—and not a bit more. Supposing it *is* Socialism? Or Russia? Can you change either one?" She left the room.

"The whole thing goes back to that fear of taking responsibility. There is a Russian saying, 'My hut is outside the village,' which means, 'I don't know anything about it.' The Communist group at the head gives the orders and each man strives to put them through his department in some fashion, assuming as little responsibility for their execution as he can. Then 'his hut is outside the village.' Every paper that goes out must wait for the signatures of four or five men—anything to avoid bearing all the blame for mistakes, to try to scatter responsibility. The result is that tractors go out without carburetors, shoes hold together for a week, and whom can you blame? Take the Clothing Trust. It sent out trousers with one leg shorter than the other. Anything to keep production up to the figures of the Five Year Plan! The workmen said, 'They'll fit, somehow.' The inspector said, 'We've got to keep up to the contract; they'll fit somehow.' The storekeeper said to the customer: 'Take what I give you and be glad you get these. There's a shortage in trousers.' And the customer said, 'I'll have to wear them. They'll fit, somehow.' So responsibility passes from man to man. . . .

"No factory director cares to take any responsibility. He always goes to the trust. Hence more paper orders! Sometimes it is pitiful. One director wrote to his trust to ask if he could give permission to the families of workmen employed in the mill to use the factory baths. And worse!"

"Why don't the well paid engineers take responsibility?" I asked.

"Because, unless they are Communists, they are afraid. Don't forget that, when the State owns the factories, politics and business mix. I am so eager to study the apportionment of responsibilities in your American factories."

In the room adjoining Nadyezhda Ivanovna was singing, from "Boris Goudonov,"

> Then be you mine
> And you shall be Tsarina

And all Russians shall be slaves
To your beauty.

Andrei Georgievitch stopped and listened. "Perhaps
it were better if I, too, could sing, if I didn't take things
so seriously—I seldom go to the opera or to the theatre.
No time! I am so busy, so tired. I sometimes think of
that place in the opera *Khovanshchino* where the choir
sings 'Give us back the good old days.' How the audience cheers, even now. . . .

"But I didn't know what things were like in those
days. I was a student—a socialist, of course. With the
revolution I saw a great chance for real work here—
not work for selfish gain but work that would help us
achieve the best in ourselves. We would be a new people. But now," turning to the newspaper, "I see the
production of rubber overshoes has fallen off ten per
cent in the last month."

The newspaper one morning announced the arrival
of thirty American engineers in Moscow, come to help
in construction work. Andrei Georgievitch spoke the
same evening of meeting them. Suddenly he turned
bitter. "These Americans, we make a myth of them.
They come here, and every one says in a hushed voice,
'Ah, the Americans come, ah, ah.' Are they better than
we Russians? If we only had the chance they have!
But, when we go abroad, what do people say? 'Huh,
here's another of those damned, stupid Russians!'"
Then he caught himself, embarrassed. "Oh, I beg your
pardon. . . . But this morning I felt bitter. Did you
see this?"

He offered me the morning paper and pointed to a

little black margined box on the front page, an announcement from the secret police that three engineers, found guilty of very serious sabotage, had been sentenced to death and that "the sentence has been carried out."

He had spoken very frankly with me of late. Perhaps he was less cautious because of his imminent departure, although he was always on his guard when speaking before Petr Petrovitch.

"Perhaps they were guilty. Do you know where the greatest weakness in this whole Soviet system lies? In the inherent weakness of its slogan, 'Workers of the world, unite!' The workers unite—what then? They can't run factories. What about the engineers? They are not capitalists, but they certainly are not proletarians. Where do they fit into the scheme? In this country, where factories are everything, the engineers have the power that will determine whether or not the scheme succeeds. Most of us are not Communists, but, I think, most of us are loyal. Yet, when the situation forces the Communists to give control of the things they most prize—their factories—into the hands of a group outside their 'Workers of the World,' naturally they watch that group with suspicion. . . .

"A monkey wrench in a machine can do more damage to the state here than many an assassination. Imagine the result of a little sabotage in one of our big power houses—thousands of dollars worth of government property can be destroyed in an instant. Such a thing is more than a sabotage here; it is a crime against the State, it is counter-revolution. Anti-Soviet elements long ago discovered this curious outgrowth of the revolution. Why shoot some babbling Commissar, who can be replaced by one talking even louder, when you can quietly flood a coal mine? Such sabotage there has been. When detected, it has been 'shot out.'"

"Doesn't that stop it?"

"Of course not. And the result has been increasing mistrust of *all* engineers by the proletarian government. We are intelligentsia, we surpass the workers in technical knowledge. Our knowledge they *must* have, but, to get it, they must let us at their machinery. They own all means of production but we, the Russian engineers, must operate them and construct others. And the result—constant mistrust on both sides. No engineer wants any responsibility, of course. It is too easy to be suspected of sabotage. . . .

"One of the Commissars said not long ago: 'We shall use the intelligentsia—even those hostile to the Soviet régime—and in the meantime try to win those who hesitate. But the intelligentsia must always feel over them the hand of the proletariat, which serves those who work honestly as a strong and friendly support, but which is heavy and harsh when it hits the head of an enemy.' His metaphors are a bit mixed, but there you have an admission that a class whose hearts do not beat with the proletariat is needed to help run the proletarian democracy. So they watch us, spy on us, suspect us. Does a manufacturer in America suspect his engineers? There you have one advantage in privately owned factories, which, would to God, we had here."

"But what about the new engineers, educated from proletarian stock?"

"The government does all it can to create this new group, rushing them through the schools, saying that practical work in the mill is more important than work in the laboratories. But one is not a master engineer after four years in technical school. They cannot replace us—yet. And there is little proof that when these proletarian lads are engineers they will still be proletarians: we get good salaries. 'Proletarian' engineers may be the solution but it is long before we shall have them."

Nadyezhda Ivanovna entered. "Can't you stop talking and let the American teach me how to play bridge? I hear it is all the rage abroad."

"In a few minutes, *milaya*," Andrei answered. He continued, "The strength of the Communist rule here lies in the factory proletariat. Thus factories take on a dual rôle. They are, economically, units for production; and, more important, they are political units. At the head of each factory is a Communist, who may know nothing about the machinery or the processes involved, and a technical director."

"Which is higher?"

"In theory, the engineer. But the workmen are regimented, and the Communist and his fellow Party members are the real control of the mill. The director says, 'We must spend a hundred thousand rubles for new machinery.' The workers may say: 'We do not need it . . . that is uselessly spending the government money. What are you trying to do—sabotage?' Or the

Communist leader may decide to send sixty workers out of the village for some political campaign. Their wages continue; yet production naturally drops and the technical director gets the blame. . . .

"Consequently, the technical men are very chary about criticising the workmen. The workmen criticise one another; that helps waste their time at meetings. But too much criticism of the proletariat may be taken as criticism of the Communist régime. The workmen become bosses. Let them boss. It is their factory, although it is our Russia. . . .

"And what happens? Some of the men in the Donbas coal-mine sabotage trial a year ago were guilty; some, perhaps, were not. No matter—make an example of them for all engineers. Production fell thirty-five per cent in those mines, while the workers held meetings and meetings and more meetings. A railroad engineer advised one railroad to junk a hundred locomotives. Then the workers set up a cry, 'This criminal waste is unnecessary, a crime against the revolution—therefore counter-revolution.' That was Khalamov, of whom Petr Petrovitch spoke the first night you were here. . . .

"Was it necessary? I don't know. Was it sabotage? I don't know. But I do know how easy it is to fall into the camp of those suspected of counter-revolution and how that delays my work. Why don't they go to the root of mismanagement, of poor quality, of bad workmanship—the entrance of politics into the factories? But who dares criticise the workers when they are the class that keeps the régime in power? Responsibility —I want none of it. Did I say I was a socialist? God knows what I am now. . . .

"So, when they have alienated their own engineers, when they smell sabotage in every suggestion we make, the government brings in those foreign engineers, pays them ten thousand dollars a year—and they make exactly the same suggestions we made earlier. Then they are applauded as masters of the most advanced American technique. But the foreign engineers need not fear politics while we, the Russians, must always be on the watch . . . the heavy hand of the proletariat."

There was a shout in the room adjoining. Petr Petrovitch burst in, bundles under his arms. "Andrei Georgievitch, Nadyezhda Ivanovna, congratulate me, congratulate me . . . uh . . . uh . . ." he was reduced to bleating. "I have won ten thousand rubles in the lottery drawing yesterday. Look, I have brought vodka. I shall go to the Caucasus . . . to the Crimea . . . perhaps I can get a passport abroad. . . . What I now can buy! . . . Nadyezhda Ivanovna, your health . . . oh, gentlemen. . . ."

Andrei was to have left for America on June 15th. He came to my room, however, about the 20th.

"Haven't you gone yet?" I asked him. We had already said good-bye.

He handed me a typewritten paper, which read, "This will inform you of the dissolution of the marriage between yourself and Nadyezhda Ivanovna Malutina." He stood silent for a minute, before he said, "She got a divorce while I was away last week, and the first thing I knew of it was this in the mail. That's the way things can be done here. Woman's rights and equality! I used to be in favor of them but this comes too close to home. Doesn't it seem like a madhouse to you, sometimes? She ran off with that old horseradish, Petr Petrovitch, and his ten thousand rubles. 'When gray comes in your hair the Devil begins to tickle your ribs. . . .' I was always suspicious of him—his nice clothes—there are ways of earning money in this country . . . carrying information—but I never suspected him of this.

"You know, our government has a lot of trouble with the people it sends abroad. Last week, when my wife left me, I was afraid they wouldn't let me go. They go to Europe and then, in the calm of life there, free from the nervous strain here, they don't want to come back. If they like luxuries, if they like rest . . . those things are not here. So they refuse to return, and all that government money is wasted and another engineer lost. Or worse, Chaliapin—and Chekov, our greatest actor. There have been many, chiefly non-Communists, of course. Why do the aviators who fly out each day to Königsberg in Germany, have to be married? So that there is something here which will bring them back. With my wife gone I have nothing to bring me back. Hostages!! I was afraid they wouldn't let me go. But those fears are groundless. I am going—the day after to-morrow. . . .

"And now I do not want to go. I am afraid of so many things that I shall see in your land. I shall be made conscious of so much that we now lack and of much more that we shall never have. Things I want —no, not silk stockings and cabarets, chocolates and forty-story buildings. I am afraid that after a trip abroad Russia will no longer be my homeland . . . it will be a place of exile."

I read sometime later, in an anti-Soviet newspaper published in Paris, a headline: "Another engineer refuses to return to Soviet Russia." There followed a brief account saying that Andrei Georgievitch had overstayed his leave abroad, had refused to obey several summons to return, and had committed suicide. The dispatch was written in gloating fashion, as if to imply that the news proved some cherished point or other.

VI

PAVEL VASSILITCH: THE WORKER

HE lives in a little town near Moscow, in a "one hundred per cent proletarian centre," where the whole population works either in the "Red World Brick Yards," in the "Dzherzhinsky Cotton Mill"—named in memory of the head of the Secret Police, or in the "Rosa Luxemburg Nail Factory"—named in memory of a German Communist. The town and its industries formerly belonged to a Russian nobleman.

For forty years Pavel Vassilitch has wheeled clay from the quarries to the mixing machines in the brick mill. The clay has browned his skin, except where the veil of small-pox left its marks, but it has not bent his back. He stands erect at sixty. The rim of hair around his bald head has greyed, and there is grey in his short black beard. He wears old, dusty clothes, a Russian blouse and cap, and is indistinguishable amid the crowd of workmen dragging their way down the dusty street at nightfall.

His wife, a shapeless fat woman, has given him seven children, of whom only a son and daughter are alive. Her face is marked with the deep lines of hard work. Her voice is sharp and loud—the sort of voice that dominates at the street corner when a crowd of housewives, in line before the store for their rations, discuss the latest gossip.

I first met Pavel Vassilitch on one of the suburban

trains out of Moscow. He was very friendly and asked for my Moscow address. He stopped in at my apartment several times and, on each occasion, asked me to visit him at his home. "There is a man I want you to meet," he always added. I promised to go and he offered to come for me.

One Saturday night we took a squeaky, poorly lighted, suburban train, bumped along for an hour, and got out with a few other passengers at the town. Everything was dark, except for a few scattered electric lights. He lived at the edge of the town, in a pair of rooms on the first floor of a two-story frame building. His wife made tea for us on a little kerosene stove.

"Has Alexei called?" he asked her.

"Yes, he said he would meet you at the *pivnaya*— the beer hall," his wife replied.

"And Sasha?"—speaking of his daughter.

"She's out with Dmitri. I don't trust that man, Pavel. He knows that she is going to have a baby, but he never says anything definite about registering marriage with her," she said sharply. "Says he'll have to find a new room before he can do it. As if he couldn't come and live here!"

We went down the main street to the *pivnaya*. A long narrow room was crowded with men seated at little tables. The walls were bare except for a few signs: "Don't Spit On The Floor," "Intoxicated People Are Not Admitted," "Vodka Not Sold. Those Bringing It Will Be Put Out." Waiters in dirty aprons waddled about with mugs of beer. A fat waitress went from

table to table peddling boiled crayfish. At one end of
the room was a little platform with an ancient painted
backdrop showing the garden of some Italian villa.
There was a piano and, as we came in, a man was
singing.

Pavel Vassilitch led me to a table where there sat a
tall thin man with drooping gray moustaches that gave
him a discouraged appearance. Pavel introduced me to
his friend, Alexei Mikhailovitch, with one phrase,
"Here's the American!" Then to me he explained,
"Alexei has been in America and the lies he tells! I
wanted you to meet him so I could find out just what
was true." Alexei seemed slightly embarrassed and
tugged at the ends of his moustache.

"In what part of America were you?" I asked.

"In *Sharpsveel—pa*," he replied cryptically. I didn't
understand and he explained, "That's near Peets-
bourg—pa. I came back before the war. I couldn't learn
your English language and I was lonesome. But what
a fool I was!" He sighed deeply.

Alexei had been in America too long ago for any com-
parisons. Pavel soon lost interest and conversation returned to life in the little factory town.

"*Akh*, the ration lines at the stores," said Alexei.
"They lengthen steadily and our old women are always kicking. That's Communism for you—we workers can't get enough bread, kerosene or even salt. As
for the peasants——!"

"They say it will be better when we have food cards.
They will be in force next week," said Pavel. "Then
there will be a definite amount for everybody."

"Food cards—the free supplements to the magazine called 'Our Achievements!' " Alexei spoke disgustedly. "Ask the American if there are food cards in his country where you say the capitalists are exploiting the workmen. They may exploit them but they don't starve them! But what can you expect of a government that confiscates even its workers' savings?"

Pavel explained to me, "Alexei had two thousand rubles saved in a bank in 1918. When our government nationalized all banks he lost his money."

"Just like any *bourzhui!* You might have thought I was an exploiter of the working class instead of a machinist who has spent thirty years at the lathe. *Akh,* everything gets worse and food supplies grow smaller. The minute the government puts its hands on anything it always disappears—just like my bank account. It's like the story——"

As he paused to finish his beer, and nibbled at the small plate of boiled peas that accompanies beer in the *pivnaya,* a young man came to our table. He wore a long black overcoat with astrakhan collar and a heavy old cap, the top unbuttoned and pushed far back over his head.

"This is Georgei Lukitch, the chairman of the factory committee in the textile mill," said Pavel.

Alexei greeted him and said, "I was just telling that story about prostitution. The 'important birds' in Moscow met one day to discuss ways to meet the increase in prostitution. 'That's for my department,' said the Director of Education. 'Give me a million rubles and I will combat it.' Everybody said that was too much.

'That problem really belongs to me,' said the Director of the Health Department. 'Give me a half a million rubles and I will propagandize against it.' That also was too much. They talked for five hours before someone said, 'We're all wrong. This is a matter for the Department of Trade. Prostitutes are goods, like bread or flour or cotton cloth. Well, we gave the Director of Trade all the bread; now there isn't any more. We gave him all the flour; now that's all gone. Give him control over rationing out the prostitutes and they, too, will disappear!' "

Georgei smiled and said, "The trouble with you, Alexei, is that you want things to happen as fast as in America. You forget that this is Russia."

"Everything is worse. Here, ask Pavel—he's not been in America. Pavel Vassilitch, aren't things worse?"

"Well. . . ."

"Before the revolution you had a whole house. Now you have only the first floor," Alexei insisted.

"Yes, that is worse," said Pavel decisively.

"But you worked twelve hours a day before the revolution, didn't you?" Georgei asked. "Now you work seven."

"Yes, that is better."

"But your wife has to stand in line sometimes five hours a day for food and clothes," Alexei pointed out. "That makes twelve hours the family works."

"Yes, perhaps that is true."

"Before the revolution you got forty rubles a month, didn't you?" Georgei demanded. "Now you get eighty-five."

"Yes," the old man rubbed his chin. "That is so."

"Look at prices! Boots cost four times as much when you can find them; everything is more than double the price," Alexei spoke with conviction. "And everything gets scarcer. They tell about the new department store they are going to open in Moscow, ten stories high, everywhere the latest American machinery and, most marvellous, needing only one man to operate the whole store."

"I didn't hear about that," said Pavel, taking him seriously.

"Yes, his job will be to stand at the door and cry, 'No goods of any sort whatsoever on hand.'"

"Sometimes you seem like a plain counter-revolutionary type," said Georgei. "Why I haven't had you dismissed long ago——"

"Have some more beer, Georgei," Alexei laughed. "I have seen workmen in other countries whose wives aren't always nagging them about decreasing food supplies and the rotten quality of the goods they buy. But the Russian workman was always a fool. Remember the old story about the gift the King of England sent to the Tsar? It was a life-size model of a flea and it walked. The Tsar, jealous, therefore ordered the finest workmen in Ryazan to surpass the English. They worked for three months and returned with the same flea, saying they had beaten the English. They asked the Tsar to look at it. He did and cried, 'Now it won't go at all.' 'Of course not,' they said, 'but we have excelled the English.' They told him to get a microscope. Then he saw that they had put horseshoes on the flea!"

"It would be better if you made concrete suggestions to help the Russian workman instead of telling old stories," Georgei said. "You don't hear Pavel complain, do you?"

"He is wise—what can one man do?" Alexei asked. "But if you want concrete suggestions—let them send better shoes to our store. A friend of mine, a quiet innocent sort of man, went into a store here. He asked for shoes and tried one on. It was just as if he had stepped into a bear trap. Nails went into his foot. He screamed and he howled. What had he done to deserve such punishment? After fifteen minutes they cut away the shoe and carted him off to the hospital. There's a suggestion—don't let factories send out shoes like those."

"You boast about America, old man. Don't mistakes ever happen there?"

"You know as little about America as the peasants that Kalenin was addressing in a village one day. 'How are things?' Kalenin asked. 'Rotten,' some peasant called out. 'Look at our clothes, bark sandals for shoes, rags for stockings, anything we can get for pants, and flour bags for shirts.' 'Yes,' said Kalenin, 'but think of the American Indians. They have no clothes at all to wear.' One old peasant lit a cigarette and said, 'Very likely true, Comrade Kalenin, but perhaps they've had the Soviet system longer over there.'"

Pavel laughed. Georgei asked with some heat, "See here, Alexei, would you like to have the Tsar back?"

"What?" Alexei asked, surprised. "Of course not! But I should like to reach the levels which I have seen in other countries where there are also no Tsars. In the meantime your Communist Party talks about what a paradise it will be in the future—and food supplies diminish steadily! 'Why do you complain, comrades?' Kalenin asked a group of peasants. 'We have no shoes,' they replied. 'Akh, fools you are,' he said. 'Whoever heard of anyone wearing shoes in Paradise?'"

None of us had paid any attention to the concert. There was the loud hum of conversation on all sides and the performers were singing under difficulties. The smoke in the room was as thick as autumn fog. Alexei rose and said, "Well, it's time for me to go and snore." He said good night and left.

"He's the best mechanic we have," said Georgei as he saw Alexei go out. "He works well, but if he talked like that around the mill I'd soon have him fired."

"Where did he find all the stories he tells?" I asked.

"Those anecdotes? They go from mouth to mouth —he comes every night," said Pavel, "and you can always hear stories like that in the *pivnaya.*"

"It's too bad he never goes to the club," said Georgei.

"It's lonesome there," Pavel said.

"Yes," Georgei replied, "we must do something about our workers' club. Dmitri, who directs it, seems to have lost interest. We were talking about that at the Party meeting on Wednesday. We can't attract the workmen out of the *pivnaya* into the club unless we can interest them. The young people come, but not the older ones."

The crowd was beginning to leave. Paval paid our bill and we went out into the snow covered street. The cold, at fifty below, was breaking a forty year record. Georgei asked me if I could stay until Monday to see the factory. I declined. "Well, I'll come up to your house to-morrow," he said as he left us.

Sasha, Pavel's daughter, was at home when we arrived. She was a well built woman of twenty, with very wide red cheeks and large reddened hands, a worker at one of the machines in the textile mill. It seemed as if she and her mother had been quarrelling. She said very little and went behind a screen in one corner of the large dining-living room where she slept. I was given a bed behind a screen in an opposite corner of the same room. Pavel and his wife slept in the kitchen. Before the silence of the winter night settled over the house I heard Pavel's wife say to him, "Sasha says that she and Dmitri are going to the marriage registration bureau Monday."

We breakfasted on tea, black bread, and sausage in the combined dining-living-bedroom. It was comfortably warmed by a tiled stove built into the wall. The floor was carpetless. The walls were whitewashed and bare except for two lithographs of Lenin, one showing him as a child of three. An electric bulb, without a shade, hung from the ceiling. In the kitchen, cooking was done on a little brass kerosene stove that stood on a table. On a wall nearby hung the "washstand," a container filled with water with a plunger beneath. Pressing the plunger released a trickle of water that splashed into a bucket below.

Pavel was busy after breakfast chopping beef with

an axe in a wooden trough, for the meat cakes for
dinner.

Georgei Lukitch came an hour later. He nodded to
Sasha who was making herself a dress on an old portable sewing machine, and began to talk with Pavel
about the factory.

"We are up to our throats in work," he began. "Moscow orders us to increase production twelve per cent before October. At present we are far from reaching
that figure. We have about six hundred workmen, of
whom only a hundred and twenty-five are Communists. . . ."

"Georgei is chairman of the factory workmen's committee," Pavel interrupted. "He controls everything
connected with the interests of the workmen. And he
heads the Party group at the mill. So he is responsible for having all Party orders carried out: he's the
most important man in the factory."

"You forgot there is also the technical director,"
Georgei continued for my benefit. "Our problem now
is to make non-Party workmen take the interest in our
problems that they should. Some of the foremen are
no better. 'Alleluia, thank God, everything's in order,'
they say so long as the mill runs. That's all they care
for. There is no discipline in the mill. We had a frightful accident last week, just from carelessness. Some
men on the day shift were repairing a machine but
didn't finish their work. They forgot to tell the night
shift, who started the machine. Steel flew everywhere.
If Alexei Mikhailovitch hadn't run in and risked his
life to throw the switch we'd have torn out half the
mill."

"I heard that Vorovkin was responsible," Pavel said.

"Yes. The court will sentence him to six months' enforced labor."

"What does that mean?" I asked.

"He must work in the factory but gets no wages for six months," Georgei explained. "We must make our workmen realize that it is their factory. The amount we spend replacing mislaid tools and parts broken because of carelessness! The director of the factory is non-Party of course and he doesn't want any responsibility. He does little to lower the percentage of cloth spoiled. So long as the plant runs he is content. But he'd better remember that the director of a mill in Shermetovka was dismissed for continually falling below the required production figures!"

"Have you carried on a campaign of 'self criticism' here?" I asked. "Self criticism" was adopted all over the Union as a means of encouraging workmen to bring to light flaws in the industrial mechanism.

"Yes," said Georgei sadly, "but it's not very successful. We arranged that workmen could hand in any criticisms which they felt were justified. We printed some in the factory paper but many were anonymous and most of the remarks were personal: 'Antonov drinks himself out of his mind,' or 'Why didn't Vanyetov appear at work Monday? Find out the girl he had in the woods Sunday night.' Those comments don't help us raise production, make our workmen more careful, or help us decrease the percentage of breakage. Besides, the non-Party workers are afraid to criticise us Communists."

"It is the same at the brick factory," Pavel interrupted, coming from the kitchen. "Our breakage is too high and the quality of the bricks is poor. We had a carload returned yesterday from Moscow."

"We organized 'shock brigades' and 'light cavalry' among the workers, mostly the Communists, and, especially, the Young Communists. They worked hard to find ways to cut costs and to improve conditions. Thanks to their work the factory director had to order Platonov to clean up the factory restaurant. It was filthy. The dishes were often used a second time without being washed. Everybody complained but no one did anything until the 'shock brigade' went into action. Yet 'self criticism' should have remedied this long ago."

"Self criticism?" Alexei Mikhailovitch came in, stamping the snow from his boots. "You might as well 'Sit by the sea and wait for weather' as to expect that to improve conditions. Workmen have no personal interest—they take their wages and they know they'll get them whether the percentage of damaged goods is high or low. One thing the revolution did—it made it impossible to fire any ordinary workman from a factory. No matter what kind of work they do they hold their jobs because they are of the proletariat and this is the Workmen's Paradise. Your Communist Party can't afford not to pamper the workmen; its power rests on them. Self criticism? Did you hear about Stalin and Rykov? Rykov was in his office one day when he heard frightful profanity coming from Stalin's office next door. He stuck his head in and found Stalin alone, swearing." Alexei gave a very literal imitation. " 'Get out of here,' said Stalin. 'Have you gone mad, swearing at yourself?' Rykov asked. 'No, this is my weekly hour of self criticism,' Stalin replied."

"You might apply a little self criticism to yourself," said Georgei. He quoted the proverb, " 'If you look in the mirror don't blame it for the spots it shows.' "

Then Pavel turned to Georgei and asked, "How are plans for the new housing going?"

"In Spring we shall start building four-story apartments. Each family will have three rooms. There will be one common kitchen for the whole house and a nursery. American engineers are coming to build them. Everything here will be better . . . everything is much better now, isn't it, Pavel Vassilitch?"

"Well. . . ."

"The town didn't have a library or a big hospital before the revolution, did it?"

"No, that is better."

"You didn't get a month's vacation with pay before the revolution, did you?"

"Yes—that is better."

Alexei interrupted, "Before the revolution you didn't have to contribute to State loans, to the Society for Defense against Air Warfare, to the Society for Automobilization, and to the Society for Homeless Children, did you? Those things amount to a month's pay."

"Yes," Pavel answered haltingly, "yes, I guess they do."

"Haven't you learned to read and write since the revolution?" Georgei asked.

"Yes," said the old man positively, "that I have done."

"There," said Georgei to Alexei. "What can you say against that?"

"What do you give him to read now that he is no longer illiterate? Communism, propaganda! Make your workmen believe that a World Revolution lies just around the corner, and that, if they will make sacrifice after sacrifice, the world proletariat will come one day to their rescue. That's what I have against Communism—if you devoted all your energies to building up Russia for Russia's sake I'd be in your Party too. But you have to keep foreign Communist parties going—and all the time Russia pays for the dreams of a Soviet State of the World, with Moscow and little Jewish Communists running it."

"That's enough," said Georgei. "Don't be anti-Semitic in addition." He rose and took his coat. "Let's walk around town," he said to me. "This old horse-radish can sit here and foam at the mouth."

As we walked through the snow-banked streets, past long rows of log houses, their chinks stuffed with gray moss, he said, "Alexei never looks far enough ahead. To be sure we make sacrifices now. Food cards will give us each two pounds of sugar a month, yet there is plenty of Soviet sugar on free sale in Latvia. We export all we can of flour, of cloth, of everything we lack here. We deny our own people in order to get foreign currency from our exports. With that foreign currency we can buy abroad the machines we need to build our own industry.

"All this speeds the World Revolution—although that old fool can't see it. Look at our position. The government owns the factories, the banks, the raw materials. Our industries pay no swollen profits to investors or owners. In a few years we shall be able to dump our manufactures abroad at any price, and always cheaper than the capitalists. Right now my mill is underselling your American textiles in Persia. We shall be the world's largest dumping nation, and the more we dump abroad the more we will increase unemployment and discontent—among foreign workmen. Revolutionary situations will arise which our foreign Communist parties can use."

We entered a little park. In the centre stood a low sprawling villa of dirty white stucco, the former residence of the factory owner. Now it was the club for all the workmen in the town.

On the first floor there were rooms with cribs and little cots where mothers could leave their children while they worked. The basement, fitted with stoves and benches, was the public bath-house. As we went upstairs a young man, with bushy black hair and very thick eyeglasses, joined us.

"Hello, Dmitri," said Georgei. "Sasha tells me that you and she are getting married to-morrow. This is the director of the club," he added, introducing me.

Dmitri nodded assent in an absent-minded way and asked to be excused. "I am very busy to-day helping the Pioneers [the Communist 'boy scouts'], who are giving a play next week."

The whole second floor had been turned into an auditorium. In one corner was a statue of Lenin. Everywhere there hung banners and posters, white letters on faded red muslin, flaunting the popular slogans before the people: "Maintain the Quality of Our Products," "Keep Down the Percentage of Damaged Goods," "Prepare a Defense Against the Capitalists Who Are Arming Against Us." Everything seemed dusty and shoddy. On the wall behind the platform, framed portraits of Lenin and Stalin hung crookedly.

"We use this room for moving pictures twice a week," Georgei said, "and there is usually some sort of a meeting on other evenings. But the men complain— you heard them last night. Dmitri should be thinking of new ways to attract crowds here. There is little culture in a *pivnaya*," he added as we turned toward home.

We came home to find Pavel's wife raging in fine fury. "I went to the store to get some beef," she was repeating, "a pound and a half. The clerk gave me a nice piece, without a bone. Then he cut off a quarter of a pound of meat and made up the weight with that amount of *ham* bone. Of course I protested but he only said, 'Citizen, we must share alike with everyone—so much meat, so much bone.' I threw it in his face and left."

"You should not be surprised at anything that happens in Soviet Russia," said Alexei, consoling her. "We're all like the peasant woman at a fair who saw a camel for the first time in her life. She looked at it for half an hour and said, 'Just see what these damned Bolsheviki are doing to horses!' "

I met Pavel Vassilitch on a bus in Moscow two months later. "My daughter is in a Maternity Home here. She expects her child to-day. Come with me while I go down there to inquire."

"Where's Dmitri, her husband?" I asked thoughtlessly.

"In jail, where he belongs—and he isn't her husband." He postponed further explanations as we entered the Home.

It was a new building, smelling heavily of drugs. A nurse in gray took his name and went upstairs, leaving us to wait in the corridor. From a distance came sounds of pain, of crying. "They give no anæsthetics in a State Home like this," said Pavel as he paced the corridor nervously. "That's why nobody likes to have to live anywhere near them."

The nurse returned after ten minutes saying: "It's a boy, seven pounds, born this afternoon. She is all right —do you want to send a note up to her?" He scribbled something and we left the building. "They never let outsiders, not even husbands, into the rooms," he said. "But everything is free."

Suddenly he turned, "You remember the day you visited my family? That same night that scoundrel Dmitri left town and took with him four hundred rubles of the club funds. He went to Crimea. They caught him a month ago and sentenced him to eight years in prison."

"That's pretty severe," I said. "A murderer last week only received three years."

"Had he been non-Party he'd have gotten two years or so. But you see, he was a Communist. He is therefore expected to have a greater sense of responsibilities and when he hasn't he must pay more heavily. And, what is more important, he took State funds."

"But what about your daughter? Doesn't he receive punishment for that?"

"No, they may do as they wish in such private affairs. But he'll have to support the child, of course."

The Moscow newspapers, which devote more space to news of happenings in Soviet factories than they do to dispatches from abroad, were emphasizing the old slogans more than ever that September: "Keep up Quality," "Fulfill the Figures of the Five Year Plan." The first year of the nation-wide plan for building up Soviet industry in five years was nearly finished. In addition newspapers were publishing reports of *chistki*, the periodical "cleanouts" of "social-dangerous elements" from factories, offices and Party. Wanting to see a *chistka* in operation, I went out to the town where Pavel Vassilitch lived.

The railroad siding was crowded with old freight cars. The factory chimney was belching forth black smoke. Across the main street hung a huge sign, "Socialist Competition Is the Accelerator of Our Industry." Georgei welcomed me warmly in his office. "*Chort*, the devil, we are working like horses. We have just finished a *chistka* in the factory and in the Party group too. We have a factory meeting to-day, at four. You'll be welcome. In the meantime, take a guide and go around the mill. We finish the party *chistka* at a Party meeting to-morrow. That's for members only. We don't believe in 'sweeping the trash out of our huts on to the public street.'"

He introduced me to a young workman who was overly anxious in trying to show me everything. From all walls hung slogans about 'Socialist Competition.' In the vestibule was a huge poster, a "wall paper," with column after column of typewritten articles and paragraphs. "We prepare one of these each month," my guide said. "The whole factory reads it." One column was labelled "Self Criticism." It contained many paragraphs, among them:

"An anti-alcohol club was organized a few months ago and nothing has been heard of it since. Is the director, Comrade Loshadyenko, spending too much time in the *pivnaya?*"

"The autobus from the station to Gryaznaya Sloboda has no stop before the cooperative store. This is very inconvenient for housewives with heavy bundles."

"Why can't the cross be taken down from the former St. Sergius' Church in which a children's nursery has just been organized?"

"The washroom on the first floor is damp and dirty. Why can't it be cleaned?"

"Some people are taking the empty spools out of their machines and throwing them on the floor. Bad accidents can result if anyone slips on them. Let baskets be provided for these spools."

The factory meeting, scheduled for four, did not begin until five-thirty. Several hundred people gathered in the auditorium of the clubhouse. On the platform stood a table decked with red bunting, holding water carafes and ashtrays. Georgei presided.

"The committee has completed the *chistka* in the Dzhershinsky Textile Mill," he began. He then announced the names of those dismissed for being irresponsible workmen, those dismissed for idleness, breakage, and carelessness, and those dismissed for belonging to "social-hostile groups." "Molotov concealed from us that he is the son of a wealthy peasant, Galidov's father-in-law keeps a private store in Moscow, and Dryanov"—a laugh arose at the name, which means "trash" in Russian—"fought in the White Army. Those 'cleaned out' can appeal to the committee." He also announced the results of the Party *chistka*. One member was dismissed for breaking Party discipline, five for continual drunkenness, and two for belonging to "socially strange classes."

"I want also to tell you about the first results of our agreement for 'socialist competition' which we signed with the Red Textile Mill in Ivanovo-Vosnesensk. We promised to cut down damaged goods by seven per cent. Comrade, we have reduced it by eight per cent." There was great applause. "We agreed to cut down the number of days lost per month by drunkenness, idleness, and disorder by fifty per cent. One year ago, in September, we lost forty-four labor-days from those causes. This past month we have lost but thirty, and four-fifths of them were due to Bubnov, whom we have just 'cleaned out of the mill.'" The applause was even louder.

"We promised to increase our production by eleven

per cent. We shall increase it by fifteen per cent before November, when the new English machinery is put in place." The applause was terrific.

Endless speeches followed. One speaker was Alexei, who spoke briefly: "You know, comrades, I have been in America. The thing that makes life go forward there is competition. Now that we have introduced 'socialist competition' between factory and factory and shift and shift, we too shall go forward. My shift hereby challenges shift number three to increase their production of cloth by fourteen per cent next month!"

Georgei spoke once more. "Comrades, in honor of the anniversary of the revolution next month our factory should send a gift to the government in Moscow. The brick factory is sending a car of bricks and the nail factory has prepared a head of Lenin done in nails. Let us send a car of cloth—and we shall have a committee go with the train to Moscow and present it!"

He met me after the meeting. "You'll have to stay here to-night," he said. "You have missed the last train. I am living now with Pavel Vassilitch, I married Sasha last month, and I am afraid there is no room with us. You'd better stay with Alexei."

"What a change I found in Alexei this evening!" I said.

"Yes, he has a different viewpoint now. Our plant was running poorly until a few months ago. Discipline was bad and the factory director, a non-Party engineer, fought with me. Then from the Party control in Moscow came orders to introduce 'socialist competition.' That is, shift and shift, factory and factory, vie with each other to improve their work. At first it was hard to arouse enthusiasm; there was no extra pay to be gained by harder work. But the idea attracted them —at least, here. Alexei and others became enthusiastic. In other places it has not been so successful."

"Are you going to introduce the 'five day week' also?" I asked. Plans were being made to rearrange working days in all offices and factories in the Union so that everybody might have five consecutive days' work and one holiday, one group being free on Monday, the next on Tuesday, thus arranging that work goes on seven days a week throughout the year except on legal holidays.

"We are going to begin it next month," he replied. "It may be confusing at first, but we are intent on using all our power to fulfill our share of the Five Year Plan."

We left the club and walked out into what had been the gardens. Everything was dusty and dirty. From one corner of the garden came cries of "out, out, out." A group of young people were playing volley ball. Behind the house we could hear the noise of the clash of clubs on hard clay; there was a game of *gorodki*—skittles—the most popular game of the villages.

"Sasha, Pavel's daughter, has been put in charge of the club," Georgei said. "She has helped organize physical culture here. She has put in ping-pong tables and she wants to get enough money together so that we can build a tennis court next year. Money is what we need; we are so poor. The average wages in the factory are seventy rubles a month; and the vodka stores still do the best business in our town."

Alexei lived near the railroad. On our way we passed long rows of old freight cars. From the distance it looked as if people were living in them. I asked Georgei.

"People do live there, the seasonal workers who come from the villages to help in the brick yards in summer." As we came nearer the wind bore testimony to the simplicity of the sanitary arrangements. "They do have to live like hogs but they are peasants and used to it. We have planned for two years to build barracks for them but we have never had enough money. Now our factory is making a profit and perhaps we shall be able to build them next year.

"This year we wanted to house them in two of the churches which we have closed. There were five churches here altogether. One is now open and that's enough. We took the copper bells from one church and sold them for enough money to build a radio loud-speaker for our club. Everybody comes to the club Sunday mornings to hear it. But there are still conservative people among us! The town Soviet decided not to use the churches for barracks because the seasonal workers are from peasant families, good Orthodox Russians, and they might therefore refuse to live in the churches. Did you ever hear such nonsense?"

Farther down the railroad stood a long line of cars loaded with bricks. "We loaded them last Sunday," Georgei explained. "The brick factory fell behind its production standard so the workers from all the factories came down here and worked eight hours that day to load these cars—all without pay. Would your workmen in America do the same if the factory owner got into a jam? Here they do it because they, the workers, own the factories." He turned back when he reached Alexei's.

"Of course you can spend the night," said Alexei, "although everything is crowded with potatoes."

"Potatoes?"

"Yes, some government trust made a mistake and gathered all the potatoes in Russia, it seems, and shipped them on to Moscow. There was insufficient storage space for them so they asked the workmen to buy all they could at reduced prices; they even had a competition to see who could buy the most. I think I won. Lord, I've potatoes under the beds, under the table—my old woman says she feels as if she slept on potatoes. She's away now for two weeks."

"I was surprised at your speech to-night," I began, after Alexei had set the kettle for tea.

He smiled rather innocently. "I laughed at the idea of 'socialist competition' when it was first suggested. It seemed like another way to trick the workmen without increasing their pay—like these 'voluntary labor Sundays' when, if you don't load bricks, you may find your name on the 'black list' at the factory. Then Georgei talked to me, appointed me head of my shift, and set another shift to compete with us. They were more experienced workers and beat us the first week. That was the last time. Now we work like horses and have the best shift in the mill. Besides, I have just finished a little invention for changing spools on the machines and the factory gave me a premium of five hundred rubles. In America the workman could patent it and make much more. But I am satisfied.

"I am convinced now that whatever the Communists may be doing they are at least building up Russia. We shall be a great industrial nation when our Plan is completed and I have always longed to see it. What's that slogan? 'Equal and surpass America!' Perhaps— I at least know what they have to catch up with and most of our Communists don't. But we are beginning —and I may join the Communist Party myself."

On the wall hung a large map of Russia showing the sites of all the projected factories, power stations, and mines that would be completed during the Five Year Plan. "I like to look at that," said Alexei. "By the way, do you hear that rat gnawing at those potatoes— there, under the bed? The devil, I haven't anything but sausage to set the trap with. We only get a half a pound of cheese and a pound of ham every month on our ration cards. That doesn't leave enough for rat traps."

As we finished our tea he said, "Perhaps this 'socialist competition' may be all talk—you can't judge by surface signs in this country. Did you hear about the American who was in Moscow for the first time since the revolution? He was shown a new factory and he asked what it would produce. 'Parts for elevators,' his guide told him. He became very enthusiastic. 'There was nothing like that here under the Tsar,' he said.

'And what parts are they going to make for elevators?'
'Oh,' said the guide, 'That's where they're going to
paint the signs, "Elevator not running"!' I do know
that my shift is going to lead our factory and our factory will surpass that mill in Ivanovo-Vosnesensk which
we have challenged."

I went to Pavel's one day in late Autumn. It was
his wife's namesday; there was a grand dinner with
roast sucking pig, buckwheat, and plenty of vodka.
Everybody was very gay and talkative. The vodka
helped Pavel Vassilitch to find words. He explained his
viewpoint to me at various times during the afternoon.

"Now take Sasha. Supposing this child business had
happened before the revolution? She'd have been disgraced. And now? A fine fellow like Georgei thinks
nothing of it, marries her,—while that rascal Dmitri
must work in prison and send her twelve rubles a
month until the child is sixteen. That's the law!

"And my son! He has a good job in Kharkov,
working with foreign machinery! Gets two hundred
rubles a month. He's been elected to the Kharkov
Soviet and he'll go right up in the Party to a position
of real power. My son—and for forty years I hauled
clay. . . .

"But I don't haul it any longer. Last month they
installed an automatic conveyor. Now I stand at the
mixing machine and do nothing except ring a bell when
the conveyor doesn't dump properly. A much better
job! I'd join the Communist Party now but I'm too
old. Our new Russia is for young men!"

Georgei overheard the remark and interrupted him: "Long ago men like Alexei went to America to find a better life. To-day America is closed; and many who went earlier became mere tools of the American capitalist class. Some day men all over the world are going to come to Russia. Here is freedom in all that really matters to an individual, here is progress, here is a chance to work for your class and not become merely the tool of some man, automatons in a Ford factory. As unemployment increases abroad and conditions get worse we shall some day be the future America for the proletariat of the world."

Alexei raised a glass of vodka and called across the table to me, "Are you returning home soon? I have a favor to ask. Alexei Mikhailovitch Shchukin is going to be a Communist to work for the future America of the proletariat of the world. Tell that to any who remember me in *Sharpsveel—pa!*"

VII

PAVEL NESTOROVITCH: THE VILLAGE PRIEST

HE is nearing seventy. At vespers, as he reads the liturgy, his white beard and long silver hair seem to catch all the light from the smoking candles and to throw his strongly molded face into sharp relief before the dim gold of the ikons around him and the green and silver robes on his shoulders. He is a priest at the church in the Spassky convent, the last of the fifty who once attended there. The convent, not far from Moscow, has been closed, but the white-walled church is open on Sundays for service and its bell tower, high up amid the clusters of blue and golden domes, still marks the hours for the little village. Eight years ago the quiet faced nuns were dispersed; but, like uncertain fledglings, they have not gone far away. They live as best they can, as women of all work, in the villages round about. On Sundays, through mud, snow, or dust, they return to their church to sing in the choir, or to soothe with prayer those secret sorrows which they never tell on earth.

Spassky Convent was built in the eighteenth century. Napoleon marched by its crenelated walls. Within, leaning on those walls, a solid row of two-story buildings, where the nuns lived, runs full way around the four sides. They are now occupied by workers from the new factory two miles off. In the centre of the huge enclosure is the cemetery; here are buried soldiers dead at Borodino, officers and ministers highly honored; and there are many graves of civil war and famine, marked by plain wooden crosses. The cemetery is weathered and worn, and goats browse amid the weeds. There are five other churches within the walls, but they are closed. "One is enough," the workers living in the former convent decided. One has been made a day nursery where the women who work in the factory leave their babies before going to work. Another is a "club," a gathering place where there are always speeches in the evenings, a radio, perhaps a moving picture. Two other churches house the firewood, and the fifth is a storeroom for the community store.

The factory workers decided long ago that the old priest should not be allowed to live within the convent. He has a little two-room house half a mile away. His family is scattered; he was married, as are most priests in the Russian Orthodox Church but his wife died in 1920. Two sons perished in the civil war, two other sons are alive but never write, and there is left only a daughter, Sophie Pavlovna, and a son, Dmitri Pavlovitch. Dmitri I knew in Moscow; he is a Communist, employed in some government office. He is an active member of the Atheists' Society and is, I think, a trifle ashamed that he still feels drawn to his father. For many reasons he keeps the fact that he is a priest's son carefully hidden; it might mean no job. When asked he replies, "My father taught school." Yet every week he travels forty miles to see his father and sister and, I believe, gives them part of his salary. They need it. For Pavel Nestorovitch has made no compromises with the revolution. He is what he always was, a village priest. Therefore he suffers all that comes from being a priest.

He is, of course, one of the "deprived." By Soviet law a whole group of the population is barred from the right to vote and from all rights of citizenship. The group includes former landowners, factory owners, the clergy—and in many instances their children. Deprivation of the franchise means little in itself, but outside of politics it is the mark of Cain. The "deprived" can secure no ration card, they are often barred from the community stores, they can hold no government position (hence Dmitri's eagerness to hide his "social origin"), and they must get along as best they can.

Sophie Pavlovna told me how they lived. "From the church my father receives little—perhaps thirty rubles a month. Everybody is so poor. Dmitri gives us some, so we have about fifty rubles' income monthly. I can earn nothing, for I am a 'daughter of the deprived.' We are taxed more than the other classes, sometimes twenty rubles a month. Were it not for what the peasants and the sisters bring us— But even they must bring it secretly. *Akh*, this government! It is the government of Anti-Christ. We are 'the deprived,' which means we may walk Russian land and breathe Russian air—but our living we must find ourselves, with everything against us. We are 'the undesired,' those whom the proletariat would crush.

"And why? What have we done? Before the revolution perhaps we lived comfortably—but father was revered, he did much good. Many times he has risen at midnight and travelled ten miles through winter cold to give the extreme unction. To this day the peasants love him for it. With them it is not difficult; it is the factory workers, the kind of trash that lives in Spassky convent. It is always peasant against worker in everything. Two years ago at Easter, just at midnight when the most beautiful part of the service begins, the workers tied a loud-speaker up in a tree right at the church. It blared forth its awful profanity just as the choir began to sing. But a peasant climbed up and pulled it down, and all the peasants swore they would kill the workers if they tried it again. Last year all was quiet."

I went frequently with Dmitri to his home. I soon found that, between him and his sister, there was an unbridgeable distance. She was nearing forty, she had never married, she had seldom moved far from the village. Had she gone to Moscow or some other city, she might have found life easier than staying to bear the hardships of her father. "I could not go and if I did, how should I have avoided the brand of 'deprived'?" she asked. "Dmitri was lucky—he fought for Soviet power in 1919 and was able to hide his 'social origin.'"

"But if it is ever known?"

"It will be serious—especially since he is a Party member. It is forbidden to hide 'social origin.' . . . But he is a 'loyal Communist.'"

I thought she spoke bitterly.

Spassky is a convenient and popular excursion point for crowded Moscow. The morning train, one Sunday, brought a picnic of "Pioneers" with their ragged red

banners and shrill bugles. They paraded through the
former convent, played games amid the tottering
crosses, and held a meeting with the local workers in
the club. Their cheers and noise clattered through
morning mass and jangled above the soft music of the
black-robed choir. At dinner at the priest's house the
invasion was the sole subject of conversation. Pavel
Nestorovitch sat silently—while brother and sister argued. They were discussing the value of the new generation.

"The new generation is arising, without reverence,
without decency—the true children of the Godless.
They know nothing of religion. They mock at us,"
said Sophie Pavlovna.

"A generation without religion will be happier and
healthier," said her brother. (The father said nothing. It was as if he were not listening.) "A generation without a parasite like the church to support will
be wealthier and freer from the superstition that is
Christianity. The Orthodox Church has had its opportunity and failed; there is no more damning fact in
history than that the church, which controlled all education before the revolution, should have kept seventy per cent of the population illiterate. And church
services have gone on in Slavonic. Nor has it ever
warred on the superstitiousness of the peasant; instead,
it has utilized it and grown fat on it. Religious festi-
vals to kill insects in the fields by sprinkling the land
with holy water! Our new generation will know that
insecticide is what counts, and not water which some
priest's fingers have dirtied.

"Ignorance and superstition! Look at that case up in the Nijni-Novgorod district a few months ago. A peasant woman while washing in the brook found a piece of iridescent wood. She took it home, claiming it was a messenger from Christ; a little later she proclaimed it as Christ Himself, on earth in another form. Did the priest teach her otherwise? No—he doused it with holy water and blessed it. The result? Crowds came from all around willing to pay to see it. When the government sent out police to interfere, they were beaten. Superstition—that is what all churches thrive on.

"There was a priest in Ryazan last year who announced that on a certain Sunday evening the archangels would come down and elevate him to heaven in full view of all believers. The church was crowded with peasants bearing gifts. Nothing happened. The priest retired for a moment, then returned to announce that an archangel had come to him and reported that the Heavenly Mind was changed and that he would be allowed to stay on earth for some time to come to carry on the good work."

"There are such false prophets and charlatans in everything," said Sophie, pointedly. "Look at your Communists. Stalin says Trotsky is a rascal and a false teacher. Even Stalin admits that there have been charlatans in your holy Communist Party."

"Individuals, perhaps—but not the entire Party. Whereas the whole church could not live without charlatanry, without superstition."

"The greatest charlatanry in the world is Communism," Sophie insisted. "It thrives on the superstition that class struggle is the normal state of affairs in the world and the stupid belief that the proletariat are the children of Creation."

"History, my dear, supports us. But what supports that belief that was so prevalent this year in Voronezh? There a whole group announced that very shortly the Archangel Michael would appear on a white horse and lead the righteous against Communism. Everyone had to be ready, so there was much church-going, praying, and preaching. Did the priests deny that such a thing was possible? No. From such a belief they gained support. But nothing supported the belief except superstition. You have all prayed long for an end of Soviet power—why doesn't God answer your prayers if you are His children?

"No, it is better to teach the truth. Remember that old revolutionary song—

> 'No other one shall free us,
> Neither God nor Tsar.
> We gain our independence
> By the work of our own hands!'

That is what we are teaching the rising generation. Free from gods and such remnants of the Tsarist régime, they will be more intelligent, more self-reliant, and better citizens for our Soviet Russia." Dmitri poured himself a tenth glass of tea.

Sophie spoke with scorn, but without anger. "And how will your Godless generation replace the charities of the church? Think of Spassky convent. Before the

revolution the nuns taught the peasants sewing, but-
ter-making, bee-raising, child-rearing. They gave shelter, medicine, and free seed. Here the peasants came
for advice. Here was the village hospital. Now, in the
name of culture, 'freedom from superstition,' everything is gone, even the model gardens. What will
your atheists substitute for these things?"

"The State will do it. Do you think the peasants
didn't pay for those things? I'll grant that life in this
village is worse, now that the convent is closed, but
that is only temporary. Our people shall have freedom
from savage superstition and the chance to receive all
the church gave—not as charity, but as the birth-
right of a laboring class."

Just then the deaconess came in, without knocking.
She brought the morning collection—five rubles forty,
chiefly from the sale of candles.

"Another fake," said Dmitri. "You sell the peasants
candles to burn before the ikons. Then, as soon as the
poor fool has gone, you run, put out the flame, and
melt the unburned portion back into new candles.
Wouldn't a soul in purgatory profit more from a whole
candle than half a candle? Everywhere in the church
you find cheating, superstition, lies. I heard last week
of a priest who told his peasants, 'You have a radio?
Can you hear Moscow on it? Without wires, too.
Well, can you therefore doubt that God, without wires,
can hear your prayers?' "

Pavel Nestorovitch took the money, marked the
amount in a little book, and said nothing. Sophie
watched him, then added triumphantly, "Well, at least

the people still go to church. The churches are open, and the people will fight for them."

"Yes," Dmitri replied, a trifle sadly, I thought, "their superstition is deeply rooted. This old generation cannot be changed, but the young—they are ours. In Yaroslav last month the Soviet decided to open the grave of your Saint Sophie. Before the revolution thousands had gone to her grave, believing her body to be miraculously preserved, and contributed half a million rubles a year to the 'sacred' shrine there. Well, the Soviet decided that such a famous town character deserved a place in the Atheists' museum. So they opened the grave. See the chance they took? Supposing they *did* find her body miraculously preserved— then that would have only strengthened the church. But science is on our side. They came to the grave. A riot broke out as the peasants defended their belief and the infallible church. Three men were killed—so deep is superstition rooted. And in the grave were found the bones—of a dog. The incorruptible remains of holy Saint Sophie! We have them in an anti-religious museum now. Do you think that thirty years from now men will die to prevent such exposures? The younger generation is ours. . . ."

The most spectacular trial for many years was going on in a town not far away. In that town of nineteen thousand there were six churches. One adjoined the hospital. The village Soviet decided to tear down the church and its bell tower and build a wing to the hospital. Notice was given to the church board. After a vain protest to the government, they called a final memorial service, which drew peasants from miles around. The service continued through the night. Its theme never varied: "Rise, Christians, defend the true Slavic faith."

The next morning, when the officials came with the wrecking crew, they found the church surrounded by peasants—peasants on the roof, on the bell tower, clinging to every possible place on the building. "Tear down the church," they shouted, "but you must tear us down with it!" The crowd was ordered to depart, but it refused. Eventually a riot broke out and seven police and other officials were killed. Thirty arrests were made on the charge of "counter-revolution" and their trial was now closing.

Dmitri had been sent to that town as agitator and came back with an eye witness's story. "You should have seen those peasants holding fast to every foot-hold on the building, their beards blowing in the wind. The damned church bells were rung for three days without a stop. And old women cursing the Soviet in the name of God. The priests, clever devils, stayed out of sight. The whole demonstration continued three days and it wasn't long before the slogan 'Defend the church' changed to 'Attack the Soviet.' It looked like a popular uprising. But we knew whose hands had directed the whole thing. That is why we attack the church—it is the stronghold of counter-revolution. . . ."

"Whatever the church does against the government is right," said Sophie. "This is the government of Anti-Christ, and Christians must oppose it."

". . . And we shall punish counter-revolution with shooting. The court decreed to-day that seventeen men, including six priests and deacons, should be shot. *Pravilno*, that's as it should be."

"God will receive the souls of His martyrs," she crossed herself. "The more you persecute the church, the more you further religion."

"We will wipe out counter-revolution in any form. Last summer the government sent out agents to collect wheat from the peasants. 'Don't give it up,' the priests said. 'God sends you wheat for yourselves, not for this government of the Devil.' This autumn we sent out men to sell government bonds. 'Don't buy bonds—God gives you money and it is not for this damned government.' Counter-revolution, always. We shall shoot it out. The former nobility, the former merchants, the wealthy peasants in the village—they are all church-goers. Why? Because the church is a counter-revolutionary force. Everything the government tries to do, the church opposes; it is remarkable how the church always says God is on the side of the anti-Soviet elements. Very well, then He also must be prepared to face the charge of counter-revolution."

"God is against your persecution of the peasantry—it's written in the Bible." Sophie took the book from the sideboard and read, " 'And there went out another horse that was red' (red—you hear, Dmitri?) 'and power was given to him to take peace from the earth, and that they should kill one another.' There's your Terror, brother. Now listen, doesn't this describe your grain collections—the way you rob the peasant, taking his wheat and paying him practically nothing for it? 'And I beheld . . . a black horse; and he that sat on him had a pair of balances in his hand. And I heard a voice . . . say "A measure of wheat for a penny, and three measures of barley for a penny." ' That's just the way you rob the peasants. They go to church for relief against government persecution; you therefore call the priest counter-revolutionary and shoot him."

"If he advises them to oppose the government, we shall shoot. Whether he leads or not, all the agitation against government policy in the village seems to centre around the priest. Queer, isn't it?"

Pavel Nestorovitch had been in the other room, dressing for vesper service. He came forth in his robes —he had been listening. "You always talk, Dmitri, as if the priest was working for himself, as if he wished to use the peasantry to make himself rich. The same chapter which Sophie read speaks also of the coming famine. Remember, the priest knows the peasantry better than any worker-agitators whom you may send out in the village. He knows that famine will follow your village policy. I do not believe one-tenth of the stories I have heard about priests engaged in what you call counter-revolution. That term is too broad. Your Communist government has the sole right to define it. But when the priest advises against submitting to grain collections, against making the peasantry equal in poverty, it is because he feels for the peasant and has his best interests at heart."

Dmitri was about to speak.

". . . Don't interrupt, Dmitri. You Communists are

young, you have met no great defeats as yet, you are self-confident. You reject and attack anything that denies that man is self-sufficient. That is one reason why you attack the church. But men cannot live by bread alone—although God knows, you've even taken most of the bread away and we must live on ration cards. When Communists, in their supposed omniscience, can explain the mystery of death and make that parting less harsh, then you will be able to destroy religion in Russia and I, too, shall be a Communist. I am not counter-revolutionary. I have always believed that church and state should be separate. Whatever God sends, so will it be. In the meantime, while you are learning the limitations of man and the part the church plays in explaining them, the service of God goes on."

And he left. The little bells were ringing for vespers.

I asked Dmitri a delicate question one day; I felt I must know the answer: "With a point of view so opposed to your father, why do you visit there weekly? And why does he so seldom take part in your arguments with your sister?"

He smiled. "It must seem strange to you, but you do not know my father. He was well-educated—not like so many priests who went into the priesthood because it was the family career, even though they could scarcely read. Before the revolution my father was a radical. It was dangerous to hold the beliefs he held and still remain a priest; the church, too, exiled its more advanced thinkers. But he taught his children one thing—the value of individual thought, the supreme right of differing from the majority. When I was a boy our house held many a revolutionary meeting. I honor him for this. He taught many peasants to read and write; he read the Bible to them and explained it in simple language. He was one priest in a thousand.

"The revolution inspired him tremendously. We all felt as if we had come through a long dark night of pain into the dawn with its peace, its quiet, its opportunities. Ah—those were the dreamy days of the Kerensky régime! There has never been such liberty in Russia before or since. *Papasha* felt that the revolution would make a liberal church, just as it would make a liberal government. He did not see with us Communists that to build any new society in such a paradoxical land as ours necessitated force, force, force— no liberal vapidities, no matter how attractive they might be, but a dictatorship. He thought the church would have a great part in building up the new Russia.

"After our Communist success he was shocked to see that we were going on without the church, that we were branding it as something to be wiped out—not only its mediævalism, but all of it. So, from a radical he has become a conservative. He became even more conservative when he saw that internationalism and not nationalism was our aim. For he believes to-day that the church, whether good or bad, is the only unity in Russia that can save Russia. And he is a Russian— you foreigners do not know what that means. 'As a Russian loves his homeland . . .' " he hummed a popular song.

"So he holds to the church, ignoring the evils which he previously condemned, for he feels that some day it will arise to save Russia. His faith is unshakable. He is wrong, of course. In the meantime, I personally don't approve of useless persecution of the church. It is dying—let it die; we Communists have too much else to do. If the priests engage in counter-revolution they must be punished. But *papasha* does nothing but his own useless work. Except on holidays he has about fifty in church each Sunday. . . ."

"But if your father was mixed up in some counter-revolutionary activity and ordered shot, what would you do?"

He spoke without hesitation—"Shoot him, of course."

We were walking through the cemetery on the way to his house. He kicked at a clod of dirt; the top of a human skull fell out. "It will make a good ash tray," he said, picking it up. "Perhaps," as he read from a nearby stone, "it *was* 'General Trubetskoi, honored by the Tsar,' but more likely it was some dumb peasant who, in ignorance, paid with his sweat and blood to maintain a place like this."

At tea, one evening in early winter, the usual argument on religion had a peculiarly local slant. The workers residing in the former convent had just voted to tear down the bell tower, on the ground that it was a nuisance, and to give the bells to the government.

"*Pravilno,*" said Dmitri, "why should they be allowed to continue their useless noise when our government can use the copper and decrease its imports by so much?"

Sophie said nothing. She was envisioning the eventual closing of the church as well. Dmitri talked on, but with what seemed a trifle less conviction; the anti-religion campaign was coming close to his home. "The church has held its people by fear, too. Why is it to this day considered bad luck to meet a priest on the road? Why do the peasants then spit three times? An old superstition—but we shall end their fear and eliminate religion. . . ."

Pavel Nestorovitch, reading a Moscow newspaper, broke the silence.

"You quarrel with the church, Dmitri, but you never explain yourself well. You confuse the church as an institution and religion as a part of a man's life. You are wrong. You know I fought long ago for many changes in our church—for the elimination of many of its evils, trying to bring it closer to the masses, to have the service in Russian and not Slavonic, trying to make it teach what Christ really taught and not mere dumb subservience to certain customs and practices. I lost— as the church lost a little later and is still losing.

"But you Communists talk about the counter-revolutionary tendency of the church; you never admit that Communism, too, is a religion, and that there is no room in Russia for two diametrically opposed religions. Communism, the new faith, must drive out Christianity, the old. You yourselves deny that Communism is a religion, for you would thereby open yourselves to the undeniable conclusion of a deadly syllogism. You say, quoting Karl Marx, 'Religion is a narcotic for the people.' I agree—it softens much of the pain of life. But if you admit that Communism is a religion, therefore it follows that Communism is a narcotic for the people!

"Communism is built on the theory that one class, long oppressed, shall arise, conquer, and build a new society. The individual and his interests are nothing; the class is everything. Communism offers an explanation of the world and its history—so does Christianity. It appeals to faith, it teaches 'the good life'—sacrifice for the class in helping it to build for the future, and it paints a rosy picture of what is to come 'when there shall be no more oppression and exploitation of man by man.' Christianity does all this, too.

"Communism appeals to those people who need an explanation in the midst of a troubled and unsatisfied life; it gives them something to work for, something to die for. Christ said, 'Come unto me, all ye that labor and are heavy laden, and I will give you rest'; Communism says, 'Workers of the world unite—you have nothing to lose but your chains.' Both of these religions appeal to things that lie deep in men's souls, Communism has its Testaments—Marx, the old, Lenin, the new. . . ."

"Rot, *papasha*," Dmitri interrupted. "We claim no Divine inspiration for either Marx or Lenin."

"I mean that Marx and Lenin play the same part in your religion that the Bible does in ours. They are guide-books, explanations of the world, rules of action. Christ came to explain the Old Testament to the people of His time. Don't you teach that Leninism is Marxism of the New Imperialist epoch, that Lenin supplements, explains, and adds to Marx? You don't claim Divine Inspiration yet. You have your leader, Lenin, dying from overwork in the service of his people—a real Vicarious Sacrifice. How is he portrayed now? As a human being with faults and errors? Isn't it counter-revolution ever to state publicly that Lenin was seriously wrong in anything he said or wrote? The beginning of infallibility! Mind you, we are only a few years removed from Lenin. His wife, his friends, are still with us. Wait a hundred years from now. . . . Oh, you Communists know well the depth of religious feeling in the human soul and are busy developing all the details of your new faith. In that Communism is a faith, as well as an economic system, lies its strength."

There was an interruption. A peasant hitched his sled outside the door and entered very subserviently. *"Batoushka,"* he said haltingly, "if it is not too much trouble . . . my wife is dying . . . if you can come . . . to the village of Palino. . . . It is eight miles. . . ."

"Have a glass of tea, comrade; you must be cold. In a few minutes I will come with you."

"You are thinking of how to better the world, Dmitri; how to make life easier. These are the aims of Christianity, too. We have had and we have used superstition—don't you? The rapaciousness of all capitalists, the evil intentions of all bourgeoisie, the infallibility of Lenin—aren't these the beginnings of Communist superstitions? You have our aims: you appeal to the same instincts—and others—in man; you begin to have our faults, you even begin to have heresies (Look at Trotsky), you have our same propaganda methods—for any religion seeks to become the Only True Religion and even Christianity has been spread by force—and finally, you put a meaning into life for every Communist. . . .

"But there we have you, Dmitri. There is where you will fail. You have the younger generation now, to train as you wish. But there is one thing Christianity has which Communism does not have—and sooner or later your younger generation will find it out. Our 'true Slavic Church' will go—I have stayed by it, with all its faults, for I believed it could unite Russia, help resurrect Russia. I no longer care and I believe it is dying. But a new organization of Christianity will arise; religion will last and every religion must have its organization—even Communism needs the Party. Against the church your fight will be successful, but Communism, the new religion, fighting Christianity, the old, will lose—for only Christianity puts a meaning in death. . . . And there we have you."

He put on his coat and prepared for his trip to Palino.

It was, for me, his valedictory. I never saw him again. Needing an operation badly, he was told at a Moscow hospital that "places are first for trade union members, for workers and peasants; the 'deprived' come second." He died before there was room for him.

Spring was late, and so was Easter. Sophie managed to keep the house and Dmitri and I went out there Easter eve. Sophie took me to church that evening; Dmitri was speaking at a celebration in the local workers' club on "Easter and other barbarian myths in Christianity." The church was crowded, but there were few children there. In one alcove lay the Easter bread and the dyed eggs which the peasants had brought to church for the priest's blessing. The service was pitched in the minor. The nuns' choir chanted softly. There was incense and candle smoke. Pavel Nestorovitch's successor seemed to be directing the worshippers, slowly raising their fervor, lifting the pitch higher and higher.

Just before midnight we went outdoors. A bell (the tower had not yet been dismantled) was booming a low monotone. Suddenly, at midnight, the little bells began—higher, higher, faster, faster. The crowd around the church lighted small thin candles. There was no other light. Everything seemed so fresh—the melting earth beneath, the wind from the pines, the star-studded sky. The little bells continued, faster, sharper.

At once the double doors of the church burst open. There stood the priest in gay vestments, holding aloft his golden cross. He slowly descended the steps and the worshippers followed, with banner, crosses, and candles. There was a silence—then the whole congregation took up the chant, now in the major:

"Christ has risen from the dead.
By death He has defeated Death.
And brought life to those in the grave."

The procession marched round the church, "to show to the world that Christ was truly risen." According to the old custom, a few fireworks lighted the sky.

Sophie was crying. "The beauty of it—and they would destroy this. I always think of Russians abroad on this night. How homesick they must be when they remember. . . ."

From the club across the way there was a roar of laughter. Following the lecture there was to be a moving picture. There were the resident workers, their children, and most of the children from the village, seeing the moving picture after the lecture. It was Harold Lloyd in "Safety Last." There was another roar of laughter.

VIII

ZOYA KYRILOVNA: THE TYPIST

SHE is a pretty little *blondinka*, who works in the State Bank in Moscow, in the barnlike room of the Foreign Section. She, like all Moscow women, has neither the delicate cosmetics nor the fine clothes that add feminine charm in the lands west of Russia. But Zoya's delicate beauty transcends clothes and cosmetics. There are few finer figures in the ballet than hers and she plans her simple home-made dresses accordingly. Not yet twenty, she walks proudly, conscious of the power of her gift. It is not given to every woman to look stunning in gingham or in shoddy cotton prints.

My friend, Seryozha, brought Zoya to my apartment one evening. They were a well contrasted pair. His height, his outdoor tan, his lean muscular face, hidden at the brow by a lock of unmanageable black hair, emphasized her demure daintiness. He had often spoken of her and hoped to marry her "when he found a room." Their mutual air of quiet familiarity told plainly that only a room, literally, was lacking to make their marriage complete.

No factor plays a larger part in Moscow romance than living quarters. Seryozha and his family of five shared one room in this overcrowded city while her family of six had two rooms. There was no place for newly weds. There is scarcely any place in the city for courting except the parks, Sparrow Hills, or a friend's room "while you tell him to run around the corner for a box of cigarettes and stay an hour."

"I want Zoya to come to see you occasionally to practise English," Seryozha said, introducing us. "She can speak a little now but if she learns it well she can get a better position in her office."

"I have been going to night courses in our bank," she interrupted, "but it is impossible to learn English that way, with thirty pupils in a class and one teacher—and him with a Jewish accent! Your English is too hard anyway. Look at 'bough,' 'dough,' 'cough'! I'm glad I'm a Russian!"

Seryozha, who was also studying English, smiled. Then he added, "Zoya has a question she wants to ask you."

Without hesitation she said, "Do you know any woman in the foreign colony here who wants to sell old dresses or things from abroad? Especially a bêret. They are all the mode abroad, aren't they? And they go so well with bobbed hair!"

"You talk styles with him," said Seryozha, laughing. "I've got some work to do and I'll come back in an hour."

She continued to talk like a running brook after he had gone. She would not try English this evening—there was too much to talk about.

In a few minutes, at our first meeting, she sketched her background. Her father was a dentist with three other children. "After the revolution father said that we all had to earn our own living. He paid for me at a 'business school' and I got my job in the bank. He sends one sister to ballet school but when she finishes there is no guarantee that she'll get a job. There are too many ballet girls now. My third sister is going to be married soon. It is funny about her!

"We have two rooms, one in which we live and another for my father's office. My sister and her fiance have nowhere to go—she has no money to spend, as I do, nor does he. So they stay home in the evening, in my father's office, and make love in his patient's chair! Of course in spring they walk up and down the boulevards but these are crowded with Red soldiers and servants."

She spoke in detail of her work. "It is awfully dull and awfully strict,—six and a half hours a day—from ten till four-thirty. We do get a month's vacation with pay but it is very hard to get any other time off. I'd like to find a place with some foreigner—he'd pay much more! A friend of mine has such a job—and the powder and clothes he brings her from abroad! But his wife is coming to Russia to live soon and he won't be able to bring her as much!"

She came frequently for a few months after this, sometimes with Seryozha, sometimes alone. Her desire to learn English gradually weakened. She never stayed long but flitted from place to place, from a lesson to a cinema, from the cinema to a party. She seemed to have no worries, no cares, except about the all engrossing problem of making her wages of eighty-two rubles a month buy the things she wanted.

She spoke always with freshness and enthusiasm and never about politics or economics. "Politics are awfully dull, anyway. There was a circle in *politgrammar* begun in our bank, but I dropped out." She cared nothing for those aspects of American life that interest most Russian acquaintances—unemployment, factory production, export and import balances, but her curiosity about the life of American women was unbounded.

She asked again and again, "Is it true that American women simply use their husbands to provide them with *things*, with dresses, jewels, and automobiles? Do they call that love?" She had read every romance about life abroad that she could find and attended every American moving picture. "American men let themselves be suppressed by your women," was part of her seasoned conclusion. "Women marry you for a home, for social position. Here we have no such thing as social position."

The Russian "world concern," the *Weltschmertz* of the Germans, never afflicted her, and the World Revolution and the problems of Communism meant little to her. Russia and its future were unimportant compared to her vacation plans. But she did know the gossip of Moscow, the scandals of the theatrical world, and the affairs of her fellow employees.

After an hour of her laughing conversation there was a knock on the door and Seryozha entered, followed by another girl. Her face, in the half light, seemed oriental, with little beauty in it but taking charm from the lights and shadows. In full light only her black hair would have attracted attention. It was drawn tight to a knot at the back of her head. She wore black, broken by a blood red amber necklace.

"This is Kira Ivanovna," he said. She nodded. As Seryozha walked toward Zoya I saw her flash an angry glance at him. "I met her on Lubyanka and asked her to come along. Let's go to a cinema." Zoya agreed and we started off to see a German picture called "To the Street."

As we walked down Lubyanka, Zoya whispered to me, "I don't see why Seryozha had to bring this Kira along. Wait until you know her—she's from some noble family and thinks that she's better than us typists. Lucky that she has a job, with that 'social origin'! These 'former people'—!"

The picture told of a girl whose sweetheart had to leave the country for some time. During his absence things became worse and worse. Finally she saw nothing to do except to "go on the street." The spectators followed the story with interest and, as usual, each title brought out a buzz in the audience as literate members read the titles aloud for the benefit of their illiterate companions. There was a steady "putt-putt" as various spectators chewed sunflower seeds and spat out the hulls. The seventh reel ended showing the heroine about to begin her new occupation. It was obvious that the eighth reel would find her meeting the long lost sweetheart. But there was no eighth reel although it had been advertised. The censor had cut it out and there came only an abrupt "The End."

"And that's the way it should end," said Zoya, answering my objections, as we sat over tea and cake in a pastry shop near by. "Why should the cinema show happy endings? You foreigners don't know what life really is!"

"Why so pessimistic, Zoya?" Seryozha asked.

"Because I know life."

As if speaking to herself, Kira added, "But there *are* some happy endings in life. . . ."

Zoya came to my apartment one evening in deep winter several months later, when bonfires were burning on street corners and those unfortunate enough to have to go out could run from fire to fire. She wore only a light coat but beneath it were two sweaters. Her dress was of flannel and her shoes laced halfway to her knees, yet her attractiveness was undiminished.

"I'm not disturbing you?" she began. "I had to go somewhere—our home is like a madhouse. In father's office are Nalya and her *parin,* her boy friend. And five of us in the other room. I'm so upset—a terrible thing happened at the bank to-day.

"There is so much ill feeling in our office—jealousy and fear of losing one's job. A member of our union committee had been threatening to report a typist, claiming that she had concealed her real 'social origin.' She hadn't, but she was afraid, and she jumped from a third floor balcony this morning and killed herself on the lobby floor. There will be an investigation and the man will be dismissed from the union. He behaved just as if he were a Tsarist official. I hate everything left from those times.

"There is the same thing even in the ballet. An old

ballerina, famous before the revolution, directs all the affairs there. She holds back certain young people and advances others who are her friends. One night she was dancing the lead in 'The Red Poppy.' Have you seen it? At the end, you know, she dies and her body is placed on a slab and covered with a red flag. Just at that moment, a month ago, two girls who were afraid for their position jumped down on her from the top of the stage, hoping to land on her and kill her. They just missed her and killed only themselves. They should have killed her. Everybody left from the old régime should be killed."

She changed the subject abruptly. "Have you seen Seryozha lately?"

"No, he seems very busy."

"He doesn't come as often as he used to," she said petulantly. "I could have taken two tickets from our office for the opera to-night but he said he couldn't go. Have you seen Kira?"

"Not since he first brought her here."

"I think he is courting her. One of the typists in our office said she has seen them together at the theatre. Well, let him! But I do feel sorry for him sometimes. He has been trying for three years to enter a technical school, for his present position in the laboratory doesn't pay him very much. Every year he applies for entrance to a school of electricity—and every year there are ten times as many applicants as places."

"And they take those whose 'social origins' are most satisfactory?"

"Of course—preferably factory workers' sons. His

father was a little merchant in some provincial town so he will never get in."

She picked up a New York newspaper and by chance turned to the pages advertising "rooms for rent." "What are these?" she asked. "You mean there are many rooms vacant in New York? Here in Moscow, newspapers advertise a hundred rooms wanted and only one for rent." She sat silent, thinking.

"If only Seryozha could find a room we would get married immediately. Rooms aren't supposed to be sold but, when some man moves out of his room he asks a 'gift' from the person moving in. Usually you can get a room only when its owner leaves town."

She talked for a half hour of rooms, and the strange situations which the room shortage produces: "There was a man in our office, in a good position, drawing two hundred and twenty-five rubles a month, the maximum wages that a Communist can get. His wife was studying to be an agricultural expert; when she finished she was offered a good position in Siberia, to stay there two years. Her husband couldn't leave his work and she couldn't let this chance go by. Of course they divorced before she went away; what sense was there in staying married at that distance? We Russians are not hypocrites! After a year the husband married a girl in our office. Now his former wife has come back to Moscow for further study——"

"Where does she live?"

"With her former husband and his wife of course. What other room could she find? In another month she will leave for a new position in the South."

Then she returned to her own problems: "If only Seryozha could find a room! I know that Kira has a room. Her father was once mayor of Moscow, with a large apartment on Tverskoi boulevard where Kira and her mother still keep one room."

She was preparing to go when Seryozha came in. He seemed a trifle embarrassed at seeing her. "I'm sorry I couldn't go to the theatre with you, *milaya,* darling," he began. "Besides, it is almost too cold for anyone to be out."

"Yes," she replied angrily, "and why are you out?"

"I heard of a room——"

"Where is it?" her anger changed to eagerness.

"On Chisti Prudi, but the owner wants a 'gift' of nine hundred rubles. I can't find that much," he said discouraged.

"No, I suppose not. Well, let's go home, Seryozha."

As they went down the corridor, I heard him say, "Wait, I've forgotten my gloves." He returned and said to me in a whisper, "I'll be back here in half an hour—wait for me."

He returned, apologizing for keeping me up. "I want to talk to you about Kira and Zoya—you know them both."

"I scarcely know Kira."

"You will. By the way, I want you to come to a party a friend of ours is giving next week. I don't know what to do. Zoya is cheerful but awfully light headed. She doesn't earn very much nor do I. Nor shall I, until I can finish that electrical school. And rooms—! How can we ever get married? We can't continue to live like this—! I know those who marry and continue to live separately with their own families and I don't want that. I am lonesome enough as it is. I could find a place ten or fifteen miles out of Moscow but Zoya wouldn't be happy there."

"Has Kira a room?"

"Did Zoya tell you? Do you think she suspects how I feel?"

"I think so."

"Well, God knows what I am to do. Russian women are as jealous as cats. Zoya is pretty but sometimes she's a tiresome little gossip and she cares about nothing but theatres and clothes. And Kira—wait till you get to know her better!"

The party the following week was at Shchukins', friends of Seryozha. Zoya, who stopped in for a minute, seemed very eager and said, "Everybody will bring something to eat or drink—you bring a bottle of wine. Some one has borrowed a phonograph somewhere and new records from abroad. We will get a chance to dance that new American step, the Charleston." It had just come to Moscow.

The Shchukins had two rooms. The wallpaper in the living room attracted one's attention even before the guests or the other decorations. It was a vivid red, with the design of the Soviet state seal, the hammer and sickle, repeated in gold. At the top was a border in black showing smoking factories. "One must be patriotic," Zoya said of it, later in the evening.

There were perhaps fifteen guests and the mumbled

introductions meant nothing. Zoya's forehead wrinkled as she frowned when she sighted Kira sitting on a divan in one corner talking with a man who wore the only Russian blouse in the party. The other men wore European clothes, with shirts whose collars fitted poorly. The women wore silks and *crêpe de chine* and most of them had silk stockings.

In the second room a table was loaded with the offerings of the evening. Almost everyone had brought a bottle of wine and the wide choice of the Moscow wine stores was on the table. The Shchukins provided bread, butter, caviare, cheese, and ham.

"These parties are such fun," said Zoya, as we began dancing, "although they don't occur very often. It's only at parties that we can dance your western style, but it is often difficult to find someone who can borrow a phonograph. And parties give the women a chance to dress up! Every woman tries to have one party dress of silk, even if it does cost eleven rubles a yard. And Soviet silk stockings—at eighteen rubles!"

She was silent for a moment as she saw Seryozha talking with Kira on the divan. She could not help noticing that he spent most of the first part of the evening talking steadily with the dark-haired girl, although she watched stealthily for a chance to sit beside him. In retaliation Zoya rushed about from man to man, joked with them, tried to get them to dance, and flirted outrageously. She stopped when she saw that he paid no attention.

Later she sat with me in another corner of the room and it amused her to identify other guests. "That man in the Russian blouse, Korsakov—he's very unhappy. He had to divorce his wife a month ago. He had a close friend during the Civil War whom he lost sight of when he came to Moscow. Korsakov married and found a little room in a basement. In those days you could find rooms. A year ago he met his old friend on the street here. He had come to Moscow to work but had no room. 'Come home with me,' said Korsakov, 'we have a bed and a divan also.' The friend stayed there permanently and everything went well until one afternoon when Korsakov came home unexpectedly and found that things between his friend and his wife were going too well. . . .'"

Dancing stopped and the party settled down to conversation. All the guests seemed to remember that there was much wine yet to be consumed. One young man with long uncombed hair was monologuing to more than his share of listeners. "That's Pisakov, the proletarian poet," Zoya continued. "He writes trash."

I strolled from group to group. In one corner some men were talking politics. In another corner a group of girls were arguing excitedly. "Of course her hair is dyed. . . . and the rotten dye they make here—her hair turned green."

Suddenly some one called, "Zoya, get up and dance the Charleston." She looked questioningly at Seryozha. When he nodded she rose to dance. She began slowly, in a far corner of the room, and, dancing faster and faster, moved to where Seryozha was sitting. When she saw him watching her she danced wholly without restraint, just in front of him.

The room was silent except for the whine of the phonograph and the patter of her feet. Several men moved forward in their chairs. The poet sat up and stared. Unconsciously he licked the corners of his mouth. As she danced in beautiful time, laughing and tossing her head, it was apparent that she wore no brassiere. She looked nowhere except at Seryozha.

Kira, who had taken the place beside Seryozha, broke the spell when she turned to him and said, "I think these American dances are stupid. Our own Russian dances are far more graceful." Seryozha turned to Kira, smiled, and unconsciously twisted about. His back was toward Zoya. She stopped abruptly. The tension among the guests ended; as if glad, they broke into nervous conversation. On Kira's face there was a smile, the smile of almost certain mastery. Had there been anything handy Zoya would certainly have thrown it. Instead, she went into the other room, poured herself a large glass of cognac, and talked with a group of men. They patted her familiarly on the shoulder.

I didn't notice Kira, who had taken the chair beside me, until she asked, "Don't you find this a trifle dull?"

"No, but all this conflicting conversation is confusing," I replied.

"Oh, they love to talk and drink. It is hard to tell whether they talk so that they can drink or vice versa." She spoke of her work, as a German interpreter in some government office, "which I can do because I had a German governess. During the revolution they arrested my father and the Secret Police turned our house into a prison. My father died in jail in the basement of that very house in which he and his father were born. Only my mother was left, for my brother fled abroad, and as all our mail is censored, he writes very seldom. We lived for a little while on some jewels which we had. Then, needing a job, I had a chance to get into this office. I have a job—that is most important. Now we are 'former people.' Everything in Russia has changed—even styles in wall-paper."

Our hostess announced that anyone who wanted to play cards would find tables in the other room. No one paid any attention to her. She shrugged her shoulders, as if content with having at least made the offer.

The wine or perhaps the example of the others seemed to make Kira talkative. "It is always best to belong to the class of government employees. No matter what happens to a government, that class goes on. Letters must be written, routine attended to, and there must be people to do these things. It's stupid, slow, and without much responsibility—that's why everybody tries to get a job in some office. I've had my place six years and I am *loyalnaya* to the Soviet régime. . . .

"You think that strange? Most of my class are not. I too was in prison, in Butirka, when there were eight women in a cell built for two—and that awful bucket in the corner! I saw a woman beaten for asking for more water, beaten by some dumb peasant soldier. Then suddenly it came to me, 'Who is responsible for this brutality?' And the answer followed—'We of the so-called upper class!' For years we set them an example of selfishness and brutality, we thought the workers and the peasants were beasts and treated them as such. The fault was ours for first thinking of it. When I was released from prison I decided to stay with this régime, to be *loyalnaya*, to atone, to try to teach . . . to help the despised proletariat to lift themselves!"

She pointed to Seryozha, who was listening while Zoya talked seriously. "Yet there are some things— you are a good friend of his? I feel so sorry for him. He has set his heart on entering that technical school. He alone refuses to admit that it is impossible. Can't you tell him—? If only he would be content with what he is, as I am at being a lowly German interpreter in the Council of National Economy with a salary of a hundred and seventy-five rubles a month!"

"And Zoya?"

"Had there been no revolution she would have made a nice wife for some merchant and her father would have given her a large dowry. You don't give your daughters dowries now. Instead, fathers like hers, from the petty intelligentsia, give their daughters a course in typing or millinery and trust them to ride the troubled sea of their life as best as they can. What good can she do Seryozha? In ten years she will be fat and ugly, like all middle class Russian women."

The party ended at two, after all the bottles were emptied. No one except the poet seemed to have drunken to excess. He was lying on the sofa exclaiming his verse to the red and gold wallpaper. "Isn't Kira unbearable?" whispered Zoya, as we said good night. "Did she talk only about herself? She's always doing that and never about other people."

I did not see Zoya at all during the spring until one day when I met her in the Bank. She said, with her old enthusiasm, "I am so glad that summer is coming. There will be tennis and swimming, and, on my month's vacation, I think I'll go to the Caucasus—perhaps with Seryozha."

"You still see him?"

"Of course, though not as often as I used to. He is getting ready for those examinations for the fourth time. And that Kira—I'd like to kill her. But I can't tell him to stop seeing her for then he will stop coming to see me!"

Seryozha had shown clearly in the few times that I saw him that he was still undecided. The room situation was unchanged. "I don't know what to do," he said. "Zoya is so pretty, so much alive. She wants me to go to the Caucasus with her, but Kira is going to Crimea and has asked me to come there. I'll make a decision by autumn about my future. If only I can get into that school!"

But he made his decision in June. Like most Moscow families who can afford it, the Shchukins had taken a *datcha,* a little frame house in the suburbs, for the summer months. They invited a few of the same group of people who had attended the party to their *datcha* one Sunday. Their little house stood amid a pine woods near a branch of the Moscow river. As soon as all the guests arrived the whole crowd went down to the river to swim.

There was a sandy bar, a hundred feet long. At one end were the men and, separated by thirty feet of beach, 'no man's land,' the women. No one wore a bathing suit and only the foreigner seemed embarrassed. The men and women stayed at their ends of the bar the entire time. Neither group particularly watched the other, although Zoya, slim as a white birch, continually tried to attract Seryozha's attention. When he dived she stood watching that strong sinewed body break the quiet green surface of the pool. At a signal both parties dressed and started back to the house.

On the way Seryozha walked with Kira. Zoya came last, walking alone. The Shchukins had dinner ready on our return. In addition, a table was laden with vodka and wine just out of the little ice house. Someone began proposing toasts to each member of the party. When the toast for Kira was called Zoya refused to drink and ostentatiously threw the liquor over her shoulder. Seryozha, sitting between the pair, whispered to Zoya, "Little fool, have you gone out of your mind?" She did not answer.

In the middle of dinner, while conversation bubbled like bottled water, Zoya suddenly turned to Kira and asked in a loud voice, "Didn't your father own a house at Tver before the revolution, Kira?"

"Yes, I think so."

"I heard a story about you the other day—that your father buried a lot of jewels and money in a house he owned there."

All other conversation ceased. "My God, what are you saying?" one man cried. "Zoya, have you gone crazy?" Seryozha tried to put his hand over her mouth.

She freed herself and continued, half accusing, half jeering, "I heard that you went up there a couple of years ago to see if you couldn't find the money and that you discovered that your father's house is now a day nursery for the children of the workers in a factory. In the very room where part of *your* wealth is hidden there are now twenty sleeping babies. Why don't you bribe a nurse to help you dig it out of the wall?"

Some of the people looked at Kira in amazement. She sat pale, expressionless. Others watched Zoya's face where there flamed the angry red of sudden hysteria.

Seryozha jumped up. "Come, Kira, let us go," he said and tried to lead her away. Kira stopped him; on her face now there was a smile, the smile of complete mastery. She said quietly, "The poor child shouldn't be allowed to drink so much. She doesn't know what she has just done."

At her words Zoya looked at Seryozha. Seeing his face, stern, icy, furious, she broke into tears, left the table, and ran to the house, where she locked herself in a room. Seryozha muttered to me, "Telling a story like that, a lie of course, in front of all these strange people here. God knows what trouble might come from it if it got to certain ears."

He took Kira back to Moscow on the first train. Zoya came out a long while afterward with eyes that showed how much she had been crying. She asked me to take her to Moscow and all the way she kept repeating, "I didn't mean it, I didn't mean it, but I do hate her so much!"

The following Saturday morning I met Seryozha and Kira, looking very happy, hurrying down Arbat. "Come with us," they said. We entered a dingy building, the air in which seemed unchanged since the time of Alexander III. A few couples were waiting in a poorly lighted corridor. "We are going to be married now," Seryozha explained, "and to-morrow we shall be married again, in church. It isn't necessary and I don't want to, but Kira— Then we shall live with her mother in one room."

"Why don't you come out to the church with us?" she asked me.

"Do come—and lend me your newest necktie," he added.

A young woman "married" them in a little whitewashed room, whose only decoration was a poster printed in flaming red showing a hand pointing to the question "Stop! Do you know about the health of the person you are marrying?" She asked their names and addresses, whether Kira chose to take her husband's name or to keep her own, and stamped a piece of paper. We left the room as the clerk said, "Well, be happy, and don't come back for a divorce for at least three months!"

The next morning I rode with them to a station twenty miles north of Moscow. Her mother and one of Seryozha's friends came with us. We walked through the woods for nearly an hour and came to a small village gathered around a little stucco church, a seventeenth century structure. The gold stars in its faded blue dome caught fire from the morning sun. Morning mass was not yet over and we waited outside. "This old church is on what used to be our estate," Kira explained. "I set my heart on being married here long ago, when I was a little girl."

The priest, in frayed and shabby robes, greeted us warmly. He began the ceremony immediately, supported by the "choir"—one woman who chanted the responses out of tune in a voice terrible in its raucity. Seryozha's friend and I were the "best men" and held gilded crowns over the heads of the bridal pair throughout the half hour's service. Kira's mother, in a simple black cotton dress, was on one side, smiling and happy. In the rear of the church stood an old man, the janitor. On his face there was only gloom.

When the ceremony proper was finished the priest led the pair to the ikonostase to kiss the ikons. Before each ikon were lighted candelabra, their gold paint almost peeled off. As the priest led the couple from ikon to ikon the janitor, his shoes squeaking loudly, followed behind, and blew out the candles as soon as the rites before each ikon were finished. "Have to be economical," he whispered to me as he passed. When we left the church the janitor said to no one in particular, "I've seen many a wedding but few happy marriages." Seryozha and Kira did not hear him for they were walking far ahead, hand in hand, hurrying toward the train that would carry them back to Moscow.

Zoya phoned me that evening. The telephone did not conceal the tears that were in her voice and probably in her eyes. She began bravely, "So they got married? In church too? How unnecessary that was—if it had been I—! Well, let her have him two months and I shall take him away from her. She is plain, conceited; he likes neither of those things."

The attempted bravery suddenly vanished and she sobbed, "Oh, if only I had had a room! What else *could* he have married her for? What else can she give him that I . . ."

One evening in autumn I saw Zoya at the opera. During the intermissions the people now parade around the marble hall in the large opera house where formerly only nobility were allowed to strut. She was walking in the circle of people, on the arm of an American engineer who had recently come to Moscow.

She introduced him to me and continued, "He understands little Russian so I can say what I please. Do you know that Seryozha failed to get into that school again? Some one in the office told me! I met this fellow countryman of yours at a party—he is so nice to me. The Houbigant lipsticks and the Coty powder that he can bring me from abroad! And silk for dresses!"

"Shall you marry him, Zoya?" I asked.

"Well, he hasn't said anything about that yet——"

A month later I saw her on the staircase in the Hotel Europa, where the engineer lived. She was very enthusiastic: "He says that if I learn English he'll take me abroad with him some time. He himself is teaching me! But he says that I must speak it well so as not to disgrace him when he introduces me to his American friends in Berlin."

IX

DMITRI PETROVITCH: THE TUTOR

DMITRI PETROVITCH did not criticise the revolution because it ended his wellbeing. He hated it because it meant his finish as a personality. Until the revolution he had been Commander of the Horse Guards of Poltava, retired on a miserable pension. In all Holy Russia there was only one such Commander and it was he, Dmitri Petrovitch Krasov. That was distinction sufficient for him, a distinction which the revolution removed, along with his pension. That gave him his position among his friends, albeit a lowly one. They were generals and pompous state officials and theirs was the rank. But the pride was his.

Dmitri faced the revolution as it came, sure that he would ride it unhurt. He came through unhurt in body. Of course, he "sat" in jail for a few months, as did all the generals and state officials now devoid of their pomp. It was really the utter insignificance of his position that saved him, although he never saw it that way. While in jail there was much conversation about the end of the revolution. If weakened Russia could not throw off the Bolshevik scoundrels—the *svolochi*—foreign aid would come from England, from France, even, perhaps, from America.

The Americans! He had a brother in America, forgotten for many years. Might Boris return to help his Motherland? It was foolish to think of that—Boris would be nearly sixty. He had spent his youth sowing wild oats with abandon. One scandal in St. Petersburg could not be paid to die, so Boris fled to America where, upon promising to stay and never to communicate with the family, he was sent a yearly allowance. He kept his promise and none had ever heard from him.

"Here is material for philosophy," said Dmitri to himself, sitting on a bench and scratching. "I, the loyal son, sit in Butirka Prison eating herring soup, once a day, the color of the eyes of a dead fish. Boris is in America, perhaps wealthy; certainly not an innocent man, in prison. I wonder if he ever knew of the honor I brought our family when I became Commander of the Horse Guard of Poltava?"

During the Civil War Dmitri found a position in the Department of Education. It was pleasant, with little work, and there was no need to go to all the tiresome meetings and to listen to all the windblown speeches about the "New Russia"—all nonsense and soon to pass. He lived in one room with a Colonel Semanov, an old acquaintance, formerly an officer in the Infantry. They argued constantly.

"There would have been none of this Communist foolishness," said Dmitri, "if we had used more cavalry at Marienburg in 1914. They could have gotten through, the Germans would have been beaten, the war ended."

"Nonsense," said the Colonel, "a revolution was inevitable." He had been suspected of liberalism in Tsarist times. "But not this revolution!"

It was not to the revolution that Dmitri wanted to lead the conversation. "Did you ever see the Horse Guards of Poltava, my company?" he asked innocently, but for the hundredth time.

"No, I was never much interested in cavalry. Now, our infantry——"

Dmitri would then excuse himself to prepare the tea.

In the circle of the "former people," Dmitri was referred to at first by his title. He would tell stories about his command but soon found that his stories were replaced by discussions on what to do, where to get money, who was in jail, how to get out of the country. "Why worry?" he asked his friends one day. "It will soon pass; then we shall welcome back the Grand Duke, there will be demonstrations, parades. Did you ever see the Horse Guards of Poltava on parade?"

Old Kupfer, a former manufacturer, was listening. Fumbling with his glass of tea, he exploded, "Fool, parade? Tell me, do you have any money?"

"Yes, thirty rubles."

"That is little. What happens when that goes and you lose your position at the Commissariat of Education?"

Dmitri stuttered, "But I had a high position in the Army and——"

"And what good is that? Fool, little fool, the revolution has taken everything from us. Everything, even our past. Our lives are as a pleasant day wiped out by evening storm. And there is no sunset. What shall we eat to-morrow?"

No one answered, for Kupfer always talked that

way. His former friends thought him a member of the Secret Police, talking thus to lead them into thoughtless remarks. Dmitri rose, put on his coat, and buttoned its three brass buttons. It was his army coat.

"And that coat," said Kupfer, "you'd better dye it or they'll arrest you for being counter-revolutionary. With those buttons, too. Only yesterday I heard one say they arrested . . ." his voice dropped low. Dmitri bowed stiffly and went away.

A life without a sunset! There was one sunset he remembered, when the sky, like blue chiffon overcast with silver net, outlined the Winter Palace, when the golden spire of the Admiralty lay like a breastpin on the bosom of Heaven. The day of manœuvres and the Horse Guard of Poltava riding before the Tsar!

The evenings were long and there was neither cordiality nor hospitality in the land. Dmitri was left to himself. Always remembering, rather than thinking, sitting alone, the idea of writing a book came to him. It should be something valuable, a contribution from the past to the future. He acted on the idea immediately. Buttoning the one remaining button on his overcoat he went out to buy a notebook and returned smiling. He wrote the title page, "The History of the Horse Guards of Poltava."

I do not know what he did during the famine years. In 1924, he was working in the Department of Education but in another position,—checking the hats, coats, and rubbers. He spoke little to anyone and never about the past. It was not that he was waiting for the end —he had abandoned waiting or hoping for anything.

In Russia, May 1st is a holiday. For the first time since the revolution he went down to Red Square to see the army manœuvres. It was a chilly day and his overcoat, although held closed by a piece of string, was comfortable. The infantry paraded, as always, shouting "Hurrah" as they passed the stands. Then came the cavalry, riding prettily over the rutted surface of the Square. The demonstration would end with the ride of the Kossak machine gunners.

With two men in blue uniform on each carriage, driving four horses abreast, several teams raced the two hundred metre course through the Square. Occasionally a wheel broke, but the team continued, for the panting and foaming horses had the carriage hanging in the air behind them more than half the time.

"So goes our Red cavalry," said a voice in front of Dmitri.

"Oh, yes, very brave—but you probably never saw the Tsar's Horse Guards of Poltava," answered Dmitri.

It was a stupid remark. Someone overheard it. That night he was taken from bed and once more sat in jail. When he came out, three months later, his room was gone, and his position was filled by another. He had but ten rubles and his coat.

He went to see Kupfer, who knew all about it and said ugly things about stupid old officers. No chance of borrowing any money there. One friend did lend him a few rubles, another told him where there was a vacant room in a basement. He secured the room, but the money was soon spent.

In some mysterious fashion, known only to those

who have had to try it, he found a few pupils to whom
he taught French. It was bad French, but he earned a
little each week and managed to live. The basement
was damp and he had rheumatism constantly. He kept
more and more to himself, never complaining about his
health, although the rheumatism, which robbed him
of his erect, military figure, completed the work of un-
linking him from his past.

I met Dmitri and knew of his past through Semanov, with whom he had formerly lived. There comes to
the doors of foreigners in Moscow, in more or less
steady stream, a host of peddlers: Tatars selling rugs;
peasant women with home-made laces, and nonde-
scripts coming almost surreptitiously with royal shav-
ing mugs, ikons, bits of jewelry, and china for which
they ask ten times the price they hope to get. Semanov,
formerly in the army, had joined this stream and came
occasionally with a burlap bag beneath his arm and
smilingly saying "I have just the thing you would like
—two letters signed by Paul, the Tsar," or, "Here is
a real Orenburg shawl!"

He brought Dmitri with him one evening. "My
friend would like to know if there are any of your acquaintances who would like lessons in French or Russian. He was a distinguished officer——"

"I was commander of the Horse Guards of Poltava,"
Dmitri interrupted.

He continued to call once a month for a time but
finally stopped coming, for I had no success in finding any pupils for him.

One day, in the rains of the Russian spring, he came again to me, not excited but showing he had important matters at hand. I had not seen him for more than a year. Now his gray beard was white and more unmanageable. His hair had receded, bringing into unpleasant prominence a gray scar on his forehead. He wore Russian boots, a pair of patched breeches, and a gray jacket shirt. But on his face, lines that once guided his smile, long unused, seemed about to break out and there was a faint glow in the ashes of his eyes.

"I came to you . . . a letter from America. You read Russian? Do you know where Chicago is?" He gave me a letter to read.

My dear Brother:—

I write this uncertain that it will reach you. Perhaps you are dead or your address unknown but I must write. Once brothers, we are now past sixty and strangers. My life has gone well—and yours, in the whirlwind of revolution?

I came to Chicago in 1894 and, with a little money, bought land. I am wealthy, beyond all my desires. Oh, Dmitri, come to me. For the sake of Christ we should again live as brothers. Too long have we been apart. The cause of our separation—that has been forgotten. Let the love which we should bear one another be the cause of our reunion. Can you not come to me? I need you.

Should you answer this I shall immediately send you money for your visa and passage and I shall arrange for your entry into America. If this seems difficult, let us meet in Berlin or Paris. Only, answer quickly.

Christ is my witness, Christ is our friend. Let Christ, whose hands surely have upheld you through the long and stormy years, at last unite our paths which have so long lain apart.

The letter was signed "Boris," and gave an address in Chicago.

"Do you want to answer?" I asked. "If so, let's send a cable."

"No, no, it is a trick of the Secret Police. It is not true; besides, America is too far. Enough is it to know that Boris is still alive, if it is he who writes. But I fear all letters purporting to come from abroad."

"Is it Boris's handwriting?"

"I think so, although I do not remember well."

"How did the letter reach you?"

"The police, they know all addresses. They have an address bureau where you can find anyone in Moscow," he replied as he went away, undecided whether to answer or not. There had already been ten years of delusions, casting shadows on future hopes. And Boris had changed if it were he; to judge by the letter he had become very religious.

The next day he returned, greatly excited.

"Answer that letter, you who speak English. Send the cable. I have decided that I will go, if only it is true. Last night I thought about it. Did you ever know that I was Commander of the Horse Guards of Poltava? Why should I not finish my years in a land where long and loyal service must be respected and honored. I shall have time to write my book there, in a friendly atmosphere. It is not so here. My friend, can you lend me some money? I shall repay you when Boris answers. Can you come to Kupfer's room next Monday night? I shall entertain a few friends."

To his party he invited eight guests. A rickety table

threatened to break under the load of wine from the Crimea; vodka in its chaste green bottles; cold fish, meats, and caviare. "The good old times" were the sole subject of conversation. There were endless toasts, proposed very quietly, to the memory of friends of the long ago, to women whose beauty now lived only in the memories of old men.

There was a toast to the Horse Guards of Poltava, proposed by Kupfer himself. Dmitri replied with a long speech. ". . . The Commander, once reinstated in honor in America, will not forget. . . ." There was no mention of the Soviet nor of the revolution except when Kupfer said, "Be sure and put the corks back in the empty vodka bottles. Otherwise the store won't redeem them and we shall lose five kopecks a bottle. The Bolsheviki have found where they can sell second hand corks abroad."

I felt indisposed for several days afterwards. On the fourth day Dmitri came, shivering slightly.

"A wonderful party, wasn't it?"

"How did you do it with the money I gave you?" I asked, for that had puzzled me.

"Oh, I sold a few things. I shan't need them and I can get a better overcoat abroad."

He had sold everything he had, furniture, books, and clothes, and there was still some cold weather to come. "I shall get along well—tell me, is there any answer to your telegram?" He was building high on this hope and I felt slightly concerned, but I explained that only a week had passed. He left, accepting an old overcoat of mine, promising to replace it with a new one "when Boris writes."

Within a day or so he called again looking like a small boy who sees something unknown and who is unable to decide whether it is pleasant or terrifying. "Here's a second letter. Read it—I can't understand."

Dear Brother:

Jesus loves the sparrows and the weather is fine. Are you a follower? Have you seen Peter Ivanitch? Tell him we have found the True Way. Thirty five stories in the air. So much nearer Heaven. Roar, roar, roar, for the Golden Gates swing silently.

How is Natashya Fedrovna? And Mama and Olya? Do they know the Light? I shall write them about my true experience, my Guidance. Do Papa's peasants still worry him? Treat them kindly for they are laboring beneath a false faith, never having seen the River of Blood which flows from Calvary. Tomorrow is Sunday. The Tsar will go to Church and wish he did not have to kneel so much.

But come to me, come to me. I shall send money. And bring a picture of Natashya—tell her I am sorry to have gone away.

Love Christ and keep his Commandments, for this is my will."

"What does it mean? If that letter was opened and the names read, I shall 'sit' again and die in jail before I get to America. Peter Ivanovitch, he was an uncle and died before Boris left. Olya, my wife, died in 1901. Mother died six months after he left—yes, he knew that. Natashya, that was the ballet dancer in Petersburg, you know. Telegraph him at once to send the money and not to write again. He may mention other names which would be very serious—he doesn't understand. But I don't understand either. The peasants? And the Tsar?"

I sent another cable. We had no answer while a month passed, with Dmitri coming every day. I think he was losing hope, although refusing to give up the illusion. Some days he asked me about American life. "Tell me, what happens to your army officers when they retire? Do they get a pension? Do they wear their uniforms? Does anybody speak Russian—I am too old to learn English? And do they know the history of our Russia? There was Michael Igorovitch, a lieutenant in my company, the Horse Guards of Poltava you know, who went to America. Perhaps I can find him—but no, there will be no answer."

One day in May Dmitri brought the answer—a letter looking very formidable and official, in typewritten English. His face was set, blank. I translated slowly, keeping my eyes turned from his face.

We have just discovered that an inmate, Boris Krasov, claiming to be your brother, succeeded in smuggling two letters out addressed to you, through the services of a guard, whom we have just dismissed.

Boris Krasov has been an inmate here since 1914. Of his past we know nothing except that, just previous to his admittance, he became hypochrondrically religious and in a frenzy murdered a man in an argument over religion. He was adjudged insane, committed here, and his mania has increased, sometimes to the point of violence. At other times he is quite normal and seemingly sane. Such, as you probably know, is characteristic of this type of insanity.

We trust that the contents of these letters, if they reached you, have not annoyed you. Please ignore any others he may find means to send you. We shall be glad to send you further information about him, should he be your brother as he has just recently claimed.

The letter was signed by the superintendent of one of the state hospitals in Illinois.

I finished translating but continued to stare at the paper, not wishing to meet his eye. Then he put his hand on my shoulder and said, "So, now I understand. Poor Boris, his *has* been a hard, hard life." He straightened up, although a twinge of pain crossed his face, and reached for his overcoat. It was the old gray army coat, patched, shredded, buttonless. He foresaw my question, "Oh, yes, I exchanged your coat for my old one. Yours did not quite fit me."

He shook hands, and refused a bank note. "By the way, should you know of anyone who wants French lessons, send him to me. Liebknecht street, number four. My room is hard to find but just ask anyone there. Everyone knows the old man who teaches French."

IN THE PROVINCES

X

AKHMED: THE INNKEEPER

FOR three days we had driven over the rocky roads that led through the narrow passes of Daghestan. Behind us were the sheer cliffs, the rocky chasms of the interior; our road led to the coast of the Caspian. Before us were the green foothills that looked on the sea. Behind us the mountains were steep, stony, treeless. It was sunset; clouds, like shapeless birds, were nestling on the mountain summits for the night. Herds were descending from the heights to their villages.

The horses moved wearily. They were panting as they climbed still another slope, for we had travelled twenty-five miles since dawn. The jangle of our teapot, tied on one side of the wagon, accompanied the noise of the clash of hoofs on stones. Our driver, dubbed "Gus" in preference to his guttural polysyllabic name, turned on his seat and said, "Two more *versts* and we shall reach an *aul*, a village, where we can stop for the night. I have a relative there, my aunt." His record was perfect: he had a relative, real or hastily created for the chance of selling curios to the foreigners, in every village through which we passed.

The horses, as if understanding, broke into a trot. We soon reached the outlying orchards of a village, passing and repassing the little irrigation canals with their precious water. A few villagers were picking apricots although fruit drying season was nearly over.

Clusters of poplar trees in the distance, the mark of villages in the Caucasus, showed us where the houses stood. We rattled by the cemetery, its tall stones graven in Arabic characters, and into a main street with its dust, half a foot thick.

The way was crowded with women returning from the grain fields up on the mountain slopes. Little girls with water jugs balanced on their heads were coming from the well. Out of a side alley came the village herds, broad horned oxen, black sheep and goats, plodding back to their owners' stables. Traffic was confused. On every door-sill sat the men of the house. Before several doors hung the meat of freshly slaughtered lambs, dripping blood on the dust below; their black caracul hides were stretched out near by. There were people moving about on the verandas of the little clay, adobe-like houses.

The day's work was done. Against the sky, in silhouette, rose the minaret of the village mosque.

Our driver shouted to the men as we passed. They cried back greetings in guttural Avarian. A crowd of men was gathered before a large brown clay building with a sign over its door reading, in Russian and Arabic characters, "SOVIET." For five minutes Gus talked with some of the men in the local language. "There's some excitement in the *aul*," he said as we started on, but he offered no further explanation.

The horses knew where they were going. They broke into the maddest gallop—to stop abruptly fifty feet farther before a two-storied house with a gate set in the first floor where the front door should be. The gate swung open and the horses walked into a courtyard. The house surrounded it on three sides. A little man, as wide as he was tall and twice as stout as he was wide, came down to greet us from the second story balcony.

"I have rooms for the night. You can stay here," he said, cordially, in Russian. "You are the first foreigners I have had in my inn."

He led us up to the balcony which ran full way around three sides of the court. Doors to rooms opened on to it: at one far end was the kitchen. All home life was concentrated on the second floor. On the first floor were the granaries, the store houses, and the stable. The court was churned up with filth. Sheds closed the fourth side of the court. With the gate barred the house was like a little fortress.

The innkeeper showed us to a dark room. On two sides against the wall there was a wide shelf of solid brick work, several feet high, covered with threadbare carpets. The young American with me felt the surface and said, discouraged, "Caucasian bricks may be softer than American, but these don't feel like it." While we unpacked, Gus and our host talked excitedly in Avarian. The innkeeper suddenly flew into a rage at something the driver said and waddled away. "There is much excitement and trouble in the village," said Gus, "this fat Akhmed had better be afraid." He said nothing more and went below to feed his horses.

Daghestan is a little district, the size of Delaware, in the northeastern Caucasus, fronting on the Caspian.

Long ago, as invasions poured from the East through the Caucasus each succeeding tribe left behind remnants in the desolate mountain valleys. Years later the armies of the Crescent conquered these mountain peoples but could not blend them; each group held to its language and to its customs. Here, too, came Tamburlain and the capital of the land, until the revolution, was called "Tamburlain's fortress." It is now called Buinaksk in honor of one who died when another army, the Red Army, invaded the valleys of Daghestan in 1919. After Tamburlain came the Persians to make Derbent their proudest seaport.

Endless invasions have made this small land a philologist's paradise. Here are no less than thirty-eight separate languages, related only in their use of gutturals. Here are Avarian, Chichenian, Darjinian, Akhvakhtian, Botlikhian peoples and even a race of mountain Jews, distinct from all other Jewry. Of some of these peoples only a few hundreds remain.

Daghestan has passed through as many hands as an old Arabic coin. To-day it is an autonomous Soviet republic, and strange foreign words have crept into the mountain dialects—words like "socialism," "electrification." Karl Marx and Lenin are new heroes in the land. Once there was another hero, a hundred years ago, when the political status of Daghestan was undefined. Then armies went forth to conquer these mountains, valleys, and poplar studded villages for the Tsar. A defender, one sheik, Shamil, arose from the Avarian peoples, the largest racial group in the country. Where he was there was the hope for a united, independent

Daghestan. Where he went there went the suspicion of hope for an Empire embracing all Mohammedan peoples.

For thirty years the armies of the Double Eagle tried to catch him. He fled from one peak to another. Whole villages were burned and, in revenge, Russian columns were crushed in the narrow defiles by man made avalanches. After thirty years he was captured. The Red flag now flies over Soviet headquarters in forlorn little *auli*, yet, at night, around the fires in their clay-brick huts, old men still tell of Shamil.

Although one village often speaks a language totally different from its neighboring village five miles off, although intermarriage was rare before the revolution, yet the men everywhere dress in the long black cloaks, the boots, and the caracul hats typical of all the Caucasus; they are swarthy and their seeming ferociousness is not lessened by the *kindzhali*, the long pointed daggers, which every man past fourteen continually wears. The women dress variously; in some villages they wear long black pantaloons. They age rapidly for they do most of the work in the house and in the fields. The men prefer to ride or gossip.

Here, for nearly a thousand years, was a Mohammedan stronghold and, since Shamil's time, a fortress of Mohammedanism militant. Before the revolution the *mullahs*, the priests, were the most important men in the villages. Mohammedan customs prevailed although, in some of the villages, the women went unveiled. Those wealthy citizens who counted their possessions in flocks of fat sheep, in land, and in speedy surefooted mountain horses, asked no greater good in this world than a pilgrimage to Mecca.

The country has its natural resources but they have scarce been tapped. There is little fertile land in the valleys and, worse, it rains seldom in summer. Water is precious. The mountain snows melt in April but the rushing torrents of spring are dried beds of rock by July. Agricultural methods are primitive and whole *auli* sometimes starve when cut off from the world by the snows of winter. Then it is that disease and plague stalk through the passes where no doctor can ride.

It is not Russia. Its people say "When I was in Russia," meaning in any village above the north Caucasus railroad. The few Russians who travel there are called foreigners while the fewer foreigners are called Russians. To this day there seems to be little love lost for the conquerors from the north. The revolution conquered Daghestan after two years of the bloodiest fighting in the whole civil war; it conquered there, as elsewhere, by winning that great majority, the landless, to united action against the landlords. Then Russian support more or less withdrew, leaving this mixture of peoples to work out its own salvation, leaving the *mullahs* to cry their call to evening prayer from the shapely minarets.

Akhmed brought a samovar and some boiled eggs. While we ate he looked curiously at our belongings and asked a few questions about our impressions of his country. "You should have come before the revolution," he said. "Then there was something to see. Now everybody is poor and everything interesting about our people has been wiped out."

Gus returned. He had found his aunt busy plastering a house she was building. "She wants you to come to supper," he announced. "Will you pay me some of my wages now? I'll go out to buy some lamb. That will be a treat for her."

"I should say so," Akhmed interrupted. "Before the revolution there was always meat in the village, but not now." He pointed to where the clouds hung in scallops. "Once those hill sides were black with herds. Many were killed or stolen during the civil war and have never been replaced. And the people who own herds to-day know little about taking care of them."

"There are many herdless families; everything was divided equally after the civil war but later the clever ones managed to buy the herds from some of the poorer peasants—like you did, Akhmed," said Gus.

"I? I don't own one sheep," the innkeeper replied, his face red with anger.

"No—but you did until your brother went to jail. Then your herd was confiscated."

Akhmed changed the subject. "Come out in the village and look around."

The village lay on a steep slope. The houses, built of clay brick, stood in tiers. The roof of each successive house was part of the courtyard of the house above. Each house had two floors, the first used as the stable. A flight of steps led to the second floor. Here was a broad veranda, littered with implements and bags of grain. Doors led to the two rooms of the house. On

the clay sides of the houses and the walls of the courtyards there were stuck long rows of circular pads.

"Ox manure," said Akhmed noticing my glance of
curiosity. "See, there are little children sticking it up
on the wall. That's one of our children's household
chores. The manure dries there and is used for fuel.
Wood is so scarce." I agreed. The east Caucasus mountains are gaunt rock and trees are rare.

"Everybody is so poor," continued Akhmed.

"It was just the same before the revolution," said
Gus. "What other kind of fuel would they use?"

"Has he been telling you about life before the revolution the whole time you've been travelling with
him?" said Akhmed. "What does he know? He was a
herd boy here."

"I was old enough to fight in the Red Army for two
years. We fought a few miles away at Devil's Valley,
where three thousand mountaineers died in two days.
But we broke through the White ranks and reached the
coast. Where were you then, fat Akhmed?"

Akhmed ignored the question. "All the old customs
of our people are gone. Once we wore handsome cos-
tumes; our women wore dresses embroidered in gold.
One dress of a wife of Shamil took twenty years to
make and the woman who made it went blind. Our
brides we decked with silver ornaments, sometimes
with twenty pounds of silver, with turquoises and onyx.
A wedding in those days lasted a week and lambskins
full of wine were piled to the roof. Drinking and fighting! Now the Soviet compels all guests at weddings to
leave their knives in a pile outside the door. A policeman guards the pile."

"No wedding was any good unless there were half a dozen fights," added Gus.

"Yes, everything is changed. Our old customs are gone. But one thing the revolution has not altered; out of the killings at weddings there grew family feuds. Those feuds continue to-day and new ones begin. Of course, stealing wives from neighboring villages seldom happens—that was always a great cause of feuds. Just last week one of the men in our village went up in the mountains to gather brush. He did not return at nightfall. He was found two days later with a knife in his back. Now his brother will wait for an opportunity to kill some one in the family that killed him."

"There were more than three hundred such killings in this district last year," said Gus.

"Is that what caused all the excitement in this village to-night?" I asked.

"No, it's something else," Gus replied, glancing at Akhmed.

The innkeeper continued: "We Avari are a mountain people. There are a hundred thousand of us. Before the revolution we seldom saw foreigners from Russia —in the cities, yes, but here in the villages came only the soldiers. Now we are all governed from Moscow. Twenty years ago, ah, we spent our life in the saddle, as men should except when they go to the mosque. What hunting there was! In the mountains there are deer, wild boar, wild goats. I have seen twenty men go out with a pack of two hundred dogs and return three days later with fifty wild boars: a hundred dogs would be killed in the fighting. Game is increasing now for few go hunting. Guns may be kept only with special permission from the police and powder and bullets are hard to get.

"We are short of everything—and Daghestan is a poor country anyway. Our rug weaving has stopped for raw materials are more difficult to secure. Food is scarce; we have had a drought this summer and corn will be scarcer than ever. Before the revolution the head of a village looked out for his people. A village was a unit, we Avari were a unit. But now—long live the Soviet!"

Men were still sitting before every house. They looked curiously at the foreigners. It takes more than two weeks in Daghestan to free one's mind from the thought that those questioning black-browed glances and those dangling knives do not imply murderous intent. Twilight was coming over the village and kerosene lamps began to shine on the open varandas. Suddenly there was the sound of music. The throb of a drum braced the cracked notes of a bugle. Down the narrow street came a parade—all children, wearing red neckties or red bandannas. They carried a banner bearing some slogan written in Arabic letters. I asked Akhmed to translate.

"It says 'Death to some robber Chinaman'——"

"Chinaman?" I asked puzzled. "What is a Chinaman doing in Daghestan?"

"His name is—uh—uh—Chang Kai Shek."

Then I understood. Relations between the Soviet Union and China had recently been broken off. Anti-Chinese propaganda had travelled even to Daghestan.

Gus left us to follow the parade. Akhmed continued, as we walked back to the inn, "That's what's wrong with our country. Our children join the Red children's organization and know more about China than they do about the great men of their own land. The Russians are a clever people. We fought all their earlier attempts to Russify us. Before the revolution they used force: that was something we knew how to meet. They forbade our language and made us learn Russian. Our nationalism thrived wherever we were oppressed. Now, very cleverly, they permit what they call cultural autonomy. Our language is freely taught in the schools. But they stress the fact that it is the Soviet Union and that our nationalism, our customs, our traditions, are worn out, 'bourgeois.' Our children learn Russian eagerly, that they may go to higher Soviet schools; twenty years ago they would have fought it.

"No one protests when some of our own people come back from Russia and say 'Nationalism is wrong. It is being so nationalistic that has kept you a weak people. Unite all nationalities and we shall be a strong Soviet nation.' What of our Avarian peoples then?—a drop in the Red Sea. These Communists are like the old Armenian wife who told her husband, 'The donkey is very sick. Take him out in the mountains, lose him, and let him die there.' He did so and returned next day. 'Did you lose him?' the wife asked. 'I should say so—we walked twenty versts and I lost myself as well. And if it hadn't been for the donkey guiding me I couldn't have found my own way back.'

"Our nationalism may be weak and sickly now, but it is the only thing that will help the Avari to find their way. The pride of a people is in those things that make it different from all other peoples. Once we dreamt of a Holy War. That is what we need—another Shamil to lead us. Then we shall unite with other Mohammedan peoples who more or less resemble us and those sly, blond, Russian scoundrels from the north shall not force us into poverty, into Communism, into the loss of all that our forefathers taught us. I talk frankly to you because I am in so much trouble already that nothing you might repeat would make any difference. But these are the things I believe."

He walked on silently. "Look at our young men! Poverty forces them to become effeminate—they marry only one wife. I have only one now because that is all I can afford but once I had six."

"You are a good Mohammedan?" I asked.

"I used to be. I went to Mecca in 1916. But now— you heard there was some excitement in our village, didn't you? It's about a new mosque we began to build." He said no more for Gus joined us, bringing two bottles of wine.

"We'll go over to my aunt's now," he said. "That parade was going to the school house. Ibram, the teacher, is making a speech to them. Is Ibram a friend of yours, Akhmed?"

The innkeeper only scowled and hurried home.

Darkness had settled over the *aul*. There were no street lights to guide us along the crooked uphill lane.

Once we bumped into a brush laden donkey, coming down from the mountain. Gus swore in rich Avarian gutturals at the woman following behind.

We went through a little courtyard, climbed a veranda, and entered a room with a very low ceiling. There was one other room in the house. A fire was burning on the hearth but only half the smoke went up the clay-brick chimney; the other half stayed in the room and the odor from the burning manure was overpowering. On hooks around the room hung pots and pans, clothes, harness, and small farm implements. In one corner of the room, opposite the fire, was a high brick bench; covered with a mattress and some rugs, it served as a bed.

Our hostess was a lean gaunt woman of fifty. She wore the costume of all women in that vicinity—a long black dress hanging in folds to her sandaled feet. The front of the dress occasionally served as a towel to wipe off the dishes. A cape, clasped to her forehead by a silver band, hung down her back. She spoke only Avarian; conversation was going to be difficult. She continued preparing the dinner.

The lamb had been cut in cubes an inch thick and the pieces were boiling with some garlic. She took rough-ground cornmeal, mixed it with water to make a thin paste, and, having cleaned the outside of a basin with her dress, she spread the paste over it. This she put near the fire and turned it as one side browned. Then she took the lamb, transfixed it on long metal prongs and broiled it over the fire. In ten minutes dinner was ready. Each guest received a chunk of un-

salted, tough, gritty gray bread and a skewer of meat.
Table etiquette demanded that the guest take a piece
of the bread, wrap it securely around a piece of meat on
the skewer and pull. The resulting parcel was swal-
lowed with its "corrugated paste-board" wrapping.

We satisfied or, rather, destroyed our appetite after
a few mouthfuls. Although our hostess insisted hos-
pitably that we eat more, she and Gus had no trouble
finishing our portions as well as their own.

Gus, between huge mouthfuls, acted as interpreter.
"My aunt says she has a son in Moscow, at the University. He is studying to be a doctor. She is a widow
and must cultivate her little piece of land alone. She
says her son sends her ten rubles a month out of the
twenty-seven he receives monthly, but she is very poor.
She asks if you would not like to buy some old rugs,
some silver jewelry, or some water jugs that belonged
to Shamil."

I laughed and said that everything in the country
that people wanted to sell us was always said "to belong to Shamil."

"Yes," said Gus, innocently, "he was a great man.
My aunt's father fought with him against the Russians."

I asked about conditions in the village. Gus translated at great length. Drying apricots and plums was
the chief industry. It was operated on a co-operative
basis; the village as a whole owned the orchards. Together the people repaired the irrigation canals in the
spring. Together they picked the fruit when it rip-
ened. Together they packed it and some of the men

took it to the sea coast in the high-wheeled ox-carts. Profits from the fruit were for the village; the whole business was managed by the local Soviet of five elected deputies. In addition each family had a bit of land and most of them had a few sheep. "But there are some men who have more than others. They buy the flocks from their poorer neighbors," said Gus. "In that way they get rich. And the older men still control the village; the younger men go off to the cities—as I did," he added with a puff of pride. "But it is better than it was before the revolution. Then one man controlled the whole village for he was the head and very wealthy. The poor had nothing and they were always indebted to him. In this village the richest man was Akhmed——"

"The innkeeper?"

Gus laughed. "He has only been an innkeeper for five years. Soviet power was not strong here until five years ago and his influence still continued. Then, when he saw he might be arrested, he declared that his house should thereafter be an inn. He sent away five of his wives, pretending he was too poor to keep them. Oh, he is very clever and very sly! He used to talk boastingly about what he would do against our Soviet power. He used to say that what we need most is another Shamil, to lead us in a holy war."

Gus talked on at great length, occasionally drawing on his aunt for additional information. The innkeeper had had his friends on the village Soviet; they controlled it and he controlled them. Contact between the Daghestan capital in Makhach-Kalai and this remote

local council was feeble. The Soviet had run things to
suit themselves. "They raised the taxes on the poor
and lowered their own. Finally, my aunt, who is very
poor, told her son in Moscow about it. He reported it
and police came from the capital; there was a big
scandal and Akhmed's brother now sits in jail. But
that shrewd scoundrel, Akhmed, escaped. He became
an innkeeper."

A howl, as from a wounded dog, cut through the
silence of the night. I jumped and Gus laughed. "That
is the *mullah* calling evening prayer." The sound,
seeming far away, was unholy, fearful. "Fool," said
Gus, "he had better save his breath, especially to-
night."

"Why to-night?"

"You will see later. Nobody will go to mosque
to-night."

"Ask your aunt who it is that usually goes to
mosque," I said.

His aunt was most vociferous and guttural in her explanations: "Only the old men go; they die off each
year but the *mullah* still has power in the village.
Three years ago he tried to be elected to the village
Soviet but there is some law that says *mullahs* shall
have no political power at all, not even the right to
vote. Before the revolution they were powerful and
took much of our money. Now we have an anti-religious course in our school. There is a young man,
Ibram, an Avarian, who went to Moscow to be educated. He returned a year ago and works very hard.
He is a Communist—the only one in the village. He

has organized Pioneers, he teaches school, and at night holds courses for the older people. My aunt says if she knew you foreigners were coming she would have asked him to come here this evening."

Our conversation was interrupted by the noise of several wagons rattling by on the road below the house. Our hostess and Gus broke into excited Avarian.

"There they come," said Gus to me, "quick, let us run over to the inn." Our hostess strapped her sandals on her bare feet.

"What is it? The event you expected?"

"Yes. Secret Police officers from Buinaksk. Everybody knew they were coming to-day or to-morrow. There has been a great scandal. The fruit crop this year was very good and the profits large. So the village Soviet, with its old men, decided to take more than half the money and build a new mosque. Yet we need roads; and we hoped that the Soviet would use some of the money to buy one of your automatic fruit sprayers from America. But they decided to build a mosque and began it last month. That school teacher protested and they threatened to kill him. He made a report to Buinaksk and the police have come now to make an investigation into such a big scandal."

"They have arrested the Soviet?"

"Not yet—the members wouldn't run away. We Avari are not cowards. But there will be a trial to-morrow and perhaps someone will be shot. The *mullah*, maybe. That Akhmed is not on the Soviet. Yet we all know who is the power in this village. If they let him escape this time——"

As we hurried through the darkened lanes to the inn we heard a voice, somewhere in the distance, singing to the accompaniment of a guitar. The voice rose slowly half tone by half tone. Then the singer descended the scale in the same way. The guitar kept up its rapid music in what sounded like quarter tones.

"What's he singing?" I asked.

"An Avarian song. It says 'Give me a bright sword and a speedy horse and I can cut down all my neighboring enemies.' "

The inn was ablaze with light. A crowd had gathered before the closed gates. We passed through to the courtyard; here there were two wagons and several saddle horses. A group of men stood on the balcony, some wearing army uniforms with scarlet topped caps, the mark of the Secret Police soldiers, and others were in civilian clothes. They were talking seriously, calmly, and smoking cigarettes.

I have never seen a man so changed as was Akhmed. He had waddled lazily when we arrived. Now he ran breathlessly from kitchen to balcony, carrying food, mattresses, rugs. With every breath he bleated, "Yes, comrade," "No, comrade," always adding the 's' which in the Russian language denotes servility. No one paid any attention to him except to give more orders or to hurry him.

Some one knocked insistently at the outside gate. "Citizen," one of the men in uniform called to the innkeeper, "open that gate—it's probably Ibram."

A man in his early thirties, dressed in Russian blouse

and trousers, without boots, entered. "That's the school teacher," Gus said. He and the soldiers went into the room next to ours and closed the door. They conversed quietly. Akhmed found many excuses for approaching that closed door. Finally he came to our room, ostensibly to see whether the mattresses he had placed on the brick piles were soft enough for us; but he kept close to the wall trying to hear what was being said in the adjoining room.

"I am an old man," he said suddenly. "I have done no wrong against my people. But it is as Allah wills." He went below to the stable where Gus was sleeping.

After an hour the conference broke up. The newcomer, Ibram, stepped into our room with one of the men in uniform. "I heard there were Americans here," the teacher said. "I am sorry I have not been able to come and see you. We are very busy to-day. Perhaps I shall have a chance to ride some of the way with you to-morrow morning."

From the stable below came the sound of laughter— as of one man laughing at another caught suddenly in a ridiculous predicament. After a little while Akhmed returned to our room. "That driver of yours—what a swine he is! Fifteen years ago I should not have let him step on my land, let alone sleep in my stable."

Then the quiet of the village settled over the inn. But that song continued, high up on the hill.

The noise outside the inn awoke us early. A crowd of villagers was waiting; there had not been so many strangers in the village since the civil war. Wanting to start early, Gus had already harnessed the horses; by driving all day we could reach the railroad and he could devote the remainder of the week to drinking up the eighty rubles he had charged us for his services.

The innkeeper was busy getting breakfast for the men in the room next to ours. We waited, and waited long for our turn; the guests were being served in the order of their importance. Gus stood on the balcony and watched the innkeeper scampering back and forth with trays of bread, eggs, and watermelon. Occasionally Gus broke into laughter but Akhmed only frowned and perspired. When he brought us a samovar he apologized, "I have only one, and you had to wait while it was in use."

We finished our breakfast and paid our bill—three rubles for everything. Gus was standing near by, greatly interested. When Akhmed had withdrawn Gus explained, "He charged you a very small amount because he is afraid. He's trying to behave as little like a skinflint as possible."

Our neighbors were walking on the balcony, paying no attention either to us or to Akhmed. Ibram, the young teacher, was with them. We loaded our baggage on the wagon and were ready to leave. "I'll be with you in a minute," Ibram said, whereupon he kept us waiting half an hour. Akhmed came down to the court. "You are soon going to America?" he asked. "What I would not give if I could leave for America right now, with you, this morning. Well, go with Allah, as do I." He glanced at the uniformed men on the balcony and went upstairs.

We rattled through the village. Its people had been working since dawn. Gus's aunt was plastering the walls of her new house. She stood on a ladder, smearing the mud over the clay bricks and smoothing it with a board. Another woman was mixing clay, water and straw in a wooden trough.

We passed the threshing floors. Here, on the hard clay, women and children were spreading the opened sheaves. A small boy sitting on a board with pegs of wood protruding beneath was being dragged by a panting ox round and round over the levelled grain. On another floor the straw was being raked to one side while the grain and chaff were swept to the centre. On a neighboring floor a man was winnowing the grain. With the wooden shovel he tossed a mixture of wheat and chaff high into the air. The wind blew the chaff away. It blended with the dust of the road and blew into our faces.

"It's too bad you aren't going to stay here," said Ibram. "There will be a trial that would interest you very much. It has been so difficult to get the villagers to accuse the Soviet members; they are afraid of reprisals. But now we have these rascals caught in their own evil deeds. They voluntarily decided to use money from the village orchards to build a new mosque. That is misappropriation of village funds, of State funds— therefore counter-revolution.

"We must be severe against such criminality. When we clean off a piece of woodland we have to tear down all the old growth that hinders our new planting. It is the same in the village. Everywhere we have had to

fight blind nationalism and the backwardness of in-
grown Mohammedanism. The *mullahs* and the former
landowners have always worked together. Do you
know," his voice expressed the greatest surprise, "when
I came here a year ago I found that all nine of the
mullah's children were being permitted to study in the
village school? I put them out immediately although
there was much opposition. Why should we use Soviet
money to educate the children of Soviet enemies?
There are many things we can do with our country——"

"Do you mean Russia or Daghestan?"

"I always speak of Daghestan as my country. We
are guided politically from Moscow but we are free to
work out our own economic and cultural future. There
is so much we can do here."

"We passed by the site of that new dam yesterday,"
Gus interrupted. "The engineers were beginning
work."

"That is one of the things we are going to do,"
Ibram nodded. "In three years we shall have built a
dam there on the Koika, thirty *versts* from here, that
will furnish electric power for all northern Daghestan.
I think you Americans are going to equip the power
plant for us. Just think what that will mean—electric
light in all these little mountain *auli,* no more hand
labor in our mines. With factories and mines here to
employ part of our population we shall no longer be
dependent on the rains of summer for our life in
winter.

"Yet, with all these things coming in the near future

there are those among us who would rather see Shamil return. They lament the passing of customs and traditions, not seeing that those customs will be replaced by the habits of an up-to-date modern people; and the traditions will be replaced by the aspirations of a country developing its wealth and spending all the profits for the good of all its people. No longer will a few men hoard the wealth of our country for the sake of foolish and useless journeys to Mecca. I always think of this when I feel discouraged by my work here.

"I have fought alone to convince these people of the advantages in our new ways; with the adults it is impossible. When they openly oppose me I can call for help from the city as I have had to do in all this trouble about the new mosque. With the young it is different. They are interested in all I tell them about the 'new life.' I introduced physical culture here; we had a soccer team and played every day until the bladder in the ball broke. I could not get another one—we are so short of manufactured goods! The old men used to watch us play. They would sneer, 'Better if you taught them how to ride and use a sword, Ibram; they will need that training in the holy war against Russia.' "

I remembered seeing a newspaper account a few weeks before, of the murder of a young Communist like this one in a village aroused to fury by his innovations; such incidents are only too frequent. I asked, "Aren't you in danger here with so many people against you?"

"There have been many attacks and murders on people like myself," he replied simply, "murders frightful in their ferocity, but none as yet in this district. In villages, especially in Russia, such men have been tied to trees and burnt, they have been blinded, they have been shot in the back. The fact that I am a native of this village has saved me up to this time. I am one of these people and they know that I would report my father for any counter-revolutionary activity as quickly as I have reported these scoundrels who planned the new mosque. But my father's sheep have been killed and his ox was mysteriously lamed last week!"

"They burnt the house of one Communist near Khunzakh a month ago," Gus interrupted.

"Yes, we are a wild people, easily angered," Ibram continued. "Some day I may be found on a lonely mountain slope, my eyes gouged out and a dagger through my back. But I think that, after this trial to-day and to-morrow, this village will be scared for many a month; they will know that I am not alone but that there is a power greater than their traditions behind me."

"What will happen at the trial?"

"We shall arrest five members of the Soviet. Some will be sentenced to the highest measure of social defense, shooting. Perhaps we shall shoot Akhmed too— he has long been a reactionary force in the village. The others will go to jail. Their trial will be public for we want to set an example for the whole country. It is by such violent but necessary measures that we are clearing our land for its new harvest. Don't you use dynamite in America to clear away old stumps and roots?"

In the distance we saw the dust raised by a train of ox-carts. "Here come carts with cement for that new dam. I'll ride back to the village with them," said Ibram and he slid from the wagon. "Ox-carts—you would laugh at them in your America but some day we too shall have cement roads, automobiles, and there will be electricity in the little *auli*."

We met the carts. Ibram found a place on one of them and waved good-bye. Gus clucked to his horses but they were unwilling to hurry. The dust flew in thick clouds and the heat was oppressive. "We need rain so badly," said Gus, as we passed a field of withered corn. "No rain now for forty days." So we jogged along—toward the blue haze beyond those little hills that marked the sea.

XI

MOHAMMED FATEEV: THE BARBER

"Thus once it befell in the city of Kazan," as a character in *"Boris Godunov"* sings when he tells of conflicts between Russians and Tatars in the proud Tatar capital long ago.

Kazan, now the capital of the Tatar Autonomous Socialist Soviet Republic, is a Volga city with a hundred thousand people, one-third of whom are Tatars. Once that people controlled all Russia. There are three millions of them in the Soviet Union, gathered here in the central Volga region, in the Crimea and in Turkestan.

A little river divides Kazan. On one side are the Russians; on the other side live most of the Tatars as of yore. There has been a daily bazaar in the Tatar quarter for endless years. It still continues, since no revolution could eliminate the oriental love of petty trading, and at the corner of the huge market square still stands a red brick mosque.

At one end of the market, when I entered it that afternoon, were the little stands of private traders; on the side opposite stood peasant wagons loaded with produce. Here were open-air restaurants dispensing *peremania,* meat and dough balls, flat rools filled with boiled barley, and meat stews of various kinds, colors and degrees of iridescence. The dozen plates and dippers belonging to each enterprise were in constant use.

Melon rinds lay everywhere. There had been no rain for six days, but there was mud in the deepest wagon ruts. Aimless winds raised little flurries of dust. On one side of the square stood a half dozen shanties, each labelled "Sanitary Barber Shop."

The market was a cross section of the complicated ethnology of central Russia. In the crowds passing by there were square-faced Chuvashi, swarthy Bashkiri, Chermesi, Mordvi and Volga Germans, but the Tatar face with its sparse, walrus-like beard predominated. An ancient bearded Tatar sitting on a box before the pile of old clothes that constituted both his "shop" and his goods had made a place for me, beside him. Along the maze of paths all around us were similar merchants with second-hand clothes, shoes, bottles and scrap iron spread out for sale on the sun-baked mud.

The old Tatar, who wore a gaudy skull cap and a long black cloak and sat cross-legged on his box, was explaining to me, in broken Russian, stranger that I was from America, how he came to be there. "I served in the Tsarist army," he said. "I fought at Port Arthur. I had a little farm when the revolution broke out. And three wives. The revolution beggared me. After the famine seven years ago, I had nothing left but my land. Where was I to get the means to work it? The government doesn't give free horses. I threw away the land. And here I am. I can earn scarce enough now to keep one wife."

Near us stood a young man, clean shaven, wearing a Russian blouse, trousers and sandals. He was listening to our conversation, curious perhaps about the

American. But the merchant's complaints proved too much for him. "A Soviet profiteer, that's what you are, Abdul," he interrupted. "You ought to give up this private trading and go back to working honestly. This way you produce nothing."

"Honestly?" the merchant replied. "Why should it be dishonest to buy and sell? Who can make a living in the village these days? My brother raises honey. The government comes and says, 'Sell it to us for so much,' offering him a starvation price. If he refuses, he can't sell it anywhere else and he starves; if he does sell it, he starves. For you, Mohammed Fateev, it's easy— you're a barber and have a definite income each week. The revolution is all right if you gain from it."

A customer appeared, an ungainly young peasant, seeking a pair of trousers.

"That pair is two rubles," the merchant said.

The peasant threw them down with the comment: *"Batoushka!* their owner did nothing but sit in them. Look, they're quite worn out, there isn't any seat." Yet the bargaining continued.

The barber turned to me, remarking, "You wouldn't believe it, but he earns maybe a hundred rubles a month from this junk."

"Junk, that's all we have here," a neighboring Tatar merchant joined in. "You Communists have turned everything into junk."

"Everything of value is owned by the government," said Abdul. "Factories, machines—even people. But the government forgets that we are just like the cabmen's horses. Some one asked a Soviet official why the government took over the factories but not the cab business. 'Well,' he replied, 'if we run short of things, the machines in the factories don't spoil. The government doesn't have to worry. But, if we take over the cab business and run short of food, the damned horses die!' So shall we all; for everything gets scarcer. For twelve years we have been living on fat stored away, on goods made before the revolution. There is nothing new."

The merchant on a neighboring box nodded. "It's just like the two Jews who were in a restaurant. They were swearing at the Soviet government. 'Why do you swear so at our government?' interrupted a Communist who overheard them. '*Oi*, we weren't swearing at the Communists; we were swearing at Nicholas II,' they said. The Communist looked puzzled until one of the Jews explained, 'He gave us bread for eleven years after the revolution, but the scoundrel didn't give it to us for the twelfth.' "

Mohammed spat in disgust. "Can our government do wonders in twelve years? You must first sweep away the rubbish from the place on which you are going to build something new. The revolution gave us Tatars the first real chance to amount to something." He went back to his barber shop to attend to a customer.

"These young fellows—they consider us some of the rubbish," said the mechant. "It is easy for them to be impudent. The revolution destroyed all that was fine in the Tatar people. Tatars were always better than Russians—that we know, even if the Russians did conquer us and change us from warriors into merchants. And, among us, all were equal in the sight of Allah, prince and beggar, fighter and trader. Now their talk about classes has made Tatars hate one another. Our whole life is upset. We shall die before we get used to it."

He waved to a passing friend and said to me: "What a fool that old fellow is! The revolution came. He thought it made him a young man. He kicked out his wife. He then married a pretty girl of eighteen. What did he want to marry one so young for? Now he knows every young man in Kazan because there are always two or three hanging around his house every time he comes home. One night he found one in a closet! He sits here in the bazaar and worries—runs home five times a day. That's where he's going now."

He pointed to another acquaintance, a man with a shaven head topped by a little skull cap, who was sitting behind a tremendous stock of second-hand bottles. "There's another old fool!" he said scornfully. "When the revolution came, he let his hair grow, threw away his cap and declared, 'There is no Allah, and the *mullahs* are all liars.' Of course none of the younger generation go to mosque, but the older generation ought not to change. Our religion was the bond that kept us a united people in the midst of the infidel Russians. That idiot of a bottle seller may never have had any such idea, but just the same he turned religious again and goes to mosque regularly now. Two years ago a runaway horse ran through the bazaar ·twice and touched nothing except his pile of bottles. They were smashed to bits." He laughed heartily. "Allah is still Allah!"

We stopped talking and watched the churning life of the bazaar. The merchant broke the silence to call my attention especially to a young man wearing the sparse mustache and skull cap of a Tatar. "Look, see that chap?" he asked. "That's Akhmed, the brother of the barber Mohammed. He hasn't been in Kazan for two years. He's a rascal, just as his father was before him. Mohammed's a good boy, but he's a Communist, light-headed, confused. He and his wife live with his mother. He talks all the time about the future of the Tatar people; yet he can't do anything about his own future or straighten things out in his own house!"

Business was not flourishing as the afternoon ended. Some of the merchants began to close up shop—which meant stuffing their second-hand wares in a bag and carrying them home. My friend Abdul showed no signs of leaving until a *mullah* from the minaret of the mosque near by called the faithful to evening prayer. Mohammed rejoined us as Abdul packed away his stock. "Going to mosque, old hypocrite?" he asked.

"Yes, dog, and it would be better for you if you did. Oh, the good old days, when it was the opinion of men that bore weight and not the babbling of irresponsible boys." Then he added some remark in Tatar and walked away.

The barber, without replying, invited me to see his shop and led me toward his own particular frame shack that had the sign "Sanitary Barber Shop" over the door. The room was swept clean but reeked with cheap, heavy perfume. The little kerosene stove in one corner held a steaming kettle. A plain chair, standing before a cracked mirror, and a shelf holding a perfume atomizer, a cake of soap and a grayish towel were the only other furnishings. The price list hung on the wall: "Shave —ten kopecks. Haircut—fifteen kopecks." Hanging by its side, in type so small that no one could read it, was a lengthy order of the Kazan Soviet "concerning the sanitary care of barber shops."

"Abdul told me that my brother passed through the bazaar this afternoon. Did you notice him?" Mohammed asked. "He used to be my partner, but I have another now who takes turns with me at the work. We divide the profits and thus exploit no labor. Are there many differences between my shop and the kind you have in America?"

"Are you allowed to take tips?"

"Tips are considered bourgeois, insulting to honest labor. Besides, no one ever offers me any! I have been a barber for only five years. Before that I was in the army—an officer!"

He was a full-blooded Tatar, born and brought up in a village near Kazan. "The population in our village was almost all Tatar and very strict Moslem. The women were never allowed to eat with the men. Men kept their heads covered always except in the mosque. Mecca was the goal of all who could afford to travel there. My father made his pilgrimage just before the revolution. After the civil war I came to Kazan. Your American Relief was here and fed many of my people—we were in the midde of the famine belt. By the way, won't you come home with me to dinner? My wife would be so glad to see you, an American.

She could tell you how the *amerikantsi* saved her life during the famine. She is a Russian. Tatars seldom married Russians before the revolution, but now—!" He insisted that I should come, and added, "After dinner I can show you around the city!"

There were no signs of any customers, and the square was rapidly clearing. A few men were coming from the mosque. Mohammed closed his shop and fastened not one but three padlocks on the door. "Thieves around here are very plentiful. Runaway boys gather at night. We've locked up most of the homeless children, but four times these runaways have broken into my shop."

As we walked through the dusty streets past piles of melons heaped at corner fruit stands, we saw a poster on a wall announcing the honor that was about to be paid to the city through the visit of a "world-famous" woman magician, "who will positively not hypnotize any of the audience, but, during the performance, the spectators will be as in the quiet of a cataleptic trance."

"What rotten entertainment comes to our city sometimes!" Mohammed commented. "I am much interested in building up our own Tatar theatre. You know, we Tatars are one of the most cultivated of the national minorities in the Soviet Union. We have our writers, our poets and our own theatre. It all interests me as a member of our City Soviet!"

The barber and his wife lived in a side street, on the first floor of a large wooden house. It stood within a cobbled courtyard where there was a well from which all the tenants had to carry their supply of water. The three small rooms of the barber's apartment were clean but crowded with furniture and in need of repair. "I tried to get other rooms, but every city in Russia is crowded and especially Kazan," Mohammed explained.

His wife was small, very blond, with the broad cheekbones that showed, perhaps, Chuvash blood. She seemed hospitable and unconcerned at the sudden appearance of a guest. "You will pardon our house?" she asked. "You know the proverb, 'Don't judge a house by the beauty of its corners but by the fineness of its cakes.'"

The supernumerary member of the household, Mohammed's wrinkled old mother, wore a long black dress, with many folds, and boots made of variegated bits of gaudy leather. Her hair was plaited and bound at the end with strings of old silver coins. She spoke no Russian, and her daughter-in-law evidently could speak little Tatar.

There was the ever-present cabbage soup with black bread for dinner, as in any Russian house. But the old woman put honey, *halva,* a sweet paste made of sesame, and a jar of watery milk on the table. Mohammed talked for a long time in Tatar with his mother, while his wife spoke to me enthusiastically about some members of the American Relief whom she had met during the famine.

Mohammed finally turned to his wife and said: "I was just telling *Mamasha* that I have heard Akhmed has come back. He passed through the bazaar this afternoon."

"What? Has he returned? Well, he doesn't come here," his wife replied angrily. "I hope he has found a job and can help support your mother. Perhaps he knows where your father is."

"After the revolution we had a new divorce law," Mohammed explained to me while his wife glared at her mother-in-law. "My father divorced my mother because he wanted to marry some young girl. The law says that a husband getting a divorce must support his children until they are eighteen, but my brother and I were past that age before my father got the divorce. So my mother got nothing, and the filthy wretch ran off and left her for my brother and me to support."

"That's the law," said his wife, "and it's unfair. Why should old men be allowed to toss aside their wives in that way? Divorces are all right for young people. We must now put up with my father-in-law's discarded wife."

"Then my brother refused to help me support my mother. He left Kazan. What could I do?" Mohammed asked.

"If your brother weren't so much of a rascal as your father, he would have helped. But he was always losing his job and complaining that he had no money."

Beef croquettes followed the cabbage soup. "I am sorry we have no wine," Mohammed said. "We can go out afterward and get some. My mother is a very strict Moslem and won't allow any in the house. However, there is *kumiss*. Have you ever tried fermented mare's milk?" he went on, pointing to the jug. "It's very good for the health."

The old woman continued speaking with Mohammed, and a note of pleading came into her voice. I thought I saw tears in her eyes.

"It would be better if everybody here had to speak Russian," Mohammed's wife commented. "It is so hard to have a mother-in-law that you can't understand."

"The old woman wants me to take Akhmed in if he comes," Mohammed interrupted. "He's her favorite son; yet for two years he hasn't sent a penny to help her and he didn't help her much when he was here. No! He'd better not come back."

But, as we were finishing dinner, there was a knock at the door, followed by the entrance of the young man whom I had seen in the market place. His mother ran toward him and embraced him. Mohammed and his wife were silent, waiting for him to speak.

"I came here from Ufa," he said in Russian.

"You can go back where you came from," said Mohammed sharply. "You come only when you want something. What is it this time?"

"I was working there, but I was discharged. Now I have nothing, and I want to borrow twenty rubles. With that I can go down to Samara and find a job."

"I don't care where you go, but you get no money from me. You ran off and left me to support your mother just as your father did before you. That takes all my money."

"I wanted to tell you—I saw him in Ufa. He is working as a stevedore at the wharf."

"And that *blad,* his wife, is she still with him?" Mohammed asked with the first show of interest.

"No, she ran away with another man. He now lives with the other stevedores."

"He had better not return. The old woman will kill him. You know how she feels toward me for marrying a Russian, but you don't know how she hates him for leaving her so that she has to live with me."

"And with me," his wife added.

Akhmed and his mother went into the kitchen. Mohammed joined them. For ten minutes they talked, the old woman's voice rising ever louder.

"If Mohammed lets his brother stay, I shall go," declared his wife.

Akhmed stepped into the room in time to hear that remark. Mohammed followed and said, in reply, "There, I told you she would say that."

Once more Akhmed asked for money.

As Mohammed hesitated, his wife began, "If you give this loafer any money——"

The old woman, through her tears, was pleading with Mohammed.

Akhmed, as if translating, said with a sneer: "She is right, brother. You have forgotten that, before the revolution, Tatar stood with Tatar." He flashed an angry glance at Mohammed's wife.

Mohammed looked dazed. Every one seemed to forget the presence of an outsider. The old Tatar woman shook her fist in the face of her Russian daughter-in-law and spat at her as well. The young woman only smiled, seized her apron in her own fist, let a corner of it protrude and, extending her arm, showed this "pig's ear" to the old woman. It is a deadly insult to a Tatar. Mohammed blanched. His mother, her eyes full of tears, did not seem to notice.

Akhmed laughed with scorn: "You're always talking about the need for friendship between Russian and Tatar; yet you permit this, and you turn your own brother out." He began to eye eagerly two croquettes that were growing cold on the table. "May I take these with me?" he asked. When Mohammed nodded, he wrapped them in newspaper and left the room.

Mohammed went into the kitchen to quiet his mother, and his wife took the opportunity to apologize to me. "It is a pity that you had to see all this," she said. "These *Bashibazuki*—they are swine! Why should we keep a lazy loafer like Akhmed? One Tatar around this house is enough. Mohammed is different —he's almost Russian. The old woman hates Russians! She thinks they made the law that enabled her husband to leave her."

To the young wife, obviously, the whole situation, racial and domestic, was irksome almost beyond endurance. "Mohammed," she called into the kitchen, "let's go to the cinema this evening. We can forget Akhmed and your father, too."

"You go by yourself," he replied shortly.

"Very well, I will—and perhaps for good." She stamped out of the house.

"Oh, my God!" As he was about to run after her, he remembered my presence. "How sorry I am all this happened; I'll meet her after the cinema."

I was willing to give up my walk with him, but he had counted on showing me the city and would not hear of anything else. As we left the house, he said: "My mother is so hard to live with! Of course she blames the revolution for the way in which her whole life has been wrecked. Had there been no revolution, we should all be living quietly in our little Tatar village. I think of that sometimes. If only she could get along with my wife! Not every Tatar can marry as pretty a Russian girl as I did. But my mother hates Russians, and I am always afraid that my wife will divorce me."

We walked down the main street toward the Kremlin that marked one end of the town. The signs on the shops were printed in both Russian and Arabic letters. The crowds on the streets were no different from those in any Russian provincial town except for the greater frequency of the non-Slavic, Tatar faces.

"I have been a member of the City Soviet for two years," Mohammed said as we passed the municipal building. He seemed eager to talk of things less personal than family affairs. "There are more than a hundred of us. A small group carries on the routine, while the rest of us are divided into committees to do propaganda work—all without pay of course. We can choose the committee we wish to serve on—finance, sanitation, culture."

"And which did you choose?" I asked, remembering the sign in his "sanitary" barber shop.

"I have been on the Cultural Committee for more than a year," he answered proudly.

We passed through the Kremlin gate, now crumbling. Inside the walls stood a dozen white-washed buildings. One was marked "Commissariat of Education of the Tatar Republic." A loudspeaker in one of the barracks was repeating a talk in Tatar from the Kazan station.

Mohammed seemed to forget his personal problems as we looked around the old Tatar fortress. Now he spoke of the Tatar people and their history. "Here the mightiest of our people gathered in the sixteenth century to hold off the Russians. I always like to come to the fortress and imagine what must have happened during that last great siege. It continued for many months. My ancestors built a tunnel from here to the river, and by night they used to sneak down for water. This is the most sacred spot in Tatar history."

Then he spoke of the Tatar people and their future. Although he was a barber, in business for himself, he felt that, as a member of the City Soviet, he was playing a small part in building that future. In everything he said—and he spoke in a lofty tone as if addressing an audience—there was a flaming spirit of nationalism. I remembered the remark the merchant had made that afternoon: "The Tatar people were always better than the Russians."

"We Tatars know," he explained, "what being a minority people in the Tzar's empire really meant. Government officials, except the pettiest, were always Russians. Russian was the only language allowed in the schools. Little attempt was made to teach us anything except how to be good Moslems, and our religion was a barrier to the achievement of cultural or social equality.

"Now, Tatars work in every government office and in high positions as well. The Tatar language is equal with the Russian. We have introduced a Latinized alphabet so that our language can be learned more easily. Arabic letters were used only because of Moslem tradition. Our new alphabet is a blow at the power of that religion among our people."

Yet Mohammed was conscious of the difficulties that still arose between Tatars and Russians, even twelve years after the revolution. When I asked whether the Russian and Tatar languages were used equally in the government offices, the cheerful confidence in his voice vanished and he spoke as if discouraged.

"We are supposed to use both languages. But there is still a good deal of false nationalism among the Russians. Of course, you can't expect all the old Russian clerks to forget that twelve years ago Tatars were called dogs. In government positions there are still many more Russian workers than Tatars in proportion to our population. We are increasing the number of Tatars every year and dismissing the Russians. Naturally that makes for bad feeling. The number of skilled Tatars is small. Few of us were given higher education before the revolution, and those few were not of the proletariat.

"All kinds of things keep us from gaining any ground on the Russian language. With the slogan, 'Everyone must be bilingual,' we have tried to introduce language courses in offices and factories. They begin with much enthusiasm, but attendance soon falls off. If a Tatar replaces some Russian in an office, the Russians quit the course and swear that they will have nothing more to do with this swinish language nor with the 'pigs'-ears' who speak it."

Mohammed told endless stories of things that happened "because we have not yet had time to work out the relation between Russians and Tatars." He spoke rapidly, as if afraid that other subjects might creep into his mind. "One Tatar peasant wrote to a hospital asking for a place for his wife, who was seriously ill. His letter was answered in Russian; so he returned the letter with another in Tatar, asking for a translation. His request lay around the office eight weeks before it was granted. They received a note from him the following week, saying, 'Thank you for permitting my wife to enter the hospital. She died two weeks ago.' You see what we Tatars must face in trying to realize cultural equality."

"And social equality?"

"You have seen that I married a Russian," he said with some triumph in his voice. "Before the revolution few Russian women married Tatars because they feared they might be only one of a number of wives and might have to live a more or less secluded Moslem-harem type of existence. Lord, it is getting late—time for me to go to the theatre and meet my wife. It has been good to talk with you," he added. "For two hours I haven't thought once about my brother or my mother."

We walked back along the main street. Everything

was quiet, and there was almost no traffic. The lights over the cinema burned brightly a half mile ahead. As we passed a corner store where a sign pointed to a *pivnaya,* a beer hall, on the second floor, we met Akhmed. He was well on his way to being "drunk as a mat," as the phrase puts it. "See, Mohammed," he said, as he pulled a vodka bottle from one pocket, "I have some friends left in Kazan." He turned to the flight of stairs.

"There is a Tatar who does our people no good," said Mohammed as we walked on. "He uses his nationality to get favors. He worked in one factory here. When he was warned for being lazy and drunk, he complained to the factory committee that he was 'persecuted for being a Tatar.' Eventually he was fired. It was the same story everywhere he worked. Finally I let him help me in my shop. He came in drunk one day and cut a policeman with a razor. He was jailed for four months and disappeared afterward."

I left Mohammed near the cinema and turned back to my hotel. Late at night I heard a small child playing in the courtyard. A woman called to him in Tatar. He replied, in Russian, "Coming, *mamasha.*"

I saw Mohammed once more, a few days later, at his shop in the market place. He was busy with a customer, and I went outside to the box of Abdul the merchant to wait until he was free. Some Tatars in a group near Abdul's pile of old clothes were talking excitedly. "There was a fight in a *pivnaya* the other night," the merchant translated. "Akhmed, the brother

of Mohammed the barber, some of his friends and some
Russians were in it. They began to throw bottles, and
two men were killed. The Russians say the Tatars began it. The Tatars blame the Russians. It is always
that way. If there is a Russian judge, it will be hard
for the Tatars. They talk about Tatar self-rule
here——"

"It's not a question of self-rule," Mohammed said
as he joined us. "Whatever sentence Akhmed gets, he
will deserve, and his being a Tatar will have nothing
to do with it."

"He hit the Russian because the *svoloch* called him
a 'Tatar dog,' " one man said.

"You're on the Soviet, Mohammed. You ought to
be able to have your brother freed," another added.

"Does that give me any extra influence? Are we
like tsarist Russians to have a corrupt government?"
Mohammed replied. "If you were as patriotic when I
talk about the need for opening schools in our villages
as you are now, when you think a Russian has done
some wrong to a Tatar, we Tatars should have less to
complain about. Besides, you don't know my
brother!"

The group gradually drifted apart. Only the merchant and the barber remained. "With all your talk
about—what's that new word you use?—'autonomy,'
the feeling between Russian and Tatar remains the
same," Abdul said slyly.

"Perhaps," Mohammed replied, "but it will disappear as time goes on. Intermarriage and education
will end it."

"Why do you pretend that the Tatars will ever govern themselves?" Abdul demanded. "You know that your Communist Party directs everything and that its leaders are Russians. Kazan is governed from Moscow just as earlier it was governed from St. Petersburg. What do we Tatars have now that we did not have before the revolution? What have we lost? Everything—our religion, our right to carry on business as we wish, the right to trade without a lot of silly restrictions that you call socialism."

"Listen, fool," said Mohammed, "are there not Tatars now in every government office? Can't your children go to universities? You may not see that things are better, but wait—ask your children!"

"They will very likely be completely Russianized. Tell me, Mohammed, does 'autonomy' mean that we are a free Tatar people?"

"Of course."

"That we can decide to do anything we wish?"

Mohammed nodded, though perhaps he was wondering to what the questions would lead.

"Then why can't we decide to separate ourselves from the Soviet Union and restore what you call 'bourgeois' trading and business? Why is it, if we are free, that a man who tried to bring about such a return would be shot at once?" the merchant asked triumphantly. "Why must the Tatar republic remain a part of the Soviet Union if we are a free people?"

Mohammed smiled as if he had heard the argument before and replied: "Our government was established to prevent one class from exploiting another. We shall abolish classes all over the world. Why should we allow them to flourish in any part of our Soviet Union? You have not yet learned that even national desires must be subordinated to class interests. No minority group may restore the bourgeoisie. Within those limits we are free."

"But we are still governed from Moscow," the merchant insisted.

"Before the revolution we were ruled partly from Mecca, partly from St. Petersburg. My father went to Mecca—but did you ever hear of the Tsar's calling a Tatar to his palace for advice? He sent a Russian governor out to us. We are now ruled from Moscow, yes, but we send delegates to tell the officials how the work should be done. My father went to Mecca, and I may go to Moscow—as delegate to a Soviet Congress."

I visited Kazan a year later. The market place was unchanged. Even the pile of clothes lying before the box belonging to the old Tatar merchant seemed to be the same. But the barber shop at the edge of the square was closed. My first question was about Mohammed Fateev.

"He left Kazan six months ago," Abdul said. "Hey, where did Mohammed Fateev go?" he called to a neighbor.

"To Kabardinovka."

"You were here when his brother Akhmed came back, weren't you?" the merchant continued. "Well, Akhmed was jailed for two years after that fight. The old woman blamed Mohammed for not helping him, and everything in his house grew worse. Finally his wife divorced him. She married a Russian who works in the post-office. Mohammed should never have married a Russian anyway. He took it too hard; he forgot that all women are alike, no matter what their nationality, and that Allah created them that men might use them. One is not worth grieving for more than another. What matter if you have this one or that one for a wife? I've married seven in my time and I know! But Mohammed left Kazan and went off to teach in some village. A fool he was, that's all! Always talking about arranging the life of his people —and he couldn't arrange his own life!"

The noise of the bazaar rose and fell. Its many languages clattered on. A poster printed in Tatar with Roman letters, which was fastened loosely to a booth near by, flapped in the breeze.

"How are things with you?" I asked Abdul.

"You know the saying, 'Better than to-morrow, comrade.'"

XII

ALEXANDER STEPANOVITCH: THE SOLDIER

THE double-track railroad from Kiev spread into a maze of sidings as it approached the last Ukrainian village before the Polish border. According to the station agent in Kiev the train waited there an hour, while baggage and passports were inspected; then it would pass the Red guard at the frontier and enter Poland. The agent had sworn that the train crossed the border daily.

The train stopped. All the passengers that Saturday afternoon except myself wore the uniform of the Red Army. I rushed into the railroad station and asked for immediate attention from the customs officials. The ticket agent waved his hand lazily and discouragingly. "They aren't here and there's no hurry. The train doesn't go until Monday."

"But the station agent at Kiev said——"

"I am only responsible for my own ignorance," he drawled as he walked away.

"Where can I stay until Monday?" I asked.

He shrugged his shoulders and pointed to the benches in the stuffy waiting room.

A few loungers gathered and offered advice. A young officer, wearing a red cap, left one of the groups of soldiers which were standing everywhere, and coming forward, asked what was the matter. I explained my predicament. Without a word he turned and shouted to a man who was about to drive off in a light spring wagon: "Hey, Makar! Take this citizen up to Valentina Germanovena's and say that I sent him."

"Very well, Alexander Stepanovitch," Makar replied.

We bounded over the sunbaked ruts of the road. "It's half a mile from here," said my driver who was the village postmaster. He began asking, with seemingly insatiable curiosity, about my destination, my travels, my reasons for coming to this village. "Very, very few people cross the border at this point," he said, "and only an occasional Polak."

The miniature inquisition was halted by an old man waving a fishing rod at us from the roadside. Makar stopped his horses. "Is there a letter for me?" the old man asked. The postman opened his bag, fumbled in it and replied, "None to-day, *batoushka,* grandfather." The man thanked him and walked down the road.

Makar's smile turned to loud laughter as we drove on. "That old one's crazy; every day he meets me and asks, 'Is there a letter to-day?' Every day I pretend to look; of course there never is. Then he goes down to the river and fishes for a couple of hours. Catches as many fish as he gets letters, too. Here you are— Valentina Germanovena," he called to a middle aged woman who was leaning over an unpainted fence before a little, whitewashed, stone house, "here's a foreigner I brought you." For five minutes he talked with her in Ukrainian and concluded, in Russian, "and you know, very few foreigners cross the border at this village." It was hard to tell whether he implied that my arrival was an event or a possible menace.

An apple tree shaded the bit of weedy uncut lawn between the house and the road. A bare-boned pig stood beneath it, rooting out the windfalls. There were two beds in the combined living-dining room of the house, another in the vestibule, and a fourth in the kitchen. On the shelf above the stove were matresses. The rooms, simply furnished, had been recently white-washed and freshly ironed curtains hung at the windows.

"You will have to sleep in the vestibule," Valentina said. "My son, my daughter and her husband, and my father live here with me. My son-in-law is assistant commander of a battalion here—it was he who sent you. My son manages the beet-sugar factory a few miles away. They are both Communists. You met my father as you came up the road. He asked for mail, didn't he?"

There were two hours to wait until dinner. I walked through the shady streets of the village. Everywhere there were soldiers. Some were hurrying on duty; others were strolling with village girls. The whole place had an air of activity, even of prosperity, albeit a bit shabby. The round faced, sunburnt peasant women wore gay colors and laughed as they passed. A column of soldiers, singing in harmony, marched down the road. Before the village store a crowd of men were chatting in Ukrainian, a language so close to Russian that it is discouraging to find that it cannot be understood without some months' residence in Ukraine.

The border of the village in the west was a high

river bank along which ran a barbed wire fence. Fifty feet below lay a sluggish little river, perhaps twenty feet wide. That was the boundary. Those low lying fields on the opposite bank were Polish soil. A half mile down the river the railroad passed through a gap in the barbed wire and crossed over a little iron bridge. At the Russian end stood a guard house painted red. On the opposite side, forty feet away, was the gleaming white shack of the Polish guard. Up the river the wire barrier was lost in a clump of woods growing up to the bank.

Straight in the west, a mile away, was the Polish village. The single track of the railroad ran to a red brick station and was blurred in a jumble of sidings. Through the clear crystal air of that late August afternoon men were visible on the station platform. Over the building the red and white flag of the Polish republic hung limp. From a near-by cluster of trees rose the single barred cross of a Roman Catholic church.

I heard a step behind me and turned guiltily. There was a soldier, in dirty khaki, with rifle in hand, asking suspiciously, "What are you doing here, comrade?" I was voluble in my explanation. "Better go back that way," he said, pointing to the village, and I went.

Valentina's family had gathered for dinner. The officer who first sent me to the house, a man about thirty, clean shaven, nodded but his lips remained firmly set. The son, Ivan, was in his late twenties. He smiled, shook hands, and led me to the rear of the house. Filling a clay pitcher with water, he poured for me while I washed. The old man, already seated at the table, was silent for some time, then suddenly asked, in a husky voice, "You come from America? Is that near South America?"

"Hush, father," said Valentina.

After well filled bowls of cabbage soup, there was a platter of broiled chicken. The bread was almost white. During dinner the Red officer began to question me. He asked pointedly, "Very few people cross the border at this point—why did you come?" I explained that I wanted to travel through South Poland and on to Berlin. "Then why did you come on a day when there is no train across the border?" I accused, cursed and damned the station agent at Kiev. "Have you any letters of identification?" I showed him nine, from various institutions in Moscow, all addressed "To whom it may concern." "Is that all you have?" he asked suspiciously.

Ivan interrupted, "Do you understand Ukrainian?"

"Very little," I replied.

Thereupon Ivan spoke to Alexander in that language, watching my face all the while. For five minutes they conversed, and curiosity began to replace a bit of the suspicion on the officer's face. "Put your letters away," he said, "to-morrow you will have to register your passport with the police." A note of friendliness slipped into his voice. "Have you ever been in your American army? You don't have compulsory service there, do you?" He asked several questions about our army and was disappointed at the sterility of my answers.

We strolled out into the village. The fields, divided

into strips forty feet wide and two hundred feet long, were almost all reaped clean. Grain was stacked high on the threshing floors, ready for Monday.

"This village is prosperous because the garrison is here," said Ivan. "That's why there is electric light. But there is too little land: a family of five doesn't have more than six or seven acres. Many of them raise sugar beets for our mill and members of their families work there. Others work around the barracks, so the village is not altogether dependent on its crops."

"The army does a lot for the village," added Alexander. "To-morrow you can come up to the barracks. There is going to be a good football game." He left, to report for duty.

We returned to the house. "Come to a dance at the school," Ivan said. "My wife has gone away for two weeks and I am alone."

The little room of the school house was crowded and stifling hot with all the windows tightly closed, to prevent "rabbits," lads without tickets, from sneaking in. A brass band from the garrison was playing but there were no other soldiers. In one corner men danced in a ring, opposite were the women, and spectators filled the remainder of the space. The hotter it became the more the band blew out of tune, the faster the dancers whirled. The little frame building shook violently all the while.

We did not stay long. Outdoors was the richly studded heaven of South Ukrainia. A cooling breeze was blowing over the newly harvested fields. The old man was sitting by the door when we returned. He grasped my arm lightly and said, "If your America is near South America, perhaps you have met a Russian named Butorin."

"Ask him to-morrow," said Valentina kindly to him. Then to me—"You won't have to sleep in the vestibule after all. There was no mattress there, so Alexander Stepanovitch will sleep at the barracks. You can share the front room with Ivan."

Half a mile north of the village, on the bank overlooking the frontier, stood the barracks, the former residence of some local nobleman. House, grounds, woods, and lawn were now used by the garrison.

As Alexander, Ivan and I approached the barracks next morning we heard shouts from the lawn. Here, on a crudely made field, two army teams were playing soccer. A crowd of villagers watched and cheered despite the hot morning sun. Near by was an outdoor gymnasium with various pieces of apparatus. A squad of young, clean shaven, heavily tanned soldiers was exercising. The grounds in other places were delapidated. The taller grass marked the sites of former flower beds.

Soldiers were everywhere. It was not politic to ask how many were stationed in the village but there must have been several thousand men, a couple of battalions. All the uniforms of various shades of khaki were old and dirty. Nothing distinguished the various ranks except little enamel discs which the officers wore on their collars, and the red caps which marked commanders of Secret Police forces. The Red army, six hundred thousand strong, has two sections, the regular troops and the Secret Police regiments. The sixty thousand Secret Police soldiers, in addition to doing special political work, guard the frontiers and the railroads.

The Polish town, with its station and its church, was clearly visible from the veranda of the barracks. The house was a low sprawling structure with many rooms, clean but shabby, and without any signs of its earlier furnishings. On the battered parquetry floor of the former living room stood close rows of cots. Almost every room was a dormitory, but one large chamber served as a library.

Here were a plain wooden table, wooden chairs, and piles of newspapers and magazines. Charts, showing details of rifle mechanisms and the use of gas masks, hung on the wall. One corner, draped with red banners, sheltered a plaster bust of Lenin. On the banners were painted slogans: "Lenin Is Our Leader," "The Red Army Is The Only Army In History Which Knows Why It Is Fighting." There, too, hung a poster on which was emblazoned "The Red Oath of Allegience":

I, a son of the laboring class, a citizen of the Union of Soviet Socialist Republics, take upon myself the calling of warrior in the Workers'-Peasants' Army. . . . I shall bear myself with honor. . . . I promise to refrain from any conduct which would lower the dignity of a citizen of the Union. . . . All my actions and thought I shall direct to the great task of freeing the laboring class of the world. . . . In the struggle for the Union, for Socialism and for the brotherhood of all peoples I promise neither to spare my strength nor my life. . . .

"We have another barracks on the other side of the village," said Alexander. I had noticed it, a long shed-like structure, from the train. "We eat there and most of the men live there but they use this place for recreation. The whole estate is ours. In the stables where the former owner kept his thoroughbreds there are now Red Army cavalry."

"To whom did this estate belong?" I asked.

"Who owned it, Ivan? You lived here before the revolution."

"To a Count Pshedovsky," Ivan replied with some bitterness. "He owned most of the land around here and some of the sugar factories as well."

"What happened to him?"

"He fled, like the coward he was, when we took this village in 1919. The night before we got here he packed up his jewels. The servants saw him running with his wife and his brother down the bank and across the ice into what is now Poland. Some of the villagers tried to follow—they did shoot his brother—but he and his wife escaped. He was a damned Polish coward. If only he'd have stayed we'd have shot him."

A shout rose from the football field as one side scored.

"How much better it is now, with this house serving real workers," Alexander said.

"That parasite Pshedovsky,—I'd like to catch him," sighed Ivan. "He was a young man and is alive in Poland somewhere. He knew we would take this town so he broke all the machinery in the mill. It cost us an awful lot to repair that sabotage."

We walked in the woods around the house and came to the barbed wire at the bank. Nothing was moving in the country across the river except a cloud of dust which raced over the road in the distance. Alexander trained his field glasses on it. "Look," he offered me the glasses, "Polish cavalry."

I could see a small squadron of horsemen dressed in blue. Their sabres and the gold braid on their caps glistened in the sun. "They wear much nicer uniforms than we do," said the Red soldier without envy. "I heard that America lent Poland forty million dollars a few years ago. I think they spent all of it buying gold braid for their soldiers. Those are their dress uniforms; they are probably coming from church. They are hypocrites! At least, we Communists are honest—we ask no God to bless us as we prepare for war." There was another shout from the football field. "How much better to spend Sundays our way than as they do over there." He waved disdainfully toward the flat Polish fields.

"The Poles never change," said the Red commander as he watched the Polish squadron disappear from the horizon. "They are a musical comedy people—always dramatic, intensely nationalistic, and forever futile."

We strolled beside the wire barrier. Three soldiers, on promenade, passed by and nodded to Alexander Stepanovitch but did not salute. "We have none of the trapperies of bourgeois armies," Alexander commented. "We have eliminated the salute and all other trappings that make the men in the ranks feel that their commanders are a class apart."

"Supposing a Polish soldier forgot to salute his officers?" Ivan laughed.

"You maintain such things in your bourgeois armies in order to define more sharply the classes that make them up," the commander continued, in the tone of a man making a public appearance. "Your officers come from the bourgeoisie and capitalists. Your soldiers come from 'the lower classes.' Do you ever tell them why they are fighting? They go to battle like misguided fools believing in the bourgeois patriotism that has been drummed into them—like that puffy Polish sort—never knowing that they die to save the investments and the economic interests of the ruling minority."

"The army is an instrument of the ruling class," Ivan interrupted.

"Here the class that rules is in the majority," said Alexander, as if lecturing to a class. "We are not ruled by a small clique of financiers and bankers. There is no military group governing here, as in Poland. Our army, both the commanders and soldiers, is drawn from the class of peasants and workers. Every Red soldier knows that he fights to defend his class and he knows too, that, while he is at the front, no greasy bourgeoisie are remaining at home to get fatter on war profits—and to preach patriotism."

We passed through a field where there were several sandbagged trenches. "These are practice grounds," the commander explained. "We take peasant boys from distant backward villages and teach them modern warfare. But that is only part of the rôle the Red

Army plays. It is also the greatest educating force our Communist Party has in the Union."

"How long do your conscripts serve?" I asked. There were several things I wanted to know. "What pay do they get—and what happens if they have left behind families who need support?"

"They serve two or three years. After they are discharged they are held in the reserve until they are forty. Of course, we are poor, we cannot pay our soldiers as much as your bourgeois countries do. They get a few rubles a month."

"Their families can receive financial help in case of need," Ivan interrupted.

Alexander ignored all interruptions. "When a peasant boy returns to his village after two years' service he will be able to read and write, he will have learned the rudiments of cleanliness and physical culture, he will know what the aims of the Soviet government are and how they will benefit him and his village. Our conscripts are on duty eight hours a day and, in addition, spend two hours daily in 'political study.' The villages are far more backward than the cities; the Red Army helps us advance the revolution in the villages, as two hundred thousand men return to them each year—two hundred thousand instructors!"

"There was a village a hundred versts south of here with a beet sugar factory," Ivan said. "The director was holding back part of the sugar and taking it to Kiev where he sold it privately—a nice bit of graft. A soldier, just returned from service, discovered it and thanks to him the director was shot. The old peasants had known about it but they were afraid to do anything."

"How do returned conscripts fit into the village life after two years' absence?" I asked.

"Most of them are awfully homesick when they first come to the barracks," Alexander answered. "Conscripts from the north are sent to the south, and so on. But new interests soon attract them. As their term ends they are eager to get home; their piece of land is waiting for them and, usually, a girl. They settle down easily. Not many of the peasant boys want to stay in the army permanently. They tire a bit of the strict discipline which we enforce although there is plenty of diversion for them within the barracks. We also provide them with other outside interests. We have a system that links army, factory, and village together —and no soldier ever feels that he is in a group apart, even if he does wear a uniform. Factories 'adopt' regiments, send them newspapers and books, and regiments 'adopt' villages. My regiment does cultural work in a village five miles from here; I go over once a week to lecture to the peasants there on international affairs."

"This is different from inland garrisons," Ivan added, "for most of the troops are Secret Police forces."

"They are the more intelligent," the commander explained. "We choose for those regiments the factory proletariat. They are more class conscious, more reliable than the peasant divisions."

"Men from the garrison participate in the government of this village; there are two Red Army men on the Soviet," said Ivan. "Before the revolution soldiers were a group apart, shut in from our national life by barracks walls."

"The state of mind of the army now is much healthier—even old Tsarist officers admit it," Alexander added.

"But how do they know?" I asked, surprised.

"We have former Tsarist officers in the Red Army. What other officers could we use in 1918 to train our army? Workers or peasants seldom became officers before the revolution. We had to use Tsarist officers. It was a big risk but what could we do? Some still remain. Of course we must control them all the time; and the positions of importance are filled only by Communists. We are training our own commanders from the ranks now, hoping that some day we shall be free of the menace of potentially disloyal Tsarist officers in the Red Army."

"We suffered heavily because there were many traitorous commanders during the civil war," Ivan added. "When the Red Army marched on Warsaw there was one battalion commanded by a 'loyal' ex-Tsarist officer. He gave orders for them to march down a certain road—to where the Poles were waiting in ambush."

"Such treachery is impossible now," Alexander replied decisively. "The Red Army is an instrument of the Communist Party, and the Party controls every place whether the man occupying it is a Party member or not. A larger percentage of new members comes into the Party from the army than from any other profession."

"That is why there can never be a *coup d'état* here, as happened in that army ridden land of Poland," Ivan added.

We reached the guard house at the bridge and turned back along the banks of a little branch of the river. Not far above the bridge we passed the old man of our house, sitting on a rock, gazing unwaveringly at the western sky, and paying no attention to the fishing rod hanging in the water. "Time to come home, *batoushka*," Ivan called. His grandfather picked up the rod and followed us.

"Have you ever met a man in South America named Butorin?" he asked me. "Andrei Ivanovitch Butorin? He would be about forty-five now."

"He is speaking about his son—my uncle," Ivan began to explain without expression. His explanation ceased as we reached the main road. A long line of soldiers marched through the dust, singing cheerily. Their song echoed through the village:

> "Hostile winds are blowing round us,
>   Forces dark are pressing.
>   We are met in fatal battle,
>   Fate unknown awaits us.
>   Yet in pride we bravely raise
>   Our banner of the working class
>   Of the great struggle of all peoples
>   For a better world, for sacred freedom.
>   To that struggle, bloody, true,
>   March on, march on,
>   All laboring folk!"

Small village boys ran alongside shouting to the

soldiers. They smiled in return but the cadence of their song was never broken.

On the way to a band concert at the barracks that afternoon Alexander Stepanovitch spoke about himself. He was the son of a Moscow factory worker whom he characterized in two sentences: "The old man spent most of his money for vodka and followed the advice of the proverb in his relations with my mother: 'If he doesn't beat you, he doesn't love you.' He's alive somewhere but I haven't seem him for ten years.

"I joined the army in 1918. In three months I was a commander, and I was only nineteen. Those were the days—! Food was scarce. Often we'd have fish soup for every meal. Gray potatoes floated around in it and for four consecutive meals I got a bowl of soup in which fish eyes were bobbing on the surface. Now a hundred and eighty rubles a month lets me live comfortably here."

For two years after the civil war he had served farther to the north on the Polish border. "Those Poles!" he commented. "Every day I used to ride on frontier guard through twenty miles of desolate country along the border. A Polish guard often rode with me, two hundred yards away on his side of the frontier. We never spoke, of course, but he would show off as all Poles love to do. He hung low and plucked a flower. We Russians are much better horsemen and I had to prove it. So I would throw my cap ahead and, hanging only with my feet in the stirrups, pick it up.

Once he stood up on the horse's back, holding the rein with one hand. I stood up too, let the reins loose and—" he described an unprintable feat. "That was enough for the Pole; he never showed off again." He and Ivan roared with laughter.

"Why do you guard the border so closely?" I asked. "Because of the Polish army?"

"No, they do nothing," he replied. "Because of individual Polaks and others. There is great profit in smuggling goods across into the Soviet Union. Six months ago we caught a crowd of Polaks working with some Russians who were bringing woollen cloth, silk, revolvers and bullets over here."

"There is propaganda smuggling also," Ivan reminded him.

"Yes, we are still at war here in Russia—not against any nation but against the bourgeoisie and the capitalists of the world. The few of them that still remain in Russia have their allies abroad. Those allies, often Russian emigrants, try to smuggle over letters, newspapers, and even counterfeit Soviet money to confuse our banking system. Sometimes they try to come across themselves. We even caught members of a Protestant sect not long ago combining business and religion. Their fellow scoundrels abroad were smuggling in cloth—and religious tracts."

The garden of the barracks was crowded. There were soldiers and their red capped commanders, workers from the sugar factory, and most of the younger people from the village. The band played languidly beneath the hot sun. "Let us find places near the platform," Ivan said. "There are going to be some speeches." We sat on an overturned marble statue that lay in the tall grass.

I wanted to continue the previous conversation and I asked, "What do you do with the smugglers that you catch?"

"Shoot most of them, of course," the commander replied laconically. "And the same with spies—many of them try to sneak in. Our Red Army is more at their mercy than any other army for we have in it people from a class not in sympathy with the proletariat who may be eager to give, let alone sell, our secrets."

"Do you catch many Russians trying to flee abroad?" I asked.

"We have very few trying to cross the border here. Any stranger coming to a frontier village is a suspect. His presence is reported to the guards. We have caught and shot groups that would smuggle a person across for three hundred rubles. People fleeing Soviet Russia now cross through the forests on the Finnish border which is very difficult to guard, or hire some fishermen to take them across the Baltic to Finland. We have to guard the border all the time however, for all our neighbors are basically hostile. The Poles could help us fight smugglers and runaways if they wished. Instead they send spies over and they let the *emigrés* have headquarters in Warsaw, although they know that *emigré* activity is directed against Soviet Russia, a government with which the Polish government is officially friendly. But they hate us."

The band music had been only an obbligato to general conversation on all sides. Now the music ceased and conversation was quieted. A commander stepped on the platform and began to speak. "The soldiers today are host to the workmen from the sugar factory," Ivan whispered.

The speaker told of increasing unemployment in the capitalistic West and prophesied that from this would come a crisis that might shake foreign nations. "When our brothers in other lands need aid in the revolution the Red Army is prepared to go to their help. Every autumn a million young men of twenty-one report for conscription. We weed out the unfit, and the class enemies. Remember, the defense of the Union with arms in hand is reserved for the working class. Let those from other classes dig ditches! We take two hundred and sixty thousand lads every year. . . .

"They are not soldiers, they are 'Red Army men.' We have abolished the word 'soldier' with its bourgeois connotations, just as we have abolished the word 'officer.' The conscripts are trained and they are ready to defend the Fatherland of the workers of all the world. . . .

" 'Workers of the World, Unite'—those are the words inscribed on the Red Flag which six hundred thousand men in khaki salute each morning as it flies along the Polish border, along the Pacific, above the Arctic circle, as it waves over little forts, where the men are relieved once a year, in the mountains next to India. The Red Army will go forward until that slogan waves over those landlord ridden fields of Poland,—and round the world!"

There was scattered applause. A man from the sugar factory then spoke briefly "on the part our factory is playing in building up the defenses of the Soviet Union" by increasing its production of sugar twelve per cent over the previous year. The programme was finished when the band played the "Internationale."

We started home. Alexander was thinking of the conclusion of the commander's speech. "It is strange that the revolution has not changed the old feeling between Pole and Russian," he exclaimed. "Our Communist movement would have much more influence in Poland if it were not that Russians lead the World Revolution."

"Polish workmen may be in sympathy with Communism but the hatred for Russia, which the old Tsarist government engendered, makes them suspicious of every Russian, even one of their own class," Ivan added.

"Is there the same degree of feeling against the Poles in Russia?" I asked.

"The proletariat of all the world are brothers," Alexander Stepanovitch smiled curiously, "but it is difficult for our people to remember sometimes that class comes first and nationality second. It is the same with the Jews—you will hear frightful anti-semitic remarks in all the villages around here."

Ivan laughed—"Yes, I heard a peasant ask a friend a riddle—'what do ninety-nine Cossacks and one Jew represent?' 'The Jewish shock brigade.' 'And ninety-nine Jews and one Cossack?' 'Oh, that's a meeting of the Cossack Soviet.'"

"Jews can rise to a high position in our army; we have many Jewish commanders," said Alexander. "But the Poles—! A long time ago the Poles controlled much of Ukraine, and they feel that they should have it now," said the commander.

"Pilsudsky dreams of a Poland from the Baltic to the Black Sea," Ivan added sarcastically, "but when he sees much of that territory covered by the Red Flag his dream turns to a nightmare. You can't trust the Poles."

"We signed treaties of non-aggression with our neighbors," Alexander spoke scornfully, "but we are not fools. We know that when some strong nation, such as France or England, wants to attack us it will send a border state against us first."

"Those treaties are just like Soviet marriages," Ivan exclaimed. "You have a wife and everything is quiet —until she changes her mind and divorces you without even telling you."

"What would you do in case of attack?" I asked Alexander, as I saw a cloud of dust moving down the road from the distance.

"The attack on us will come by air and by gas and will be aimed at our large cities," Alexander replied. "No army can ever conquer Russia by invading it on foot—Napoleon learned that and your foreign armies of intervention a century after him. Distance is our ally against old fashioned invasion. We have concentrated our defense"—he emphasized the word—"on airplanes and gas and if we are forced to attack, it will be by the large bodies of troops trained to move quickly." The cloud of dust rolled by and revealed a column of light horsedrawn carts, each carrying a machine gun. "Forces like those," he continued, pointing to the squadron. "Distance becomes our enemy in any trench warfare. If our railroads break down a front is useless, no matter how heavily fortified."

"Our weakness is not in the army," interrupted Ivan, continuing his rôle of prompter, "but in the industry that supports the army. We are building that now—that was what the workman speaker meant this afternoon. Just give us five years!"

"We are the only proletarian state and are hated in every land abroad," Alexander spoke with the deepest sincerity. "The capitalists could crush us by uniting in an economic blockade against us but they will not do that for they are too greedy for the profits they can make in business with the Soviet Union. They may pray for the end of the only country where their fellow men are not exploited in mines and factories but" —a note of triumph crept into his voice—"after twelve years of continuous existence we have those capitalists at a great disadvantage. They know now that another war is the greatest menace to their continued class domination."

"Out of the last war came proletarian Russia," Ivan adopted the same tone of voice. "What would emerge from the next war?"

"Supposing that Soviet Russia was defeated this year or next by internal or external enemies?" Alexander asked. "What would happen to all the land and wealth of prostrate Russia? The Poles would go after the Ukraine, the Japs would map out their spheres of interest in eastern Siberia—every nation would seek to control part of the tremendous wealth that is ours —and out of the collapse of the Soviet Union would come another world war." He laughed, "That is our fortunate situation now. The capitalists abroad must help to continue the existence of the Soviet Union for from its collapse would emerge a world war to shake them from their positions of power, a war which would bring Communism close to home, perhaps even to their own country. In the meantime we can build our defenses in peace—and wait for the coming of the World Revolution."

There were many questions I wanted to ask but one in particular: "If a revolution broke out in Germany that seemed near success, but the issue finally hung in the balance, would the Red Army march to its aid?"

"We could not just now. But in a few years—remember our slogan. We do not deal in empty words, 'Workers of the World, unite!' "

Alexander returned on duty after tea. The quiet of dusk came over the village. The old man joined us beneath the apple tree. "If you meet Andrei Ivanovitch Butorin abroad—" he began.

"He is talking about his son, my uncle," Ivan said. "My grandfather was a railroad clerk here for many years before the revolution. During the civil war his son, an officer, joined the Red Army, then turned traitor and joined the Whites. He retreated with them from Kiev and passed through this village. He ran into the house, said good-bye, and went that way—" he waved toward Poland.

"I walked with him down to the river——"

"Lucky you were not shot for it, *batoushka.*"

"He promised that he would return when there was peace," the old man murmured. "There has been peace for nine years."

"Someone wrote that he had seen him in Prague," Ivan continued, "and that he was planning to go to South America with some other *emigrés.*

"He will come back or he will write," the old man insisted.

In front of a house near by two women began to dance to the music of an accordion and to the song of the crowd around them.

> "Oh, Moroz, our Moroz,
> Worthiest Cossack,
> For you, Moroz,
> All Ukraine is weeping."

"They are singing an old song about a Ukrainian leader who perished in battle with the Tatars," Ivan explained. "We Ukrainians have always been a fighting people. If there was a war with Poland now—! I'd like to get that Pshedovsky who ruined our factory."

The singing faded with the twilight.

Alexander and Ivan came to the station before the train departed the next morning. I was the only passenger in the lone carriage but they rode with me and with the accompanying squad of soldiers over the short distance to the frontier.

"I'd like to go across with you," said the commander, "to see what those Poles are really doing."

"You'd have to take off that red cap," Ivan replied laughing. "The Poles shoot people in hats like that." The train reached the bridge at the frontier in five minutes. The guard climbed off and waved. Alexander and Ivan shook hands and said good-bye. The train crawled over the bridge and stopped again. A smartly dressed group of Polish officers came into the car and said *"Passport, pan."*

We moved slowly on toward the Polish village. For a long time, looking back toward Russia, I could see the old man sitting by the river bank, his fishing rod fallen into the water, his eyes turned toward the west.

The Polish customs examination was thorough. The inspectors even opened two cans of caviare and poked through it with knives while most of the village population, a great many of them Jews in derby hats, stood by and watched. The train to Przemesyl did not leave for several hours.

I sat on the station platform. There, in the distance, the Red Army barracks stood high above the yellow clay river bank. Over it floated its red flag. The Polish village lay dormant in the hot afternoon sun. A flock of geese waddled through the mud of the village street and a few pigs rolled in the ditch. The peasants were no better dressed than their Russian neighbors. Everywhere there were rags, dirt, and squalor.

I turned suddenly for someone had spoken in English. There stood a man, middle aged, in bright blue blazer, white flannels, modish sport shoes—a pleasing contrast to the poverty of the village.

"I heard that you have just come from Russia," the stranger said. "Tell me, were you long in that village across the river? Is there any food there or is there famine?" He fired a dozen questions at me. Then he asked, "Were you at that house?" He pointed toward the barracks. "In what condition is it now? And the grounds?"

I described the place as best I could and added, "The Red Army uses it now for a recreation centre. Formerly it belonged to a Count Pshedovsky——"

"Yes, and do they speak of him in that village? What do they say?"

I repeated the most innocuous of Ivan's remarks.

"Very interesting," the stranger replied. "I am Count Pshedovsky. I am now in the Polish diplomatic service and get home only once in three years. My home is in Warsaw but I always come out here to look at *my* house up there on the hill."

XIII

SONYA PETROVNA: THE VILLAGE DOCTOR

She was thirty, perhaps. Her face, round, with high cheek bones, was almost Mongolian in cast. She spoke to me in stilted English one afternoon on the boat from Sebastopol to Batum. She had spoken English as a child but this was her first chance to use it for a long time—did I mind? Her husband was a teacher in the village where she was the doctor. We talked most of the afternoon, the husband sitting by, smiling, never once asking for a translation. I overheard him saying to a friend that evening—"*Vot*, it is my wife, Sonya Petrovna, who is cultured. She was speaking with the foreigner in his own tongue the whole afternoon."

"You never know who these foreigners may be," replied the friend.

In our four days together I learned that both had graduated from Moscow University in 1922 and had gone directly to a village in the Tambov district, strangers in a strange province. They were now on vacation. They seemed a curiously matched couple; she was obviously well born; it was not necessary to hear her speak English, French, and German to know that. Her husband spoke only Russian. It was she who knew the social graces. He was far less at ease in the comparative luxury of the little first-class dining salon than was she.

After dinner one evening she went into the small forward lounge, to the piano. She played for an hour, stiffly, but unconscious of all around her, as if she were conversing with a friend of days long gone by whom we would never know. As for her husband, I have never seen a man so proud. He seemed to understand little of what she played but he knew what that playing meant. He walked around the forward deck, in European clothes, a trifle uncomfortable with his shirt now tucked inside his trousers. The passengers were gathered there in silent groups, listening. "My wife—" he said. Then he went inside and stood beside her. She stopped abruptly in the middle of something or other.

I gave them my Moscow address when we parted. When they came to the city before Christmas, they asked me to visit them sometime in their village. "We would have asked you on the boat but—" looking at her husband—"we were not sure. One must be so careful."

The local train pulled up to the station at dawn. An old and bearded peasant, recognizing the foreigner, said he had been sent for me. We had some tea and boiled eggs in the station buffet. When my companion found me unwilling to buy a bottle of vodka, in spite of repeated hints, he led the way to his sled. As he tucked me into the hay in the bottom of the sled he explained, "Easier to use this through the mud than a wagon. A wagon would never get there—you're sure you don't want that bottle of vodka?"

Everywhere there were signs of spring. On distant fields lay an occasional dirty patch of snow. The main street of the village was a stretch of squashy mud. Across the way a peasant was pulling and tugging to free his horse from the ooze and only getting himself in deeper. At the horse-tie, in front of the tearoom opposite, was a row of sleds and a few carts. The peasants plodded through the slime, their boots muddy to their knees.

From the crest of a little hill we saw our way before us. Our road ribboned across fields of untracked khaki mud. Everywhere there were villages, little clusters of thatched houses, like clumps of russet toadstools. The pearly morning smoke drifted lazily from a few rusted chimneys. Nowhere was there anything green—all was brown or gray under the blue and silver of the morning sky. Small rivulets of slate colored water ran down the road. The only sounds were liquid: the gurgling water, the swish of the sled over the boglike road, the squash of the horses' hoofs. The smell of *makhorka,* peasant "tobacco," drifted back from the driver's seat. In a Russian novel my driver would have turned and cried passionately, "Russia, Russia, *Matoushka.*" Instead, he lamented without ceasing, "You'll be cold —it's too bad we didn't buy that vodka."

An hour's nap, and the landscape was unchanged. Everywhere the same brown fields rolled off to the east, with scarcely a tree in sight. The risen sun fired a church tower a mile down the road. "That's where we're bound for," said the driver. "Sonya Petrovna has waited for you a long while. She expected you in winter. That's when the village is good. None of this mud and little work to do!"

Their house stood opposite the hospital—a shack of logs with a small bedroom, a dining and living room, and a huge kitchen. It was as clean as a maid, polishing and scrubbing all day, could make it. Boots were exchanged for slippers on the porch. The dining room held a little table and a bookcase filled with medical texts. There was a steaming samovar waiting, and home-baked black bread, jam, and butter. When breakfast was finished the doctor and her husband excused themselves. "We live busily in our village," she said. "Ivan Andreitch will be in school all day and I must be in the hospital all morning. When you are rested come over to the clinic."

The hospital was really a group of buildings, standing amid a little grove of trees. There was one big structure, of board slabs, a few small houses, one two-story dwelling, and some sheds in the rear for laundry and storage. In the muddy courtyard before the main building were thirty or forty sleds. I entered the waiting room. On benches, on the floor, everywhere, were people old and young. Some were on rude crutches, some wore bandages, some lay on the floor, quiet in their pain or, more likely, asleep. At a small window new comers signed for their turn. At another little window they lined up after consultation and were handed whatever medicine had been prescribed. Every so often a door opened and an interne in a dirty white apron called out the name of the next patient.

I found the doctor at her desk. She was questioning an old woman who was plainly frightened.

"How old are you?" she asked.

"Seventy, perhaps, next St. Michael's Day."

"Where does it pain you?"

"Everywhere, *barishnya* (young lady)."

"Everywhere? In your head, chest, your stomach too?"

"Yes, young lady, everywhere," and she looked the picture of misery on earth.

"Now, now, where mostly?"

"Well, in my belly."

"How long has it pained you?"

"Since Christmas. . . ."

"Why didn't you come before?" She spoke sharply.

"My son-in-law wouldn't bring me until now. I live thirty miles away."

"Well, have you done anything for yourself?"

The woman hesitated.

"I mean, have you talked to the *znakarka* (medicine woman) about it?"

"Yes. She told me to mix some herbs she gave me with raw dough and put the mixture on a rag and wear it on my stomach. She gave me something to drink, too. Lord, I almost died!"

Sonya Petrovna called an interne. "Take her inside and examine her." A clerk called out the number of the next patient. For two hours they passed before her. There were a dozen cuts and abrasions, twenty cases of skin diseases, some of them, on babies, frightful to look at. There were three women who asked for abortions and were told to wait. One old man was brought in with pneumonia and sent to the ward. There were a few children with infected eyes. There was a small baby with diphtheria who had been carried twenty miles by his mother, on foot through the mud. "You leave the baby in the ward. We'll take care of him." "But I must stay too," said the mother. "You cannot. There is no room for you. He'll be all right." Then to me, in English, she added, "He'll die to-morrow. They always wait too long before bringing them."

At one o'clock the last patient for the day had been interviewed. She counted a total of sixty-five for the morning. "An easy day," she said, "let's go to tea. I have three operations this afternoon—one for appendicitis and I must do two of those abortions."

Fifty to a hundred patients, from thirty miles around, come to her hospital every day. Those from the village itself or from near by come for the slightest cause. "They like the sensation of having someone look after them," she explained. "But those from a distance wait too long. They try their own remedies first. Or the husband says, especially if it's the mother-in-law who's sick, 'Why should I take the time to drive you to the hospital, a whole day there, a whole day back, when you're only mildly sick?' That's where the local charlatans have their hold. And what they do!— put the baby in the hot oven for five minutes to cure rickets!

"And abortions. Every week there are more. The women are revolting; they will not bear twelve and fifteen children, half of whom die, and work in the fields as well. The government says we must do them on request, but I only do them when they already have three children."

The hospital, run by the local Soviet, has a yearly budget of sixteen thousand rubles. It has a ward of twelve beds, an operating room, and supplies a limited stock of medicines as they are prescribed. Everything is free, and Sonya Petrovna is paid one hundred and fifty rubles a month. The clinic is open six days a week, from eight until one. "If anyone comes after that time I have the right to charge him, but what can these people pay? No! My husband earns a hundred rubles a month. Before the revolution I should have thought two hundred and fifty rubles a month small, but now we can actually save enough to take a vacation every two years. And I have another doctor to help me. You'll meet him, a German."

She showed me the other buildings. The twelve beds in the ward were filled and another dozen beds in the corridor also. "What can I do? This is pneumonia weather and the village Soviet is so poor." The operating room was without screens. "The flies in summer are a nuisance—but there is no money for screens."

"Why not charge the patients a small sum?"

"It must all be free; they complain of taxes enough as it is. If they had to pay they wouldn't come here."

I declined an invitation to the afternoon's operations and went to the school. It was like all village schools: the floors heavily tracked with mud from the unbrushed boots; the science laboratory with a half dozen pieces of pre-revolutionary apparatus; the museum with a few stuffed birds, some of the local rocks, and a few old stereoscopic pictures of South Africa, their holder broken. When school was finished, some of the older boys went into the courtyard to play a game very much like our "pitching pennies."

"They all want to learn so badly," said Ivan Andreitch, as he took me around the village, "but the village is so poor." From where we stood we saw the broad expanse of the market place, now a field of churned mud, rimmed on three sides by little board huts. Before some of the doorsteps the men were repairing harness, whittling yokes for their carts, or sitting and talking. On the fourth side of the square rose a huge white church; gaping cracks ran up its plastered sides. The little gilt stars on its blue dome needed repainting. In the centre of the square was a shack housing an antiquated hand-drawn fire-engine, and by its side a watch tower. A flock of rooks flew in and out of the place where the watchman should stand.

"Poverty! Yet we sent six from here to universities last year," continued Ivan. "All from 'dark people'— parents who can't read or write. About seventy per cent of the population is illiterate. We can't bother to teach them for we are too busy with the younger generation. There is an *izbatch,* a peasant reading room, in the village, but no one goes there except the children. The parents are supposed to go and someone reads to them; they say it's too boresome, always propaganda."

We were plodding through the mud of the market

place. Ivan pointed out the sights of the village: the lone brick building which housed the store on the first floor, the Soviet headquarters on the second; next to it was the liquor store and, next to that, the police station. The village policeman was sitting on a bench before his headquarters, playing a guitar while a few young lads sang a popular *Comsomol* song:

> "We are blacksmiths,
> And with our hammers
> We forge the happiness
> Of all the world."

Ivan interrupted and said that I was a foreigner who had come to register my passport with the police —the eternal Russian custom. The singing stopped, while my passport was inspected by everybody. Suddenly the militiaman said, "The Devil! Come tomorrow—my office hours are from nine to twelve," and the song went on.

"*Akh,* what do we have? Uncultured people, illiterate, dirty—and this mud," Ivan sighed as we turned to go home. "How I hate this village! Oh, to be in Moscow where there is life! Here in the winter it is so quiet, so quiet! I almost go mad. I never noticed it until I had been to Moscow. If only I could persuade my wife—but no, she insists she will not leave the village. I'm sick of it. I was born in a village. I have lived all my life in a village except those four years in Moscow. Sonya Petrovna lived in Leningrad, but no one can dislodge her now from this damned 'bear's corner.' "

"We shall go up to Andrei Maximovitch's this evening," said Sonya Petrovna. "He is the principal of the school. There you can meet the village intelligentsia."

There were half a dozen men: the *agronom,* the village agricultural expert; the other doctor, Schuler; the principal; another teacher; and one man who sat silent in a corner and was introduced without mention of his occupation. The wives and three women teachers were in one corner, talking by themselves. The conversation was sporadic. There were many questions about America. The *agronom*—he said it proudly—had been in Germany as a prisoner during the war. He was interested in automobiles. "Just think," he said, "there never has been an automobile in this village, or anywhere near it, yet I have heard that every workman has one, in America."

The principal interrupted: "True, never has there been an automobile here; yet the air route south goes over the village and the peasants now consider airplanes something of everyday occurrence."

The man in the corner added, "And it is a lie that all the workers in America have automobiles, that workmen there are not dissatisfied. Here those stories are spread by enemies to try to make our workmen restless. Under Communism every worker will have an automobile, and more."

There was an embarrassed pause in the conversation for a moment. Everyone seemed glad when the first samovar appeared.

Someone spoke of the village budget for next year.

The principal commented, "We must get along on the same amount of money we had this year; we cannot raise the taxes." Schuler, who had been drinking steadily, rose and almost shouted, "Ah, the Devil, why can't we get money out of these damned peasants? Anyway, what's the use of curing them in the hospital? They only live to have more children, and that means more for you to teach. Close the hospital! Let them die! Your country won't miss them."

Again the conversation halted. Schuler sat down and poured himself half a tumbler of vodka.

"His grandfather was a German who settled in Russia," whispered Sonya Petrovna. "He always considers himself a German, although he can't speak the language. Every day he curses his grandfather for having come to Russia, and he does nothing but drink."

The stranger in the corner rose, bowed and left. The tone of the conversation changed. In five minutes it was rattling like a cart on a sunbaked road.

"That was the president of the village Soviet," Sonya Petrovna whispered, "a worker sent out from Tambov, the only member of the Communist party in the village. A representative of the Secret Police, too. He has a lot of power in this village of course. It was best to ask him to-night to meet you. Usually he doesn't associate with us, except to watch us."

Schuler was talking. "That Petr—what's his patronymic?—that chap that just left. Isn't he the village correspondent here? *Svoloch* he is, the city newspapers keep a chap in each village to spy on honest people and report to them. *Akh,* your country is hell!"

I heard of a peasant from a 'bear's corner' the other day who came to town and asked a friend what *selkor* meant. The friend said *sel* means 'village' and *kor* means 'correspondent'—one of those cursed Soviet abbrevations meaning 'village correspondent.' 'Ah, no,' said the peasant, 'in our village *selkor* is the name given to the sawed-off rifle which the soldiers brought back from the trenches with them and with which they now shoot the village correspondents.' " He laughed, but he laughed alone.

The *agronom* quickly changed the subject. He began to talk of Germany, a land he greatly admired. It was obvious that he had aired his views to this same company a thousand times.

"This Schuler is a dangerous man," whispered Sonya Petrovna, in English, "we can't trust him. He always tells stories like that and worse, yet nothing happens to him. Probably he is *agent provocateur.*"

". . . But the thing I admire most in Germany," continued the *agronom*, "is the honesty of the people. You can put a suitcase down on the platform in a railroad station and come back half an hour later and it will still be there."

"Yes," said Schuler, "we Germans are not like you Russians. Do such a thing here and the suitcase will be gone and the platform with it."

"There is always petty thievery among the peasants," said the principal, "but they are as illiterate in morals as they are in letters. It is our task to teach them. How often they commit crimes of violence without any reason, especially if they are drunk. That

Maximov murder here last year—Maximov and Duratchkov were coming down the road and Maximov picked up a horseshoe. They quarrelled about who saw it first. Maximov took it home and that night Duratchkov came drunk, killed Maximov with a knife, brained his wife with a chair, and took the baby by the foot and smashed it against the wall. The two older children ran out screaming. All for a horseshoe—worth ten kopecks!"

"Your peasants are animals. They are stupid brutes. Now our Germans . . ." interrupted Schuler.

"They are animals, comrade—illiterate, yes, but they are not dumb nor stupid," the principal continued. "Remember one of our peasants once bested even the Kaiser. You know the story of the King of England, the Kaiser and the Tsar at a military review? They quarrelled about whose army had the most intelligent soldiers. They decided to settle the quarrel by asking one private from each army the same question— 'How do you know there are no people on the moon?' The English soldier replied, 'If there were people on the moon, the moon would be a British colony by now.' The German replied, 'If there were people on the moon our professors would know it; they would write about it and we could read it.' But the Russian said, 'Sure, there are no people on the moon. If there were, some one would be spitting on us all the time!'" The crowd laughed—all but Schuler.

The principal added, "Our peasants are our greatest problem. They have a combined cleverness and a naïveté that make them very cunning, childlike—but aren't children often thoughtlessly cruel? We must educate their children so that their good qualities are magnified, and we must try to eradicate the bad qualities. That is not the work of a year nor ten years. With the younger generation lies the hope of Russia."

The second samovar had been emptied. Although the party was invited to stay and play *preference,* the card game of the provinces, everyone chose to go home.

We sat around another samovar at Sonya Petrovna's. The first warmth of the year was in the wind. The rooks in the trees around the hospital croaked and cackled restlessly. There was no other sound save a dog barking in some far off village.

"How quiet everything is—I love it so," she said. Ivan did not answer. Suddenly, from next door, three boyish voices began a song:

> "The flames of burning Moscow glared,
> The smoke spread o'er the city moat,
> And on the far off Kremlin walls
> He stood in a gray overcoat."

"Do you know of whom they are singing?" Sonya Petrovna asked. "It's an old song about Napoleon. The grandfather taught it to the father and now the father has taught it to the son. It's always that way in the village; now young Antichrist will teach it. . . ."

"Young who?" I interrupted.

"Oh, yes," she laughed, "the revolution has even changed names. It is no longer fashionable to use the names of the prophets and martyrs of the Church for your children. Now there are new names: Oktyabrina,* Carmagnola, Revolutsia, Electrifikatsia—those are some of the new names for girls; the most popular girl's name, though, is Ninel, 'Lenin' spelt backward; and boys' names—Marat, Vladlen (short for *Vladimir Lenin*. But the tinker next door went one better and called his son 'Antichrist.' He heard it somewhere—probably doesn't know what it means...."

"Young Antichrist is going to be embarrassed if our custom of using patronymics continues and he calls his son Antichrist," Ivan added. "That young hopeful will then be Antichrist Antichristovitch."

The household rose at four on Saturday, bazaar day. I went out on the porch to brush my teeth and absent-mindedly left brush and paste lying there. While seated at breakfast we heard great commotion in the courtyard. Ivan Andreitch had gone out to bring in firewood and he was shouting as he came in the house.

"That rascal Antichrist was watching you. You left your tooth paste out there and he was eating it. Said he thought it was some kind of American candy...."

In unending line peasant carts jogged by our window. From the porch of the house we could see three roads, each marked by peasants bound toward the bazaar.

"They come from thirty miles away," said Sonya Petrovna as we plodded to the market place, knee deep

*The Bolshevik Revolution occurred in October, 1917, by the old style calendar.

in the mud. Everywhere there were carts and sleds. Following an old custom, the sellers had divided themselves off according to what they were selling. In various corners were calves and colts; wheels, wagon yokes, and harness, all home made; cheese, butter, poultry and freshly slaughtered veal. Peddlers with wood carvings, with bark sandals, roamed about; small boys played games, and idle men crowded the vodka store. With every minute new arrivals floundered into the already crowded square.

"I shall be busy to-day," said Sonya Petrovna. "Bazaar day is always the busiest for me."

I asked about the food shortage and prices.

"There seems to be plenty of food, doesn't there? Prices are low enough and living here for us is very cheap. Yet the peasants themselves have little; there is almost no flour. What you see them selling, in many instances, is the last they have. The last chickens are slaughtered, the last calf. The eleven years since the revolution have drained the surplus out of the villages; that is the greatest danger now. And there are no manufactured goods. Whatever money the peasants get here to-day will go for vodka. Wait until eight o'clock and you will see."

The bazaar began to break up shortly after eight. The line before the vodka store lengthened. Each man came out with two bottles. One he opened immediately, in peasant fashion, pounding the bottom of the bottle until the cork flew out. A few drops were always spilled at the same time. Small boys gathered around and tried to catch this overflow in cups. The second bottle was given to the wife, who put it in the sled. In half an hour the market place was bedlam. A dozen fights were going on in various corners. One old bearded peasant was pushed face down into the mud and emerged, an animated mud pie. The militiaman strolled about. "The jail wouldn't hold all if I started arresting those who should be arrested," he said. So the fights continued.

Sonya and I walked home. "Vodka is the curse of the peasantry, but it is their only outlet: vodka momentarily takes a bit of the drabness from their life. If we take it away, they cook up some stew in their samovars which can be made into excellent stills, and that is worse. Vodka, and the lack of soap! Look—" she pointed to a mother, whose long dress trailed the mud, carrying a crying baby. The mother lifted the hem of the dress, dirty and mud draggled, and wiped the baby's eyes. "I'll have that baby to cure in a month or so," said the doctor, nonchalantly.

"It seems sometimes a losing fight—culture against this overwhelming sea of ignorance. Ivan longs to leave the village. To me the village is foreign, the work hard and results never visible, but I must stay, I must stay in the village." She changed the subject. "It isn't that the peasant is dirty and can't get clean. It seems to me that dirtiness is his natural state and he is uncomfortable any other way. Be sure and come over to the clinic this morning."

The line at the clinic was longer than before. Schuler and Sonya Petrovna were working together; Schuler was yelling at the patients, and taking joy in embarrassing them. A young girl, perhaps sixteen, came in, with a boil on her shoulder. He stripped her to the waist, with four men in the room, while she reddened and would have run. He turned, leered at me, and said, "You see, some of them are nice animals."

There was a knock at the door. The interne brought in an old woman, unconscious, her hair matted with blood. They revived her. The first thing Sonya Petrovna asked was "How did this happen?"

"*Baryshnya,* I fell over my wagon."

Sonya Petrovna probed the wound. "There are bits of glass here; you fell right on a vodka bottle, didn't you? Don't lie—who hit you?"

"God's word, I fell."

"Take her out," said Sonya Petrovna, "we can't do anything for her." The old woman cried louder and finally confessed that her husband had hit her with a vodka bottle.

"We must always find who commits assault," said Sonya, "then we report to the militia and they arrest the man. Usually it's the husband who does the beating but the wife always protects him, no matter what he does to her. This chap will get fined."

All morning and all afternoon the carts and sleds left the bazaar, homeward bound. At twilight they were still moving over the roads, into the pastel palette of the spring sunset. With almost every cart it was the same: the unsold calf or the newly purchased colt trotted behind; on the driver's seat, bent, as with the fatigue of all the world, sat the woman; the reins hung limp. And in the straw in the cart was the husband, lying on his back, dead drunk, his mouth gaping at the blue and rose of the sunset sky.

The next afternoon I drove with Sonya Petrovna to a village ten miles off. She was going to open a children's nursery there during the coming summer where the women might leave their babies while they worked in the fields. She seemed highly enthusiastic, for the village Soviet had appropriated five hundred rubles and she could hire a student nurse from the city. "I come over here every other Sunday to lecture on child care and feeding," she explained. Fifty mothers met us and for two hours the doctor was busy. Then we turned home.

"And now that you've seen how we live and work, what do you think of it, *amerikanyetz?*" Sonya asked suddenly. "The worst part of my work is being under Schuler; he's in theoretical charge, although he does nothing but drink and curse his grandfather. I didn't have to take on this maternity work, but I felt I must; I always seek work and more work, and I must stay in the village. You don't hear me talk about politics, do you? I know little of them. I am a doctor and nothing else. Ivan Andreitch will argue politics with you.

"We are poor, yet the government does for us doctors all it can. We are not behind the West in knowledge and, I think, far ahead of the West in ambition; but we have so few resources, such poor equipment. We do things here with tools that would make your doctors sick in the stomach, but we pull our patients through—some of them." She paused, and I thought she was crying. "And we try hard enough. The government gives us six months' holiday with pay every few years to go to the city and study the latest methods and discoveries. So I work on in the village.

"The city against the village, the age-long fight of Russia as a nation, of Russians as individuals. How to flee the village is the motivating force behind so many of my people. In our family, between Ivan and me it is just the same. But I must stay here. He does not understand. I have been trying to find myself for six years and I can find myself only in my work—the harder it is, the better. That's what the revolution did to me. Here it is quiet, there is little political broil, only dull monotony. But I have come to value quietness, monotony, as the greatest good in life. You see . . ." she was about to tell me a story, but we were home.

The afternoon before I left she asked me to walk with her. We climbed the muddy path that led to the cemetery behind the church. It was the most bedraggled of graveyards; tall, withered unmown weeds from the year before made it look even more forsaken. We came to one mound, better cared for than the rest. The wooden cross was new; the name on it was Ivanov, the commonest name in Russia. Sonya Petrovna knelt in the mud. For five minutes she prayed, then suddenly rose, crossed herself, and turned briskly toward home.

"My only brother lies here," she said calmly. "You are leaving to-morrow and I should like to have you know. . . . Ivanov is not his name, but not even my husband knows what our real name was. It was known well in Petersburg before the revolution. It makes no difference now. My father and my mother were shot in August, 1918, on that first night when the Red Terror claimed five hundred executions in one evening. Our rank was such that my family would be chosen first. With our estate gone, with everything gone, all I had left from the past was my young brother. I got in to Moscow University; entrance was easy then. My brother lived with me, for I had a few jewels which we very secretly sold. I met Ivan, a peasant boy, and married him. In that marriage lay my safety. But the continued safety of my brother and myself lay in the village. Ivan so loved me that he gave up his dearest ambition—to live in the city. That is what the revolution did to him. . . .

"We came out to this village, where, at first, I was the only doctor. Then my brother came down with tuberculosis. I fought to save him, but I had to do it alone. We had no money to send him off. It was up to me to preserve the only link I had with all that is past; I thought that some day if Communism ever passed, my brother would be able to take his place and to become as great a man as his father was. How far away, how unreal it seems now! Well, I failed. He died. And with him died—oh, so much—but nothing more valuable than my confidence in myself. I had to save him, and I couldn't. That is what the revolution—" She paused. We were back in the village; on the doorstep near by little Antichrist and his three brothers were making mud pies.

XIV

IVAN IVANOVITCH: THE SHOEMAKER

HE came aboard the Kama River boat at Chistopol, in one of those swarms of peasants with their boxes, bags, bundles and babies which make the foreigner think sometimes that half of Russia is on the trains and boats and the other half asleep in the waiting rooms. He towered above the rest of the mob as it surged up the gangplank and met the crowd rushing off. Freight handlers, their little harnesses on their backs, charged the impasse. Every one pushed and swore and fought, as if the boat were stopping for only a second.

It was, to be sure, important to make this boat. On the little hills the leaves had fallen, and from the water in a week's time the wild ducks had taken flight by the million, leaving only a few stragglers riding the shallows near the shore. In another week the harbor "ark"—a kind of floating wharf—would be towed off to some quiet little tributary, there to wait until the spring floods had passed. This would be the last boat to Perm until April opened the ice-bound river.

After an hour the boat swung away from the "ark" in a wide circle. "Now this town is cut off from the world except by wagon for six months. A whole day's ride," said the other first-class passenger to me. He was a bank manager in a little provincial town. We moved inside to the first-class dining saloon and ordered breakfast—fried eggs, cold sturgeon and tea.

As we waited, the tall peasant who had already caught my attention came into the saloon. He was gray-bearded but erect as a stone column. His shirt was new, his black boots squeaked. He walked forward, unburdened and proud. His wife followed, carrying their bundles, dragging their boxes. Her cotton print dress was uncreased, her gray head scarf neatly tied.

"See, Akulina! Didn't I tell you?" the husband said. "Come on—isn't it fine? Look! Just as I said, clean tablecloths, and those are napkins. Look at the mirrors."

He turned and spoke to us, while his wife hung timidly behind. "See what the revolution did—here am I, Ivan Ivanovitch Laptev, shoemaker from the village of Samorodina, travelling first-class——"

"Hush, Ivan," begged his wife.

"Before the revolution, who rode up here? Landlords, *bourzhui,* exploiters of labor. And, if we came up here, what happened? 'Take yourself, your dirty paws and your running noses down to fourth-class where you belong.' Comrades, I am travelling home from vacation first-class. Won't you have something to tell the old women in the village, Akulina? Waiter," he cried, stamping his heel, "bring vodka."

"You comrades will join me?" he nodded to us.

"The old fool is probably drunk," said the bank manager.

"Hush, Vanya," his wife whispered; "don't disturb

the gentlemen." She sat down on a basket, near the door, and folded her hands nervously in her lap.

"Gentlemen? There are no gentlemen left in Russia —we are all comrades. Berries of the same field. And what are you sitting there for? Our first-class tickets give us the right to sit on first-class chairs. Oh, Lord, I forgot that crate of chickens which Petya carried on board for me—wait, I'll bring them up." He disappeared down the narrow corridor.

"Here is another type of Russian peasant for you," said the banker. "The basic desire on this broad Russian plain is to rise above the great mass of undistinguished people round about you. The Communist Party gives to many a chance to do it. Here is a chap who has found another way—temporarily at least."

There was tremendous confusion in the corridor, and the language was incandescent. A half-dozen sailors were trying to hold back the tall shoemaker as he dragged a crate up the stairs. "I tell you I paid for first-class passage for myself and my wife, and my chickens come with me," he protested.

"Now what do you think our cabins are, comrade? Chicken-coops? Bring them down below. It would be better if you and your wife came with them—" The sailors were victorious. The chickens went below. Ivan's wife had moved nearer and nearer to the edge of her basket, trembling, ready to spring and flee at the first unfriendly voice.

The peasant returned five minutes later. Curious, he strolled toward us and stood a little way off, listening to our conversation. Suddenly he noted my foreign accent. He came forward, bristling. "Are you a foreigner? A Polak?" He failed to hear my mumbled "No." "Well, you had better go home to your Polish pigpen and tell your fellow *'Laki* that we are ready to fight them at any time. I was in the army twenty years. Right at the court, in the personal bodyguard of the Tsar. I saw him every day. So near I could spit on him."

"Ivan!" his wife called in a frightened, weak voice.

"Of course, we didn't think of such a thing in those days. Then it was, 'Yes, your well-born excellency,' to every officer. Now, it's 'comrade.' I waited twenty years for a chance to fight the *'Laki* and never got it. We did fight the Germans, and Germans are almost as bad as the Polish swine. I've got a son in the Red Army. I am too old to go to war myself, but, if you filthy *'Laki*——"

"Quieter, comrade," said the banker.

"You aren't a Yid as well?"

"Quieter, quieter, comrade. This foreigner is from America."

"*Amerikanyetz?*" His jaw dropped. He stiffened and saluted, as if he were on morning drill. "An American —well, this is the first time I have ever seen one. I have heard so much about Americans! I'm not interrupting?—'An uninvited guest is worse than a Tatar.'"

He turned to his wife: "See, Akulina, how fine it is in first-class. They even have Americans up here."

"Oh, I am so glad," he went on, speaking to me again; "tell me about the class struggle in America and the *bourzhui*." He reached out to finger the material of my trousers. "Are they from America? We do not have that kind of cloth here. How much do they cost? And those shoes? How much—hey, comrade waiter, bring vodka! We haven't nice clothes in this country, but we do have vodka. You must go home and tell the American workers that the Russian workers are their friends, and that, when the World Revolution breaks out in America, we will send them plenty of vodka."

The waiter brought a carafe of vodka and three small glasses. "The devil, comrade, why did you bring such small ones?" Ivan asked. "Are we ladies, to drink from thimbles? Bring big glasses, the kind you use for tea, and more vodka. What you brought wouldn't fill one big glass.

"An American? There are so many questions I want to ask you. Do you know Henry Ford? Is he really going to send tractors to us? How nice it will be when everybody has a tractor! Then work will be easier, and we all shall have more free time for culture. The government did send a tractor to a village near ours. It's broken now, and we can't find any one who knows how to repair it. Perhaps you could come. There was a big scandal about that tractor. Some of the Soviet officials used it one day to carry them to the fields when they were going to shoot rabbits. They shot a lot because the noise scared all the rabbits out. Then they ran into a pile of stones. It was no way to use a tractor. One doesn't need culture to see that."

The waiter brought the large glasses and another carafe of vodka. Ivan poured out generous helpings and took his at one gulp. He reached for my fork and scooped up a bit of cold fried egg from my plate. I offered him a piece of sturgeon. He took it and turned, saying, "See, Akulina, your husband is eating with the American." But his wife had disappeared.

"Where has that *baba* of mine gone? The revolution has spoilt women—you never know where they are now. They won't bear as many children as their husbands want—they go running to the hospital for abortions. And they take part in village meetings. Of course that's quite right in some ways. Our Lenin said, 'Every cook must learn to help run the government.' That's all very well, but some of the women then forget how to cook. *Akh,* when I was young, girls were girls. Where do you see a pretty girl *now?* The girls in Peters—" he caught himself—"in Leningrad. What stories I could tell you. Women in those days knew only one thing. And us, with our handsome uniforms! That wife of mine—she's not pretty, but 'You don't drink water from the face'—and she can work hard. Where did she go to?"

He noticed that the bank manager had not touched his glass of vodka. "What's the matter, comrade? Do you want to give the American the idea that we Russians can't drink? If he should go home and tell that——"

"I don't want to drink and become a babbling old fool," said the banker.

"Neither do I. It would be a misfortune to drink as much as that. Besides, I never had the chance. In my day a man wasn't drunk until he had finished three yards of glasses standing in single file, or until he could no longer spit past his lips. During the war we had prohibition here. That was very bad, but it did bring in *samogon,* home-brew." He described in detail how to make samogon with chopped potatoes and a samovar. "The result will be eighty-per-cent alcohol," he concluded.

"They have prohibition now in America," said the banker.

"No vodka? No wine? No beer? But they must have samogon! Well, we got our vodka back after the revolution; so, when the World Revolution begins in America, you'll get back your vodka." He changed the subject. "Where did that *baba* go? Pardon me, comrades, I'll go hunt her. In the meantime, you order more vodka. You're sure you don't want this?" He took the glass from the banker, drank it and walked out to seek his wife.

"With types like this how can you generalize about the Russian Revolution?" said the banker. "All you foreigners judge Russia on the basis of the cities you see, forgetting that a hundred and twenty-five million peasants are living in their little villages. Their life goes on quietly, and the effects of the revolution spread slowly among them. There are as many types as there are individuals; you must not speak and think of the 'Russian peasant' as a category. The peasants defy generalization. What are you going to do with a specimen like this? A former soldier in the Tsar's guard and proud of it—now a village shoemaker. Ask him whether he is better off than before the revolution, and he will answer in accordance with what he has to eat, with what he can buy. Ask him if Russia is better off, and he will judge by precisely the same personal standards."

Ivan Ivanovitch returned, roaring with laughter, slapping his thighs. "That *baba,* where do you think I found her? Down in fourth-class, sitting on a bale of fish by the engines. She says that she is more at home down there—that it was lonesome up here. Well, 'Every one goes out of his mind in his own way.' And us, with first-class tickets! Let her sit there— 'Women are long on hair and short on brain.' She has found some friends to chat with, and she can watch those chickens. I'll stay up here and talk with the American. When I told some friends down below that you were here, they said I was lying again. There are so many questions that I want to ask you."

He was out of sight all the afternoon. The boat stopped a half-dozen times, and crowds continued to pile aboard. It grew chill at twilight with a forecast of the snow that was to come. The fourth-class passengers stayed out in the air, on the open stern of the deck below—anywhere to get away from the odor of the engines, of the bales of dried fish and of their three hundred fellow passengers. They lay all over the available space, drinking tea from battered kettles. Those who were not so lucky as to have any tea in basket or bundle put slices of apple into their glasses, added hot water and quenched their thirst with that. There were wisps of conversation, bursts of laughter.

On the narrowing shores the day's work was finished.

Small herdboys were driving the cows home. Peasants jogged over the dusty road, carting their plows back from the fields.

Suddenly a voice on the deck below began to sing:

> "From behind the leafy island,
> Out to where the wavelets run,
> Come the sharp-nosed Cossack galleys
> Glistening bright beneath the sun."

Another joined and another in this old folk song. The singing spread in part harmony through all the boat and over the water. It swelled to crescendo on the stanza telling how the Cossack chieftain, in drunken nonchalance, threw his bride into the river.

> "Volga, Volga, Russian mother,
> Fair beyond comparison,
> You have never seen a present
> From the Cossacks of the Don."

The sound rose and fell, as with the waves; then there was silence.

The few passengers on the top deck gathered at the stern. A blind beggar, below us, began to sing while his small son played an accordion.

> "Once they asked you, 'How's your wife?'
> And you answered, 'Well; alive.'
> Now they ask you, 'How's your wife?'
> 'Which one, comrade? I've had five!'

> " 'Mother of six, get up right now,'
> Every dawn her husband said,
> One morning, in her sleep, she cried,
> 'Father of three, go back to bed!' "

The crowd below laughed and offered the pair black bread, apples and tea.

An argument down there grew louder. The noisiest voice was Ivan Ivanovitch's. "But I tell you," he said, "the government must take grain from the peasants. Tell me, comrade, aren't we better off than before the revolution? You had your choice. When the White armies were here, you could have joined them and overthrown the Communists. But the Whites would have put back the landlords and you'd have lost your land. You had that choice—and now you have your land, haven't you?" There was no answer as the beggar began again:

> " 'You have your land—you're happy now?'
> The worker to the peasant said.
> 'We have our land; yes, that is true,
> But, comrade, you take all our bread.'

> " 'The fields are yours.'—'Their yield is yours.'
> 'Oh, that's what's meant by evolution.
> The trees are yours.'—'The fruits are yours.
> Long live your Workers' Revolution!' "

"The government makes you sell grain to it so it can build factories," continued Ivan.

"The factory workers get the best of everything," a voice interrupted. "Our grain goes to them, and what do they send us in return? What do boots cost now? Twenty *poods* of rye, and before the revolution they cost seven. Look, I wear bast sandals. I should like to have boots like the workers in the cities," the voice continued bitterly. "No, it is the same as before the revolution. Then we labored for the landlords—now the factory workers in the cities take all we produce."

"But aren't those workers often our sons?" asked Ivan, addressing himself to a seemingly divided mass opinion. "Aren't they our brothers?"

"Yes, and just think of all the government has built and is building," assented one man.

"Comrades, it is all nothing but promises," objected another. "What new factories have been built in this district? Not one. How many of you have ever seen a tractor in your village? All promises and lies, lies, about what has been done. I heard of a peasant who went to town and bought a pair of spectacles in a store. He put them on and walked around. In a little while his head was aching; so he sat on a bench. He happened to look at his foot and discovered that it was swollen to five times its size. He ran to a doctor, but the doctor could see nothing wrong. Suddenly he said, 'You fool, it's those glasses—take them off.' One day Kalenin came to the village and made a speech about the great increase in the number of factories. 'Hey, Mikhail Ivanovitch,' the same peasant cried, remembering, 'take off your glasses.' "

"Well, the government isn't to blame; it's the foreign *bourzhui*," said Ivan.

"You're drunk, comrade."

"He may be drunk, but he is right," said a third voice. It had grown darker, and faces were indistinguishable. "If the foreigners would give us credits abroad—they have all the money—then we could buy things. But they hate us. And why? They ought to try to help us get some of the things they have, since they have so much more than they need."

"We shall get nothing," replied the first disgruntled voice. "They say Kalenin was out in the villages making a speech. 'I want to tell you about the new roads we are building.' 'You lie,' some peasant called out. 'And how we are opening factories.' 'You lie.' 'And how we are building Socialism.' 'You lie,' the voice cried again. 'One moment, comrade. Why do I lie?' Kalenin asked. 'Because, Mikhail Ivanovitch, there isn't any bread.' 'See here,' retorted Kalenin, 'what do you want? Socialism—or bread?'"

"The government will give us everything," said Ivan. "But we must be patient. Electrification, industrialization—they will come, but first many evils must be liquidated."

"What big words you use, comrade! Read them in some newspaper? What nonsense you talk! You know that any government always takes and takes from its people—taxes, grain or men. We should do things for ourselves. Why should we rely on the government? I was travelling last month to Kazan. You know how dark the railroad coaches are at night with only a bit of candle in the lantern."

"And they lock that in so that we peasants can't steal it," a voice interrupted.

"The *kontroler* came through for tickets. The coach was crowded, and some were sleeping in the baggage racks. When the *kontroler* climbed up to waken one peasant, who had taken off his boots, he hit him in the face with his bare foot. 'Whew, you stink, comrade. You ought to wear stockings,' the *kontroler* said. 'Where shall I get stockings?' asked the peasant. 'I am so poor.' The whole car began to talk, just as we are doing now. Some one finally said: 'Well, the government ought to furnish us with stockings. We could put them on before we got on the train and turn them in at our destination.' 'And how many pairs do you think would be turned in? In America things like that don't happen—you ask that *amerikanyetz* you were speaking of. There they are a cultured people. And we are Russian peasants.' "

Interest seemed to flag. There was only a jagged cut in the sky to show where the sunset had been. It was growing colder. The banker and I turned indoors. "Who said we had no freedom of speech in this country?" he laughed. "Of course we let the peasants talk; what harm can that do? They only talk and talk——"

"A lot they know about Soviet Russia down there in fourth-class," said Ivan Ivanovitch as he sauntered to our table in the dining saloon late that evening. "Stupid? You could burn a village between their eyes and they would see nothing! Most of them can't read or write. I learned in the barracks."

"Where have you been travelling, comrade?" asked the banker.

"I am the head of a bootmaking *artel* in our village; six of us work together, and twice a year I take our goods to Kazan to sell them. Then we divide the profits. I sold our boots this time for fifteen hundred rubles. That's not much to be divided among six. We had to do our work in the fields this summer as well. In the autumn we do better. We live well with that income and with our land."

"How much land have you?"

"In our village it's one *dessiatine,* three acres, to a head. There are six in my family; one boy's away in the army. Six *dessiatines*—that's enough land. My brother got into an awful mess about land a little while ago. They redivide all the land every five years, you know. They were going to redivide on the first of last October. My brother's wife expected a child to be born two weeks after that. Stupid he is, he can't read —he asked his wife if there wasn't any way to hurry it so he would have another head in his family to be counted for a share of land. His wife said 'No.' He's a clever one—he went immediately to the county Soviet fifteen miles away to register a new baby. 'What's its name?' the clerk asked. He thought a minute and said, 'Nikolai Petrovitch.' Everybody congratulated him, and he treated them all to vodka. A little later they divided the land, and he got a share for his son. Then his wife gave birth to a daughter! *Akh,* what a scandal! He had to pay a big fine—but he kept the land!"

Ivan Ivanovitch then turned to me and asked, "How much land do your peasants have in America?"

"There aren't any peasants—they are all *fermeri,*" said the banker, thinking, perhaps, that I might not realize Ivan's failure to differentiate between farmers and peasants.

"If they all live separately in America and not together in one village as we do, they must be awfully lonesome," Ivan commented. "But it would be nice for each one to have his own automobile, as you say everybody has in America. But roads, hey, I'd like to see any one drive an automobile in our village! Perhaps Ford will come here and give us roads! When we were in Kazan this time, I took my *baba* in a taxicab. It was the first time she had ever ridden in an automobile. She was scared. She said she didn't trust the driver but preferred horses because one horse always knows more than any two Russians. *Chort!* the devil! how dry I am, and I haven't any more money!"

The banker ordered more vodka and asked, "Does your wife keep your money?"

"Yes, most of it. 'Never tell your wife how much money you keep in your box: she knows already,'" the shoemaker replied, and then, as if afraid of laughter, he went on: "You see, she says I'd spend it all. She's clever, like all *babi*. And she can work. She and the children tend the land in the summer; up to a year ago she used to do the plowing. My second son helps her, but soon he will be old enough for his service in the army—I don't know what I'll do with two sons in military service." A moment later he remarked: "They say that there'll be war soon, that the capitalists will come and try to crush us. Is America planning war against us? I read in the papers that all capitalistic nations talk about disarmament, but none of them mean it; they won't fight one another, but they won't disarm because they will want to crush our Soviet Union some day.

"Of course, the Americans would beat us—though what would be the use of that? It would be better if they sent Henry Ford over here. But let the *'Laki* try to stick their noses in here! My wife asked me this afternoon, 'If he is *amerikanyetz,* where does he come from?' 'From America,' I answered. 'Is it near Finland or near Poland?' she asked. Those are the only foreign countries she has ever heard of. All she knows is what's around her own village."

"But how do you know so much, comrade?" the banker asked with a smile.

"I can read. I wanted to start a library in our village, but we couldn't raise the money. 'Better to spend the money on a new bridge,' everybody said. But I see newspapers occasionally, and I travel to Kazan twice a year. I can understand the newspapers, too—all the new words, although there are a lot of people who use those new foreign words like 'rationalize,' 'administrative-technical,' just to show how clever they are. Comrade, what does that word—uh—uh—'*hydro-ostanovka*' mean?"

"A stopping-place for motor boats."

"Well, these cursed new words! Some bureau in Moscow sent out a questionnaire to a village Soviet when I was a member, in 1927. It asked, 'How many *hydro-ostanovki* are there in your village?' We talked a whole night trying to find out what that damned word meant. No one could tell, but I did know the word 'hydra' and explained what that was. So we answered: 'None. The last hydra in this district was destroyed with the other landlords and exploiters in

1918!' The city always forgets, you see, that we peasants are backward, stupid people."

"Doesn't the city send out teachers?" the banker asked.

"Not to our village—we live in a real 'bear's corner.' Far away, where almost all are illiterate. We have a school but very little money to run it. Of course, in the army I lived in the city; I am different. But what can you expect from the others? Last year a village near ours got an order from the city. 'One place in the Peasants' Rest Home in the Crimea has been reserved for a peasant from your district,' it read. 'Please choose him and send him by July 15.' "

I had seen that home the summer before. Peasants from all over the Soviet Union are brought there for a vacation in a former royal palace by the Black Sea. It is always shown to foreigners.

"None of the people in that village had ever heard of a 'rest home.' They didn't know what it was, and there was great noise at the village meeting. Rest? It sounded too much like 'arrest,' something terrible. Who could be spared from their village? They decided to send old Gabriel Semyonovitch. 'He's ninety, and, if anything awful happens to him, he won't be missed. His grandchildren have to keep him, and they are so poor anyway, it will be a blessing.' Gabriel wept and cried and swore he wouldn't go. Finally the villagers loaded him on a cart and carried him to the railroad. It was a job to put him on the train."

"Did he come back alive?" the banker asked, laughing.

"He got off at the next station and walked home two days later. So those who had chosen him in the village meeting decided to send no one, but for a long time they were expecting some punishment from the city. They planned to say that they had sent some one and that, if he hadn't reached there, they were not to blame. *Akh*,"—he waved his disgust—" 'dark people'! And in America all the people can read and write, can't they? And you must have Peasants' Rest Homes everywhere. What I can tell my village when I get back! This has been a great day, but there are so many questions I still want to ask. We have to leave the boat early to-morrow morning and then drive forty miles. Ha, that's a good idea," he said, jumping up. "Wait, I'll come back in a minute."

He returned and sat next to me. "I have a great favor to ask you. Will you come to my cabin for a little while?"

"Perhaps your wife is asleep," I replied. "It's getting late."

"No, and she doesn't need to sleep: this is her vacation."

Boxes and bags were piled all over the cabin. The woman sat on a crowded bunk, fingering a little crystal radio set in her lap.

"I wanted to talk to you alone," said Ivan, "and to ask one very great favor. By the way, you aren't Jewish, are you? My wife heard your foreign accent and said you were, because all the people that she ever heard speak Russian with an accent are Jews. I said you weren't—a Russian peasant can always tell a Jew.

"Did you hear about the time Trotsky and Zinoviev were walking down a village street? A crowd of small boys following after them shouted, 'We know who you are.' 'Listen,' said Trotsky to Zinoviev; 'even here they recognize us. The revolution has made us famous everywhere.' The boys continued to shout, 'We know who you are.' Trotsky stopped, turned and asked, 'Who are we?' giving them a handful of coppers at the same time. The boys took the money and ran off shouting, 'A pair of Yids!' Lenin said that we must liquidate anti-Semitism and treat Jews like human beings, but it is hard to do it."

A waiter brought tea and an omelet. Ivan's wife spread the supper on the broad side of a wooden luggage-box and added bread and cheese from a basket. Cordially but shyly she said, "Please eat."

"*Akh,* you forgot to get any vodka," Ivan interrupted. "Probably on purpose. Wait, I'll get some." He rushed from the cabin.

We sat in silence. "Have you a large family?" I asked.

"Yes, two sons and two daughters."

More silence. "Do you go often to the city?"

"I was in Kazan once, but it was before the revolution."

She fumbled at the shawl tied round her head, opened it and retied it. Suddenly she turned and asked: "Is it true—what my husband says you said—

that in America there is no vodka? It would be fine to live in America!"

Ivan came back. "Did you ask him?" he inquired. Then he explained to me: "My wife wanted to know whether there was really such a country—without vodka. And do you go to church in America? I don't here, not since the revolution. The revolution made me intelligent. The church helps to keep us ignorant. The old women go—my wife goes—but what can you ever do with old women? Yes, citizen, religion is one of the chief enemies of our country."

"So you say," said his wife, "but what about vodka?"

"Yes, religion and vodka. The two of them keep us poor. But without vodka life would be awfully lonesome. And religion and vodka are connected. When do the peasants do most of their drinking? On Sundays and other religious holidays. Eliminate religion, Sundays and holy days, and you will diminish drinking in the villages." He poured two full glasses of vodka.

"I have a very great favor to ask of you. But wait, see what I bought in the city." He pointed proudly to the little black radio set, which would have cost about two dollars in America. "I paid thirty rubles for it, and yet I don't know whether I can make it work. It will be the only one in our village, and people will come to see it even if it doesn't talk. But I want to prove to them that I can hear Moscow on it." His face lighted up. "Do you think I could hear America now? Well, I suppose you have machines in America with which you can hear what's being said in Moscow. It will be nice when we have such things in our village. They promise us electricity next year——"

"They have been promising it for five years," his wife interrupted.

"I tell her everything will be different by and by."

"And worse," she replied positively.

"*Akh,* 'Live a hundred years, study all the time and die a fool,'" he quoted. "So many people don't see that things are better. Do we live badly? We have land and we have money from bootmaking—in all perhaps a thousand rubles every year. That's a lot of money in our village. Those who have only land earn, in money, about two hundred rubles a year.

"Had there been no revolution, I should still be in the Tsar's army. That was a fine army, remember, but the wages were small. When I heard they were dividing the land in our villages after the revolution, I deserted and ran home to make sure of getting my share. Had there been no revolution, I should have no land. My son would not be an officer in the army because no peasants became officers before the revolution. Now he may become a general. Akulina, your son a general! I should not have been on the village Soviet. I should not be the one who can explain in our village all that the government is doing."

"Are you a member of the Party?" I asked.

"No, if you are a Party member you have to take a lot of responsibility and the work eats up too much of your time." He changed the subject abruptly. "I am so glad to meet an American. My friends in the village won't believe me. So I have a great request—by the way, tell my wife how every family in America has its own automobile. It would be nice if we all had automobiles; then we could drive all the time, even to Moscow."

"And you would never get any work done," his wife commented.

"*Akh,* work is only part of life, and, 'If luck is going to find you, it will find you even when you're sleeping on the stove.' We need so much here—but chiefly culture. Tell my wife how it's true that in America all women can read and write. Shame on you that you won't learn. We organized courses for adults in our village last winter at seven o'clock every evening. Just before seven all the old women would run and hide in the woodsheds. We must liquidate illiteracy!

"But I can't understand one thing about America," he continued. "If you have culture, why do you allow the priests to go on deceiving the people? Here it is the priests who were responsible for our ignorance. We must liquidate religion. Yet it continues in America, although everybody says you are a nation with culture. But I am very much interested in what goes on in America, and I have a big favor to ask."

He stopped and poured himself another glass of vodka. After taking it in two swallows, he continued haltingly, "Won't you write and tell me all that goes on in America and about the American workers and *fermeri?* See, I remember that word." He was watching my face and misinterpreted my smile. "But there is no need to write. Rather, just send me one postcard from America to show my friends in the village, and they will then believe all I tell them. I shall write to you and tell you all that is new in the village of Samorodina, Andreev County, Perm District."

"Yes, a lot happens there," added his wife.

XV

TATYANA ANDREEVNA: THE MUSIC TEACHER

TATYANA ANDREEVNA came to tea one evening looking just as my host had described her, "awfully bourgeois." She was middle aged and wore rusty black like one of those ladies who answer to the title "Madame la Propriétaire" in a French *pension*. She was conspicuously corseted and the lace collar of her dress, standing stiffly on its bone supports, mimicked the rigidity of her body. Round her neck were three golden chains. From one hung a cross, from another a locket, from the third a gold ring. The three ornaments jangled an accompaniment to her awkward little steps.

She hung her sheepskin coat in the hall and removed her felt boots. It was deep winter in a remote Russian village, with thirty degrees of frost. Here, in the house, with the tile wallstoves heated till their doors turned cherry red, there was comfort. A brass samovar steamed; its polished sides reflected the light of the kerosene lamps. Outdoors there was only cold, treacherous in its seeming mildness; and there was silence unbroken save when some ghostly voice from a passing sled called to the horse.

"This is my daughter's music teacher," said my host, Semyon Pavlitch, the village postmaster. She bowed nervously, alternately wringing her hands in front of her and putting them behind her back. She ignored

302

me and, approaching the postmaster's wife, began a rapid conversation about some village scandal. It was as my host had said: "You'll find her very nervous when she meets you, a foreigner. Ever since she knew you were coming, a month ago, she has been here daily to ask about your arrival and to remind me to be sure to introduce you."

Suddenly she turned to me. "I am so glad to meet a foreigner. They come to this village very rarely——"

"Tatyana Andreevna, that isn't so," said the postmaster, laughing, "there was a Latvian here about seven years ago."

She paid no attention to the interruption but rippled on, like a running brook, "Do you speak French? It is the one foreign language I know. *Je parle français un*—" she began but retreated into Russian,—"*nemnoshko*—a little. I seldom get any practice. No one else in the village——"

"Yes," said my host, "we are very proud of her. Most of us are *'dark people'* here." His seriousness seemed assumed.

"I was very fortunate. I have been abroad." She waited for the effect. "You see, I married a Frenchman in 1912 and we went to France after our wedding. Here is his picture." She offered me the locket on its golden chain. In it was the picture of a middle aged sad-eyed man, with lengthy drooping moustache. "He died from typhus in 1918. These cursed Bolsheviki— their revolution cut off all our medical supplies. We should have fled to France earlier but my father was then alive. We could not leave him. Then the plague took Pierre and my father died the following month. Pierre, how learned he was, the most cultured man in the village! And so *gentil!*" From there on she tried bravely to break into French but each time she returned to Russian. My host, however, solemnly asked her to translate each French word.

Her husband had been a middle aged Frenchman who drifted somehow to this little village in southern Russia, fifty miles from a railroad. He had taught French in the village school and he had managed to get half a dozen pupils from the wealthy landlord families round about.

She continued, breathlessly: "He had not been home for many years. Therefore, after our marriage, he took me to France. Ah, how beautiful it is! Paris! The Eiffel Tower! Such stores and boulevards! Then Rouen, Chartres—the cathedrals! You have seen them? I became a Roman Catholic as the result of my visit to Chartres. I find more beauty in that religion than in our backward Russian Church. There is no Roman Catholic church anywhere near here, so I continue to go to our local Orthodox church; but I always imagine I am in a Roman church.

"We stayed only three weeks in France. My husband's people were very nice to me, but they felt that perhaps he had made a mistake in marrying a foreigner. Of course the French are more cultured than we Russians. Their traditions are so much richer. His family knew that, had he stayed in France, he might have become a great professor; but he was so adventurous, so eager to learn about the world!"

Semyon Pavlitch's wife refilled our tea glasses continually while we listened as Tatyana Andreevna told every incident of her trip abroad. She spoke with the air of one telling a story for the hundredth time. We heard what the conductor of the Russian train had said when she explained to him that by riding third class they would have more money to spend in the stores of Paris. We knew what the customs guard at the German frontier looked like. We learned what they had eaten for dinner on their first night in Paris in that July so long ago.

"Of course, had I stayed longer I should have seen more and I could have learned *plus de français*——"

"What does that mean?" Semyon Pavlitch interrupted.

She ignored the question. "But I remember everything that happened and everything that was said."

"It must be fine to have such a memory," said my host.

"Yes, there are people who could spend many years abroad and have nothing to say when they returned. My husband was like myself; he always remembered life in France and spoke of it."

She fumbled at the three little curls that hung over one ear, and her stubby fingers twittered and fluttered. "I still consider myself, in many ways, a Frenchwoman. After my husband's death I wrote his family several times. They felt that they should share in his estate, as if the revolution had made us rich. It was very small; his mind was not on the things of this world. Of course, had he stayed in France he probably would have become a very wealthy banker. After I refused to divide the little that was left they wrote no more. But I should like to visit them in Paris, *la belle Paris!* Our blood gets warmer, our hearts beat faster when we reach France."

She began to retell her first impressions of Paris. My host interrupted her: "Won't you play something for us?"

"I should be delighted," she answered. "When I was in Paris I went to the Opera once. They played *'La Bohème'*—French music is so wonderful! And do you know, during the first week of our visit there were orchestras playing and people dancing in all the streets. It was so *joli,* so *gai!*"

She sat at the piano. "I shall play first *'Rêve d'Amour'*—you can just feel the spirit of France in it." There followed half a dozen waltzes and mazurkas, of the sort that children play at their first conservatory recital. Each piece was accompanied with nods and grimaces. She concluded with the *'Marseillaise.'* Then she rose and bowed politely as though acknowledging the applause of some great audience. "How I should like to study in the Paris Conservatory," she said. "Pierre loved music so much. He would ask me to play every night."

It was growing late and a rising wind was blowing fine snow against the windows. We were silent for a moment. Somewhere, in the far away, a dog was barking at the moon. As she prepared to leave, she said, "You must call some evening. I have so many pictures to show you—awfully interesting things."

She wrapped the sheepskin collar high around her face and slipped out into the night.

"Now, what do you think?" asked Semyon Pavlitch. "Come, have some more tea—we've drunk only six glasses. You know the saying 'drink tea like a Moscow merchant,' twenty glasses at one sitting. We have relief now, with her gone. *Akh,* what playing! She has been teaching music in the school for thirty years and she always plays those same pieces. But she'd be hurt if we didn't ask her to play.

"It's the same with that cursed France. I think I've heard her story a thousand times, but she'd be insulted if we didn't sit and listen to it. With you here, a stranger and a foreigner at that, she's overjoyed. You wait—you will hear nothing but France, France, France! Before the revolution, France was the great model for our aristocrats. Now that they are gone, who cares? All the nobility spoke French but no one speaks it any longer. The people who spoke French in Russia before the revolution are now speaking it in Paris! I'd rather have my child learn your English. The revolution wiped out everything connected with France, even the huge debt we owed them. Imagine a stupid Russian cheating a Frenchman out of money!" he laughed heartily.

"Tatyana is not of the aristocracy?" I asked, surprised at the idea.

"Oh, no, her father was a village priest who died during the revolution. She lives with a sister, Vera. You will have much in common with Vera, but she isn't liked in the village. She never mixes with us and keeps herself aloof. I know why and sympathize with her, but the village thinks it's because she married a Shuisky—they had an estate near here and they were real aristocracy!"

I went to Tatyana's house a few evenings later. She was dressed as she had been earlier except that she now wore an old pair of high heeled shoes. She had also added powder and a bit of crimson rouge that was applied off centre: on one cheek it was thickest near her ear; on the other side it was concentrated near her nose.

"It is so difficult for us to live or to dress as they do in France," she said, greeting me. "You will pardon the simplicity of our house. Oh, yes, this is my sister, Vera."

She introduced me to a woman of forty. Her golden hair, combed back tightly, framed a face which, in the dim light of the hall, looked Asiatic. She was simply dressed, graceful in all her movements. Her face was young, with a calmness and repose that added to its beauty.

Their house had several large rooms, all of them crowded with antiquated furniture. A huge grand piano occupied most of the space in the living room. Photographs in worn frames hung everywhere. A little red lamp burned, unwavering, before the ikons in one corner. Everything seemed old, dateless, as if, in these rooms at least, time stood still.

Vera Andreevna introduced me to her daughter, a pretty child of fifteen, who curtsied and sat bashfully in one corner.

Tatyana came from another room carrying a strap-bound box. "Please excuse me while I set the samovar," said Vera, withdrawing. "My sister will entertain you."

"I have so many things I want to show you," said Tatyana, as she placed the box on the table. From it she drew out snapshots of her husband in the garden, on the lawn, in the woods. There were photographs of his family, his parents, his brothers and sisters—in the woods, on the lawn, in the garden. There were pictures of her husband and herself in Paris, in Chartres, in Rouen. All were beginning to fade, but she handled each one as a tender memory, proudly passing them on in endless succession.

Vera returned as I was looking at two pictures of other people: one, an old priest with two pretty daughters and a second, a young Russian officer and his bride, Vera Andreevna, by his side. "Please give me those pictures," Vera asked, somewhat embarrassed. "They do not belong here."

There followed a large pack of picture postcards from France, railroad timetables and theatre programmes from Paris, even several labels from wine bottles. "These things make Paris all the more real for me," explained Tatyana Andreevna. "Tell me, is it really impossible for us to get passports abroad now?"

"It is very difficult and very expensive except when travelling on government business," I answered.

"I have some money saved and I should like to go and spend my last days with my husband's family—if they are still alive. Of course, I haven't seen them since 1913 and then for only two weeks. But *les Français* are such hospitable people—it is so pleasant to be among them."

"You might find many changes in the sixteen years that have passed," I remarked.

"Yes, if I could have gone abroad in 1919 . . ." I thought I saw Tatyana glare suddenly at her sister, "Life is so different here since the revolution. I teach music in the school and I have four private pupils, but what can you do when there are only three pianos in our little village? And why should these Russian peasants need music? They are swine. My sister teaches the Russian language in the school—it's very dull, isn't it, Vera?"

"At least, I have plenty of students," she answered. "Everybody wants to learn to read and write."

"She teaches two night courses for illiterates too. How backward Russia is! Who ever heard of having to hold night courses in France to teach adults there to read and write?"

"Tea is ready," was Vera's only comment, as she withdrew to fetch the samovar.

In addition to home-made cheese, butter, and jam, they had purchased what few delicacies the village store offered: a can of stuffed peppers, some biscuit, some cheap candy. "Almost everything is sold on ration cards," said Tatyana, "and everything gets scarcer. The peasants nearly starve here, some winters, for this is a district where the land is very poor. Sometimes they kill their horses for food. Who ever heard of French peasants eating horse-meat?"

Vera Andreevna smiled and said, "But we live comfortably enough."

"We do have two salaries each month, mine and my sister's, a hundred and fifty rubles together. We keep a cow and a few chickens."

There was little conversation during tea until Tatyana said, "How nice tea time is in France—seated by a little table beneath an awning on a terrace. And breakfast! Chocolate and *croissants!* Sometimes you can buy cocoa in our store here, a substitute of course, made from oatmeal. But it tastes just like oatmeal."

Vera and her daughter cleared the table after tea. Tatyana went to the piano. She showed me a collection of French popular songs of pre-war days. "My husband used to love to sing these. He had a fine voice —had he stayed in Paris he might have sung in the opera. It is when I play that I feel the loss of Pierre the most. Ah, these bloody Bolsheviki and their revolution—what they have taken from me!"

She played some songs, very badly, smiling and tossing her head all the while. "I should die without music. Pierre always had me play for him in the evening." She stopped and seemed about to cry. "How everything has changed! The revolution, that awful typhus, the death of my father and mother. I was left alone and was seriously thinking of going to France. I could have found his relatives somewhere. Then Vera wrote from Moscow and said she wanted to come home, to the village, to live."

"You have not always lived here?" I asked, turning to Vera Andreevna.

"No," she answered without expression. "When the revolution broke out I was living in Moscow with my daughter. A year later I came to this village."

"Her husband was an officer, a Russian," Tatyana explained. "He died in 1917 after the first revolution. The soldiers were mutinous. No one knows whether he died from a German bullet or from a shot fired by a rebellious Russian."

Vera listened, her face immobile, then changed the subject. "Play some more, Tatyana, or let us play some duets."

"Very well, I have this book of French songs. Do you know them?" She ignored the suggestion of duets. "There is something so *spirituelle* about French music." She played until it was time for me to depart.

As I left, Vera said: "Come to see us again before you leave our village. We live so far away from everything and strangers are so rare."

"Yes," said Tatyana, "be sure to come in the evening when I am here. I am often delayed in the school in the afternoon. *Bonne nuit, monsieur.*"

I passed their house one afternoon. Some one was at the piano, playing with the technique and the expression of a musician. Outdoors, with thirty-five degrees of frost, was no place to listen to a concert. I went to the door and knocked. The music stopped. Vera Andreevna opened the door, embarrassed.

"Pardon my calling unexpectedly, but I heard music such as I have seldom heard in the city, let alone in a Russian village. Were you playing?" I asked.

"I was playing, but you flatter me. Won't you come in? Tatyana should be here soon."

"Won't you play some more?" I asked.

"No, I very seldom play." She seemed tense, uneasy, excited. "I am very glad you came; for I felt I had to talk with you."

"I wish you would continue what you were playing. The last time I heard it was in the opera in London," I continued.

"In London? You have been there recently?" She seemed to pale. "And is there still opera at Covent Garden?"

"Yes, but how do you know——?"

"Tell me, are there still boat races on the Thames? And the Derby at Ascot?" She laughed at the look of amazement on my face, for she was speaking in English.

"Where—but where have you learned these things?" I stuttered.

"I was in England for four years before the war. It seems so long ago and I have almost forgotten what I learnt. My English has become rusty." She changed to her own language. "You have reminded me of so many things. Tell me, do the lindens still flower in the spring in Berlin? I read that some bombs destroyed them. And Bayreuth—are the operas still given there?"

All I could say in amazement was, "Have you been all over Europe?"

"I spent eight years abroad, until 1916. But I wanted to ask one thing about life abroad—how do

you educate girls of fifteen now, after the war? I have
such a problem with my daughter. We have lived in
this village for ten years, and she does not remember
ever having seen a train, an automobile, or even an
electric light. You can see what few opportunities we
have here for any cultural education. She has read far
beyond those of her age in all the Russian classics. I
have taught her to speak French—we never use it
when Tatyana is present—and she reads a little German."

"You should teach her English," I said.

"What is the use? Very likely she will never get a
chance to use anything that she knows. How can I
talk to her about the theatre, about so much that your
daughters abroad know intimately? I don't know what
to do. I was reared in the old way while my daughter
must live in a world which considers that the wrong
way. She has never been out of the village since we
came. Everything is so expensive, and I have no
money to take her to Moscow. Besides, what she
would see there might spoil her for any contented life
in the village. A Russian village is exile, once you
have known the cities. But I should like to show her
so many things that I knew. I am so puzzled!"

Twilight was coming on, although it was scarcely
past mid afternoon. We looked out through the window silently. Everything was very still. The snow on
the shed roofs across the street reddened in the
shadows of the dusk. A typical village woman in yellow sheepskin coat passed by, returning from the village well. Buckets, slopping water, swayed from each

end of the wooden yoke that hung over one shoulder.

"What will she become if she stays in the village?" Vera continued. "What is there for her here? Who will there be for her to marry? Before the revolution there was life in little towns like this one. Now these places are dead—there is a blight on them and the people who could understand the way she has been reared, as a lady, have gone from here. I do not know but that they have gone even from Russia. We live so much in the past. You know my sister. You have seen how all her life is concentrated on those few years before her husband died. I was abroad at the time and never met him. I, too, live in the past, but I always remember that my daughter must live in the present. So I speak to her only about the present; I seldom talk of the past—and never of the future!"

Her daughter entered and bowed. She asked permission to go sledding on the hill in a neighboring meadow and ran away gleefully with a crowd of boys and girls.

"What do you teach girls of her age in America? Here she learns about socialism, strikes, labor organizations, and Karl Marx. She comes home with questions about things I never studied nor even heard of. It is so difficult—to try to teach her at home the best of what I learned. They do not teach religion in the schools now; so I must do that. I teach her things for which they have no use in our Soviet land; but at the same time I must watch her receiving an entirely different sort of education in the school. I wonder what this blend will produce. How will she fit in this new world?

In a few years she may want to leave this village. If she wants to go to Moscow what shall I say? She is so inexperienced!"

That thought seemed to burden her, for she sat silent. Abruptly she turned, "But why should I be speaking to you, the first foreigner I have met in twelve years, about such uninteresting things? Perhaps because I know you are going away and we shall not meet again; I shall not have to face you knowing that I have told you these things. Life is lonesome here, isn't it? I see no people and I have never spoken to anyone about what I think. No one would understand. Now tell me of life abroad.

"Pardon, Vera Andreevna, but what took you abroad?"

"My husband was an officer in the Tsar's army. He had a minor rank at our Embassy in London, then in France and finally, as the war began, in Germany. I have seen 'society' but now all that seems more remote than if it had happened in another world; rather it is two worlds removed. My story is known to the old inhabitants in this town—Semyon Pavlitch, your host, could tell you.

"My father was a priest here, fairly well to do. He served also on the Shuisky estate near here—you know that name? There was none higher in Russia before the revolution. To be connected with that family now, as with the Romanovs, brings only trouble. Better to be an Ivanov—that's Johnson in English, isn't it? When I was only seventeen I fell in love with the young count. He got his father's permission, and we were married.

"Tatyana always considered it wickedness on my part, as if there was something shameful, improper in marrying above my rank. She did the proper thing. She lived on here, teaching music, taking care of our parents as they aged, and then marrying her middle aged Frenchman who came here after he had been dismissed from some private family or other. She never wrote to me while I was abroad. I have heard that her husband was cruel to her. He drank a lot and used up most of her money, but she said nothing. You have heard what she says now!

"When my husband died and the revolution took what little I had, my position was critical. I was connected with a family marked for extermination. I had no money with which to flee abroad and, worse, I had a small child. So I wrote asking if I could return here, and Tatyana was so good—she let me come back. Her husband had just died. It is her privilege to speak and to live in the past. I have the present and my daughter has the future. Won't you play some of your American music for me?"

While I was playing, Tatyana came in. She asked me, imperiously, "Have you been here very long?"

"He's been here only a few minutes," Vera answered. "He has been waiting for you."

"I am glad you came," she beamed. "It is such a pleasure to entertain foreigners. There is much that you and I have in common, *monsieur amerikanyetz*. You know life abroad and life here! I know life here and life abroad. Tell me, I meant to ask the other evening, is living cheap in France these days? How much is the railroad fare from Moscow? Vera, have you prepared dinner? Perhaps our guest will dine with us."

I declined.

"By the way, did my sister play the piano for you?" Tatyana asked, as Vera went into the kitchen.

"No, I asked her to, but she wouldn't."

There seemed to be a look of satisfaction on Tatyana's face as she rose to help set the table.

The night before my departure Semyon Pavlitch arranged a little party. The village intelligentsia attended; the agricultural adviser, some of the teachers, the internes from the hospital, Tatyana and Vera Andreevna—"the first party she has come to since she returned to the village," whispered Semyon Pavlitch to me. The evening was passed in conversation: countless toasts served as an excuse for continual drinking. "How dull everything is in a place like this. How we envy any one who has been abroad. And how glad we are for even a wisp of information from the world outside our village," said Semyon Pavlitch. "I always think of that when I send the mail out twice each week—would to God that I might crawl in the bag too." The evening closed with music. Some one had an accordion, and Tatyana was prevailed upon to play the same pieces she had performed earlier for us. Again she finished with the *"Marseillaise"*!

I was leaving early next morning for the sixty mile sled ride to the railroad. As Tatyana said good-bye she asked: "Will you do me a favor? If you can get to

Rouen, will you look up this address for me?" She was crying as she stuffed a crumpled bit of paper in my hand. "And from Paris will you send me a postcard—of the Eiffel Tower? I lost the one I had. *Bon voyage* —come, Vera, we must be going." Vera said simply, "Good-bye."

They passed into the cold quiet night.

My host and I talked into the morning. "Do you realize what you have seen in the case of those two sisters? In what manifold ways the revolution has affected our people! Had there been no revolution— my God, one never dares to think what would have been had that never happened. There is more in a revolution than economics and politics!

"Tatyana's husband was a little wretch, cruel to her, disliked by the whole town. He came here hunting for a 'warm place' and found it by marrying this old maid. He never attempted to conceal his belief that the Russian people were the lowest of God's creatures and that the French were the masterpieces. She worshipped him and believed that this opinion in itself proved the wisdom of the French and of her husband in particular. She spoke little about her trip to France until after her husband died, although we all envied her because she could go abroad. That's the great desire of every Russian; part of our national feeling of inferiority. You know our saying—'It's always better there, where we are not.' It was apparent on her return that his relatives considered her a barbarian and him a renegade, and wanted never to see either of them

again. Being childless made her very unhappy but it
is a blessing—imagine a child with that rotten scoundrel for a father!

"She felt that the coming of Vera and her daughter
kept her from returning to the France she thinks she
knows. Do you believe that, Vera or no Vera, she
would ever have gone back there? What else could
Vera do since she had a small child? There was little
food in Moscow for any one. For people named Shuisky there was a special diet—jail food—and death.
She had to return to the village. You would have
thought that it was her right. Yet she felt she was im-
posing on Tatyana for, in those days, it was every one
for himself.

"Tatyana soon realized how her sister felt and took
advantage of it. Besides, her sister had a child and she
had none. What more could Vera want? You see, being the postmaster and a resident of this place for
forty years, I know all that goes on, although Vera
has never said a word to any one here. The village
thinks her proud, scornful. It believes that her contact with nobility spoiled her. It did; it condemned
her to slow death here. It is Tatyana who talks of life
abroad; it is Tatyana who teaches music and plays
the piano, while Vera sits silent."

"But Vera could do both infinitely better," I said.

"Of course. But she knows that to do the one would
deprive Tatyana of her sole diversion and to do the
other would deprive her of her sole means of liveli-
hood. Tatyana is not stupid—she is aware of this and
takes advantage of it. Vera remains quiet and teaches

TATYANA ANDREEVNA: THE TEACHER 321

Russian to little peasant children, grateful for the
peace that enables her to bring up her daughter. There
is something in her face—has she found the secret of
eternal repose? Or is it a mask behind which she laughs
at us as she must be laughing silently at her sister?
But her daughter—she's the best looking girl in the
village, isn't she? I wish I had a son who could marry
her."

XVI

VLADIMIR FOMITCH: THE MILLER

LUKINO, the village in which he lives, rises like a heap of brown leaves from the flat fertile plains of the south. I was driving to it one July afternoon, when he appeared, in time to solve one of those problems which beset the foreigner travelling alone in the provinces.

All day, since leaving Stragonov, my driver had been complaining about money. Since my desire to cut across country to Saratov by wagon came just at harvest time, when every horse and man is needed in the village, he felt that I should pay him twice the sum we had agreed upon. Now he refused to travel one verst beyond Lukino—unless I promised to pay four times the amount.

"I'll stop at Lukino then," I said. "Is there a place to stay?"

"There's a *chaynaya*, a tea house, with some rooms. Will you pay for a night's lodging there for me?"

"I will not, unless you continue to drive me as you promised."

"Then I shan't drive another yard," he said, stopping his horse.

"Well, we'll sit here, comrade," I said, slightly worried. Lukino, visible in the distance across the fields of yellowing wheat, was still a good hour's drive.

Without answering he drew from his pocket a dirty sack of cheap tobacco, a piece of newspaper, and rolled himself a cigarette. Having lit it, he let the reins fall and hunched forward, a perfect picture of round-shouldered patience.

On the road behind us there were sounds of a horse and wagon. A peasant, bareheaded, was driving toward us in a light wagon, whistling as he gave his horse the rein.

"Is anything the matter?" he asked, as he pulled up sharply.

"Nothing much," I replied, "except that this citizen refuses to drive any farther." I explained the situation. Immediately the driver began to defend himself.

"You agreed to drive him, didn't you?" the stranger spoke sternly. "Now, keep your word. Trash you are, 'not worth a candle to God nor a poker to the Devil,' " and he added several phrases of crackling profanity.

"Yes, yes, yes, Vladimir Fomitch," my driver said humbly. "I was only joking!"

"Well, drive on. Or better, let the foreigner ride with me. You follow behind and bring the baggage."

I climbed upon the seat beside him. He was a man nearing sixty. His face, with eyebrows that were an unbroken line across his brow and a moustache that swept into his gray beard, showed amazing strength. He wore a gray blouse and "store" trousers tucked into new boots.

"To think that I should meet an American," he began. "They are as rare as christened Jews or flying horses. Here I meet you just as I am driving home. I knew we would have a guest to-day—our dog barked in his sleep early this morning and the wood fell down in the stove while it was burning. You must come to my house—'An unexpected guest is better than two invited ones!'

"There was an American who travelled here during the famine. He bought things from the peasants and paid with *dollari*. Later the bank told us the *dollari* were no good. You come to my house—I have one of them—perhaps you can tell me why."

He insisted on offering the hospitality of his house for as long as I cared to stay in the village. "The *chaynaya* is filthy and sometimes the air is so thick there that you could hang an axe on it. Stay with us —'One who sits on the stove is no longer a guest but a member of the family,'" he quoted the proverb. "There are only my wife and my sons," he added.

His was the only mill in the neighborhood, operated by a little stream which our road crossed and re-crossed. He had been a peasant before the revolution and, in 1918, had bought this mill. "Now, because I employ two men at my mill I am called 'kulak,' an exploiter of the peasantry," he said bitterly. "The government officials hate me—they tax me four times as much as the 'poor' peasants. You see, I buy grain from the peasants and pay more than the government collectors. I sell it to private dealers in the cities. The government threatens to stop this—why can't it mind its own business? It is always 'hunting fleas in strange nightgowns'!"

As we approached the village through the fields where everyone was busy with the harvest, we passed the ruins of a large stone house, almost hidden by weeds. The miller waved toward it and said, "That's typical of all the village—ruined by the foolishness of the peasantry. It was the house of the landlord. During the revolution the peasants ransacked it, burned it, and killed the owner. What did they do with the things they took from the house? One of them used the top of a beautiful bed to make a stall in his house for his calf! Now there is no money in the village, there are no goods in the store—and to buy what there is you must show a receipt that you've bought Soviet bonds! And, as a *kulak,* I'm not allowed to buy at the store. I must get everything sent from Saratov!"

"But why do you say the foolishness of the peasantry ruined the village?" I asked.

"If they hadn't been so eager to steal the landlords' things and support the Bolsheviki there would be no Soviet power. Oh, they know it now. '*Akh, akh,*' they say, 'life is impossible!' They forget the old proverb, 'If you show someone else to be a fool you say, "Ha, ha," but if you're shown up as the fool yourself you cry, "*Akh, akh!*"' Grain collectors now come in winter and take most of the wheat the peasant has hidden for himself. They got four hundred *poods* from me last year, and I know who the pig's snout was that told them where it was hidden. Landlords never stole grain from you!"

His mill was on the other side of the village, past the white stucco church and the log school. All the peasant huts were of logs, their chinks stuffed with mud and moss, roofed with mouldy thatch. The village street was almost deserted, for everyone was working in the fields. A lone carriage came down the road, driven by a young man. He stopped when he met us and said, "I'm coming down to see you this evening. That's all."

"Very well," the miller answered, subserviently, it seemed to me. As we drove on he swore, *"Chort,* the devil, what brings him here? That's Serge Sergeitch, the *agronom,* the district agricultural adviser. A fool, that's what he is, and a Communist as well. You said you weren't a Communist, didn't you? He drives from village to village, giving advice, poking his nose into other people's business, and talking about bettering village life, about all working together. What rot! 'Each for himself and God for everyone!'—that's what I believe. 'Take what God gives you and guard what you have'!"

He continued impatiently: "He talks about changing the landholding system, about tractors and machines. At the same time he experiments with plants. They say he has crossed a tomato and a pepper. What's the use of that? Eat one of each together and they'd taste the same. He may be able to change plants but he can't change peasants. 'It's easy to spit over a wagon but try and spit under it!' The new village he dreams about. The 'struggle for a new life' he always talks about. Where's the money coming from for these things? From the peasant pockets! He had the village meeting agree two years ago to buy a seed cleaner. All of us had to contribute. It broke after six months. If you want to raise better crops, don't plant your seed during the new moon—that's the best advice!"

We crossed a bridge and turned toward a little frame

mill. It was unpainted, as are most village buildings. Near it stood a large frame house, and, behind, several grain storehouses. We came to the door of the mill where several peasant carts were unloading wheat. The crackle of the grain and the whir of the stone wheel were cheerful sounds.

A quarrel was going on between one of the peasants and a workman at the mill. "But why should you raise the price of grinding?" a young peasant said. "Just because you are the only mill around here—I'll report this to the Soviet."

"You will, will you?" said Vladimir Fomitch. "Go ahead, *svolotch,* and I buy no more grain from you!" He carried my bag into his house. His wife, a woman of forty, didn't change her expression when he said, "I've brought a guest, an American."

"You always bring guests; well, welcome to our bread and salt. You can have dinner now. Andrei and Petr are still in the fields. My sister and her husband came to-day, too," she added as an afterthought.

"Your relatives—they always come! Well, *ameri-kanyetz,* you'll have to stay at the *chaynaya* after all. Marousya," he turned to his wife, "Serge Sergeitch is coming this evening."

"I knew he was in the village. I saw Guryi——"

"His pig's face goes everywhere!"

"Why is Serge coming? Is anything the matter?" a worried look crossed her face.

" 'Know a lot and sleep little. Know much and age fast!' " he replied. "Let's eat."

Their house had two large rooms, furnished with

home-made unpainted tables and chairs, and entirely carpetless. A coverless table stood in one corner of the living room, beneath the ikons. Most of the room was filled with bags of grain and storage boxes. Sleeping accommodations were in the kitchen, atop the stove.

The miller, his wife's relatives, and I sat down to dinner. "You sit in the holy corner, beneath the ikons," said Vladimir to me. His wife brought a wooden bowl filled with cabbage soup, and five small wooden dippers. Each one was supposed to take a dipper full, eat it, and dip in for more. I apologized immediately for having "a very infectious mouth disease and might I have a plate and spoon?"

Conversation, chiefly between the miller and his brother-in-law, was partly about crops, partly about American farm methods. "They let a man alone there —he has enough troubles, with drought, insects and frost. Why should the government add to his worries?" At the close of dinner, when the soup bowl was empty, he left the table, after wiping his mouth on his sleeve, to attend to someone at the mill. Then his wife said to her sister, "I am afraid for Vladimir. He does not realize that his power in the village grows weaker——"

He returned and said, "Remember those *dollari* I told you that that American brought to our village. Here's one—what's wrong with it?"

He showed me a gray-green bill which read, "The Confederate States will pay to bearer——"!

The *agronom* came shortly after dinner, as the miller and I were sitting on a cart outside the mill. He turned directly to business, disregarding the miller's attempted cordiality. "There have been complaints from some peasants again that you are overcharging for grinding their grain. I've warned you before. Just because yours is the only mill around here is no reason for robbing them."

"Robbing them? If you'll bring my taxes down I'll lower my charges, Serge Sergeitch. Because I work harder and earn a little more I am branded as a *kulak* —and have to pay higher taxes. You and your idea of Class! You have a grudge against me. Because I pay the peasants more for their grain than your government buyers and because the peasants, therefore, listen to me, you want to get rid of me."

The *agronom* disregarded the charges. "I want to ask you also—what did you tell the peasants before the last village meeting?"

"I told them to vote against your crazy proposals to buy more expensive seed. Why should they spend their money that way? Isn't our flour good enough? And the peasants listened to me, didn't they? 'The egg doesn't teach the chicken,' Serge. You are a young man—go back to your garden and experiment with plants. Let us live our own lives."

Vladimir's wife came toward us but he sent her back saying, "Run along—'wherever two fools are quarrelling you will always find a third one watching.'" Then he asked, "Why are you so opposed to me, and to the few of us who make a little money in this village, Serge?"

"Because the Soviet government works with the

poor peasants, not with you *kulaki*. We are trying to raise the whole level of the village, while you and your friends try to rise at the expense of the other peasants."

"How are you going to raise this level?" the miller asked mockingly.

"We shall change the system of landholding——"

Vladimir laughed, "You might just as well say that human beings could move faster if they had three legs. Therefore, let's get a third leg. 'The ocean is only knee-deep to drunken men and fools'!"

The *agronom* paid no attention but continued, "We will have all the land in the village owned as a unit. It will be worked by machines and the crop divided among the people. And, mind you, there will be no room for you *kulaki*—you will have to get out!"

"*Nu, nu*, Serge Sergeitch, you are a young man. I am old and shan't be here much longer. Improve the village after I am gone. How will you get the peasants to agree to your new system?"

"We will make them agree if necessary——"

"With force?"

"The workers in the cities must have bread. We need bread for export. The villages must raise more. They cannot under the old methods. Yes, we will use force if necesary."

"You can use strange methods with your plants and cross beans and peas, but you cannot make new people out of the Russian peasant," the miller answered. "What happened last winter? The peasants refused to sell their grain to the government and I couldn't buy all of it. The grain collectors came and they beat it out of the peasants." He turned and explained to me, "They dug up manure piles, pig pens, everywhere that grain might be hidden. If they found any, they took it, at their own price. That's using force."

"They did get the grain, didn't they?" the *agronom* smiled.

"And what happened this year? You keep a register of how much land is planted and you know. The peasants used the one weapon which you Communists cannot meet—they cut their sowing. Why should they work hard to grow excess wheat if the government is coming to take it?"

"I know who advised them to cut their sowings, too," the *agronom* commented.

"The harvest in this district will be less than ever this year. That's the way your Communist policy increases harvests! The peasants are not like the factory workers. Each peasant has a bit of land and he feels himself what you call a capitalist. He has no use for Communistic ideas and if you use force on him——!"

"We do not need to use force. We shall tell the peasants the benefits of the new land holding scheme and when they see it work they will support us," Serge said convincingly.

"Yes, when sand turns to stone! Peasants are not plants, I tell you. Why did you Communists win in the Civil War? Because, in a choice between Communism and the return of the landlords, the peasants

chose Communism. They would not give up the land
they took during the revolution. Now you want a
new land division, in which the peasant gives up his
land and the government becomes the landlord. Isn't
that feudalism?"

"Perhaps, but with it will come new schools, new
roads, bigger crops."

"The peasant would rather have his land than all
those things," said the miller. "Perhaps you can force
such a change. The Russian peasants can't revolt—
you Communists know that—they are too scattered,
too disorganized. You can send troops against a village that revolts and you keep special regiments made
up exclusively of factory workers just to fire on the
peasants. No regiments conscripted in the village
would do it. But I tell you, if you change the land
system, you bring on the end of Communism, just as
sure as four times ninety and nine times forty are the
same thing."

"We shall see," the *agronom* said quietly. "In the
meantime, any more complaints about overcharging at
your mill and I shall report you to the county court.
You know how the court feels about *kulaki.*"

As he prepared to go he offered to drive me to the
chaynaya. "And I can take you thirty versts on your
way to Malinova, to-morrow," he added.

"You may find it difficult to get another horse," the
miller commented, and went with me to the house to
get my bag. "He always comes and threatens me," he
whispered, as I groped around in the dim candle-light
for my belongings. " 'Planting cabbages in other peo-

ples' gardens'! Why can't he look out for his own affairs?" I stumbled as I left the room. "A good sign," he said. "'If you stumble in a strange house you will be sure to return.' Good-bye."

The *agronom* spoke about his work as we drove down the dark road. He had been stationed here for three years and was the only Communist for some miles around. "It's people like this miller who hinder my work," he said bitterly. "His hold over the peasantry is strong although many fear and hate him. He even cheated his own brother! The poor peasants would support me but the miller lends them money and rents them agricultural machinery. They will not testify when he cheats them. He's like a lynx—he doesn't soil his own tail. But when we reform the village he will be the first to go!"

I had had enough politics for one evening and changed the subject. "Vladimir Fomitch spoke about agricultural experiments you were making—" I began.

"He laughed at them, I suppose? Most of the peasants do. I am trying to cross wheat with rye. Think what extra wealth our villages will have if we get a grain that will grow up in the north, where only rye grows, but which will produce a flourlike wheat."

"Are you having any success?" I asked.

"None as yet—it is very difficult. But I like to think of the extra food our country will have if I succeed. The peasants laugh at me. People like the miller help to keep the old superstitions alive. 'God gave us such plants. Why should you try to change them?' It's the same when I tell them anything new —about putting poison on the fields to kill the field mice, for instance. 'God sent the mice—why should we interfere?' they say. 'Besides isn't it a tradition that many mice mean a good crop'?"

We drew up at a two-story frame building. An oil lamp burned in the room on the ground floor. "Here's your inn," said the *agronom*. "You'll find it pretty dirty, but who can clean the dirt out of a Russian village? There is much we must teach the peasantry!"

The innkeeper showed me to a little room, furnished with a bed, a table, and a chair. I soon fell into a half doze to be awakened by voices in the corridor, before my door. Unexpected guests had arrived.

"Which room shall we take?" said one voice.

"Let's take this," answered another.

"No, not that room—there is a foreigner sleeping there and, besides, I slept there a week ago—the bed was lousy!"

I spent the rest of the night on the table.

Russian proverbs say, "A Russian hour is a long time," and, "Much water flows by the mill in a Russian minute." We were to start next morning at six but it was not until nine that the *agronom* came for me. A peasant was driving his wagon, an old man, whose wrinkled face seemed to show dirt ingrained, wearing old ragged clothes and bast sandals tied with rope that helped to hold the burlap, which served as leggings, in place. He chewed sunflower seeds incessantly.

Our road led out of the village through the fenceless fields. Everywhere the peasants, up since dawn, were busy. Russian peasants do not live on their land but near it. Their houses and barns are gathered together into a compact settlement and their land lies around their village for five miles on each side. Every five years at the village meeting the land is divided among the souls of the village, each person receiving equal shares of so much good land, so much fair land, so much poor land.

Here the individual strips were often only forty feet wide and several hundred feet long; a family of ten might have fifteen acres, divided into thirty such strips, marked only by boundary poles or stones scattered on all sides of the settlement. Some of the strips had been harvested. On others the women, with bright 'kerchiefs round their heads, bent low and, swinging to the rhythm of a song, cut the grain with little sickles and bound it into sheaves. On other strips the sheaves were being piled on wagons.

The men, most of them in bark sandals and homespuns, carted the grain to the threshing floors on the outskirts of the village, where the sheaves were spread out on the hard clay. A flat board, with wooden spikes protruding, was hitched to a horse; a small boy drove it round and round over the grain. Elsewhere men and women were winnowing the grain with wooden shovels. Everybody in the village was in the fields.

"Do you see things like this in America?" Serge asked as we drove down the treeless road. He waved toward the flat steppe which, in the far distance, looked like the sea. "If this land could be worked with machines, as you do in America——"

The driver turned on his seat and said, "I'd like to ask the American a question. Do you have a machine in your country that reaps, threshes, and bags wheat at one operation? Serge Sergeitch said that you do but —well, 'Travellers have the right to tell strange tales.'"

"I wish you could speak to a village meeting and tell the people how farming is done in your land. They raise only twelve bushels to an acre here, although we have excellent soil."

"But that's as much as they have always raised," the driver interrupted.

"Is that a reason why they should not raise more? My work is to tell the peasants how to raise bigger crops, to use cleaned seed, to use more manure——"

"Some of the peasants say 'Manure betrays God. It only helps weeds and grass to grow,'" the driver commented, continuing to chew the sunflower seeds. The "whutt," as he spat out the hulls, punctuated our conversation.

"But they continue to work the way their fathers, their fathers' fathers and their grandfathers' grandfathers have done it. Look at that man—he might be in the fifteenth century—!" We were passing a strip planted with potatoes on which a peasant, with a thick stick fastened to a horsedrawn wooden frame, was slowly turning up a row of potatoes.

"Won't the gradual introduction of machinery into the village help you?" I asked.

"How can we use machinery in a village now? Can you use a tractor on strips of land as small as these? You couldn't turn it around. At the bottom of our problem is the landholding system. Not until we abolish these small fields can we make any progress in the village. Yet the tradition of 'my land' is deeply rooted in the peasantry. They don't see that their poverty is their own fault—that they can improve themselves. We'll make them! What good are modern industrial cities if our villages remain in the seventeenth century? Sometimes I like to think of the village of the future——"

"Are you never discouraged?"

"Yes, when I think of the twenty-seven million peasant families in our land, just that many separate fortresses of tradition and ignorance united to hold us Communists back."

We passed a line of peasant wagons, each one piled high with bags of grain.

"Where are you going, comrades?" the *agronom* asked.

"To sell our grain at Vladimir's mill," one old peasant replied.

"Why don't you sell it when the government grain collectors come. They will be here next week."

"Are we fools? They pay ten kopecks less per *pood* than Vladimir does." They laughed and moved on.

"There you see why that *kulak* has power here," said Serge.

" 'A pig in a golden collar is still a pig,' " the driver suddenly interrupted.

"Guryi here is Vladimir's brother," Serge explained.

"Can I help it? I had nothing to do with arranging that. I have had nothing to do with him for ten years. I keep away from him—'If you lie down with dogs you get up with fleas.'"

"What did he do to you?" I asked.

"During the revolution he wanted a calf that I had taken from the landlord's estate but what was wrong in that? Everybody was taking something. I wouldn't give it to him, so, at the next village meeting, he saw to it that I got the worst pieces of land. Then a year later, when I was getting poorer and he richer, he took my wife——"

"Come, Guryi, you know you don't regret that. She had a sharp tongue and you always beat her," Serge laughed.

"Beat her? Of course I did. 'Beat an overcoat, make it softer; beat a wife, make her dearer.' 'Love your wife like your soul, shake her like a fruit tree, beat her like an overcoat.' No, I didn't mind her going but why should she go to my brother?" "Whutt," "whutt" went the sunflower seed husks.

"If ever I get him jailed, will you take your wife back?" Serge asked, laughing.

"Of course not, but I hope he gets punished. I got even with him last year when I told the grain collectors to rake under the manure pile behind his house. They found four hundred *poods* of grain. Now every time you tell the peasants to do one thing, he secretly tells them, 'Who knows more about farming? That boy, or you men who have worked the land for sixty years?'"

Serge nodded. "If I could end the influence of such men in the villages in my district I could raise wheat production. But he is very sly——"

"I heard in the village that he is going to adopt another son," Guryi interrupted.

"You can't sell and buy land openly in the village, so Vladimir Fomitch 'adopts' young men who have a share of land," the *agronom* explained. "Later they go to the city and the land is his, in exchange for a little money. How can you stop that? I am the only Communist in this 'bear's corner' and there would be many protests from the peasants if I had him arrested openly. He lends them money and machinery. They stick to him like clay on boots. No—we must go to the bottom of the problem and revise the land system. I suggested such a thing here and was laughed at."

"The peasants do not want to pool their land and divide the crops," the driver said. "They are afraid that then there will be no crops. That's what Vladimir told them."

We drove on through the hot summer day. At early evening we came to our destination and stopped at the *chaynaya*. Here Guryi, Serge, and I sat at tea. When Serge left the table for a minute Guryi said to me, "Do all your peasants have tractors as Serge says? I don't know whether to believe him or not. It's the same when he talks about 'a new village.' Perhaps he can make the peasants change. When he started with his plants everybody called him a fool but now in the village where he lives they half think that he is a wonder worker. So I believe him when he talks about bringing machines to our village and making us all richer. It will be fine when we have machines."

"What will you do then?" I asked, curious.

"We shall sit under the trees and watch them work."

Two years later the central government was pushing the "collectivization movement." What Serge Sergeitch had hoped for was now the aim of an aggressive government policy. The villages must be "collectivized," their land must be pooled. Newspapers were reporting great success in persuading the peasantry to adopt the new plan.

I could think of no better place to see the "movement" in action than in the Saratov district, near Lukino. I came to Straganov, a day's ride away, one evening in the late fall. A village meeting was in progress and the school house yard was packed with peasant wagons, while their owners crowded the little room. On the platform there were half a dozen younger peasants, Serge Sergeitch, and several others in the black leather coats which showed them to be factory workers. A young worker was speaking.

"I have pointed out the benefits of forming a *kolkhoz,* a collective. Now we will vote. How many are in favor of revising the land as was done at Lukino?"

No hands were raised. A voice near me said, " 'Each priest chants in his own fashion'—it's fine to be a worker from the cities as he is and get a vacation to come out to the villages to advise us!"

"Well, comrades," the speaker continued. "I shall point out the disadvantages of not forming a *kolkhoz!*

The government will co-operate naturally with those villages that follow its policy. Consequently, we cannot guarantee kerosene for your store——."

"*Akh,* thieves," some woman's voice cried.

"——nor textiles, boots, or sugar."

"There are little of those now, comrade," a man shouted.

"There will be none this winter. Nor can the government afford to keep an *agronom* here, nor a veterinary,——"

"And you'll close the hospital, too?" half a dozen shouted.

"I did not say that——"

"You are seeing the force used which Serge Sergeitch mentioned," said a voice in my ear. It was the miller.

"Hello, Vladimir Fomitch, what are you doing in this village?" I asked, surprised.

"I came to see it ruined, just as I saw Lukino ruined two months ago. Watch!"

"Now, how many will support the new land division system?" the speaker concluded.

More than half the hands in the hall were raised, followed by a babble of questions. "Can we live in the village even if we don't join the *kolkhoz?*" "What about *kulaki?*"

"Come with me and I'll tell you what has happened," the miller said. "It is a long story——"

I pleaded fatigue for I wanted to see the *agronom.*

"Well, let me drive you to Lukino to-morrow." I agreed and we parted.

I had no chance to speak with Serge Sergeitch after

the meeting for half a dozen rings of gesticulating peasants surrounded him. He did call out, "I received your letter and I'll be in Lukino to-morrow." I left the hall noticing that, as the peasant groups walked away, there was little conversation and no laughter among them.

Early next morning Vladimir and I started for his village. Every turn of our wheel brought another tale of woe. "I no longer have my mill. It was the peasants' desire to seize that which brought this whole collective movement to a head here. All spring Serge was talking about it. 'We will farm the land as one piece, the government will send better seeds, a tractor, machinery. We will have a mechanical churn, we will take over and operate the mill. And we shall divide the profits according to the work that each man does.'

"The peasants wavered. Then workers came from the city and threatened just as you heard them last night. 'If you don't—!' Finally the peasants agreed. The *kolkhoz* was formed just in time for autumn sowing; Serge Sergeitch is the director. A tractor has come and my brother Guryi has been made its caretaker. No, he doesn't drive it. He cleans it and sees that it is put in the barn at night. But the new seed hasn't come. And when the peasants entered the *kolkhoz* they said, 'The government takes our land, it will take care of us now!' So they ate their spare grain, they slaughtered their cows! Why turn those over to the *kolkhoz?* There will be a terrible meat and milk shortage! That was more than Serge bargained for. The peasants have had to put their land, their machines, even their chickens into the collective. I wonder if Serge is going to collectivize the rooks?"

"And your mill?"

"It now belongs to the 'October Revolution *Kolkhoz*' as they call our village. It was decided at a village meeting that any who did not care to join could stay in the village and have some land, but the collective took the best. The land they gave me won't grow five *poods* in a year!"

"How do they arrange the labor in the village?"

"Every person is supposed to do so much per day. A record is kept and the profits will be shared accordingly. The women are supposed to take turns keeping the school and the new library clean. There was a frightful hairpulling the other day about whose turn it was!"

I took a box of cigarettes from my pocket and offered him one. He took it eagerly. "This is the first 'store' cigarette I have had for some months. I am barred from the store here and the taxes took most of my money. I am alone now. My wife has left me and my sons. What will happen to me? They will probably decide later to kill all whom they choose to call *kulaki*. The peasants have gone mad."

"But why did they agree to form this *kolkhoz?*"

"Force, force—and promises. I heard of a village in the Tambov district where the soldiers threatened to poison the wells unless the peasants agreed. Of course they agree—most of them. Oh, the Communists are clever. They have been able, up to this time, to decide whether a man should be allowed to earn a living in the city; but a man could always earn a living here in the village whether he liked Communism or not. Now every right except that of walking on Russian soil and breathing Russian air is taken away from such as myself even in the village. How can we fight back? We're like the Jew who said, 'That soldier hit me three times with the butt of his gun but I got even—ha, ha—I hit him fifteen times, *fifteen times,* with my cap.' "

We drove on through the day, while he continued his unceasing lament. As we neared Lukino late in the afternoon we saw before us, on the side of the road, a wagon bogged in the deep mud. On it were several crates and a piece of machinery so wrapped in burlap that its nature was invisible. The driver, Guryi, the miller's brother, was tugging at the horse.

"Hey, help," he shouted at us while we were still some distance away. When he saw that it was his brother who was coming he was silent.

"Would you really let a *kulak* help your *kolkhoz?*" Vladimir asked mockingly. "How wonderful! Next you'll be getting black milk from white cows! What are you hauling there—parts for your tractor? I thought it wouldn't be long before it was broken."

"Our tractor isn't broken; these are parts for a new seed separator," said Guryi sharply.

"Well, you get no help from me. Should I let my horse tire himself to drag for your damned collective? But if you want to I'll drive you into the village." Guryi climbed on our carriage and we started off while Vladimir continued. "It isn't machinery that grows crops—it's perspiration. The peasants won't work as hard now that there is no individual responsibility. Do you think they will work as hard, Guryi?"

"It isn't my job to think. I tend to the tractor," Guryi replied shortly.

"Yeh, and it's broken, isn't it? I know when you're lying and you lie when you say those are separator parts."

"You lie yourself. You'd like to see it break. You know that with it we'll have a harvest that will give each peasant family four hundred rubles income; twice as much as when you were the power in the village and could exploit them."

"They will have—when goslings grow to turkey hens. 'All who snore aren't asleep,' fool. All who have joined your *kolkhoz* aren't enthusiasts. They know that the government has promised much. It has become the feudal lord in the village. Where is it going to get all the money to keep its promises—for tractors for every village, for parts when they break, eh, Guryi?"

"The peasants know now that the government is their friend and not *kulaki* like you."

"Their friend? Did I not lend everything I had whenever a man was in need?"

"And at what per cent!" We were nearing a field where there stood a pair of horses. Guryi slid off his seat and turned away without a word.

"Say 'thank you,' brother—thank even the Devil," Vladimir shouted after him. " 'You never know when you may need his help again.' He is a fool and all the peasants are fools. They expect now that, in bad times, the government will take care of them. What if a famine comes—when the government is sending all its grain abroad? Good-bye, Russian village, good-bye Russian peasants! But earlier it will be good-bye, Vladimir Fomitch."

A tractor was plowing the broad fields. Near the village fifty men were busy sowing grain with horse-drawn machines. The village had changed little in appearance: if anything it was shabbier. A new school had been built and the *chaynaya* no longer had a private individual's name over the door. On the front of the store was a sign, "Friends of the Revolution," painted in red, and a column, in black, headed, "Enemies of the Revolution." There were citations in one column of those who had bought state bonds, those who had paid co-operative dues. The column in black listed those who had not and Vladimir Fomitch's name led all the rest.

"I'll leave you at the *chaynaya*," he said. "I have another house, a hut where I used to store grain. There is only room in it for my horse, my plow, and myself."

Serge Sergeitch was breakfasting on substitute tea, made from dried fruit, black bread, and cheese when I met him downstairs in the morning. He greeted me warmly. "I am so glad you have come. Here is the fulfillment of my dream. We have dropped the old land system and we are going ahead—but I am so busy."

"Are you really making progress? I heard some criticisms yesterday."

"Yes, you rode over with Vladimir Fomitch, didn't you? He didn't tell you everything, very likely. He told you his wife left him? She went to Guryi but he wouldn't have her. And his sons left, of course. We wouldn't have them in the *kolkhoz*. But did he tell you how he lied to the peasants?

"When we began to talk *kolkhoz* here six months ago the peasants were undecided. Immediately Vladimir, the priest, and a few *kulaki* talked against it. The rumors they spread—! 'Members of the collectives will have to sleep on one long bench in the school house, men and women together, under one long blanket!' 'Only those who work ten hours every day in the year will get any firewood for winter.' 'There will be no profits, the store will give you a bit to eat and a little to wear, and that's all you get. Remember how the government makes you buy bonds. It will make you work the same way.' 'All women will be common property in the *kolkhoz!*'—and endless rot like that!"

"But what did turn the peasants your way?" I asked.

"I told them of results on other *kolkhozi*—how incomes have been raised from 200 to 400 rubles a year. I brought a tractor here and they saw how deep it plowed. And I told them that the mill would be theirs——"

"Was that the final argument?"

"No, but it bore weight. Finally, we had to threaten them with force, as you heard last night. Perhaps the first few years will be hard but the new village is going to develop best when we have a new generation. They will know only land owned in common!"

Guryi came into the *chaynaya*. New boots on his feet could not balance the sad look on his face. He nodded to me and said to the *agronom:* "The tractor broke while you were away. I don't know what ails it. In a horse I can tell whether it is stomach ache or glanders. But this damned machine—! The mechanic had new parts sent from Saratov." He turned to me as he was leaving, "I was hauling them yesterday but I couldn't admit to my brother that my tractor wasn't working well."

"I don't believe the fool mechanic knows how to operate a tractor," Serge replied impatiently. "Or else he was showing off. It's funny, but the young man whom all the village girls used to run after was the one who played the accordion best; now it's the man who drives the tractor. We are starting many tractor schools for we need lots of operators. But with all the machinery we do not promise the peasants an easier life. At present we are not well organized and they must do more work than they would ordinarily do in the autumn. But our crops will be bigger. We are using science and not superstition."

"What about those who do not belong, who cannot belong to the *kolkhoz?*"

"They must shift for themselves. We cannot be sentimental. If we cannot revise the land system of Russia then sooner or later Soviet power will fail— that we Communists know. We have used force this time but later the example of successful *kolkhozi* will begin to attract peasants voluntarily. And we shall have all of Russia collectivized by 1933. Once more we shall be a great wheat producing nation; and the villages will not lag far behind the cities in progress."

He finished his breakfast and rose from the table. "I'll be busy here to-day—if you want to look around, make yourself at home. And ask questions of anyone."

"There is one question I'd like to ask. What happened to your agricultural experiments?"

"I stopped those. Here is the most tremendous laboratory in the world—the Russian village. It is more interesting to change the ways of people than to change the habits of plants. We are trying to bring our peasantry from the sixteenth to the twentieth century in three years."

"And if you fail?"

"Only a country-wide famine now can make us fail. But if we fail in the villages then Soviet Russia fails. But we must succeed, no matter what happens to the old generation."

The first snow of winter in Moscow was blotting out even the lights of the apartment across the courtyard. With it came the quiet that winter brings to Russian city and village. There were only the sounds of the "whisp" of snow against the windows and the crackling of the birch logs in the tiled wall-stove. The government wine store had recently put on sale a stock of wine taken from the cellars of the Hotel Europe in Leningrad and was selling Richebourg burgundy, 1904, for less than two dollars a bottle. With that, with the fire, and with the silence there was a comfort not often found in the Russian land.

Suddenly I heard voices in the courtyard. The janitor was arguing with two men. "I never heard of such a name," he said. "Why should I take you to where he lives even if I knew? What would I get for my trouble—you peasants would run away, like satisfied piglets from a trough, without even 'thank you,' let alone a tip. . . . ."

"But we want the *amerikanyetz,* comrade," one voice said.

"Oh, that one? Why didn't you say so in the first place? It's too cold to be outside talking. He lives on the second floor." A door slammed shut.

In a few minutes there was a knock on my door. Vladimir and Guryi entered. They wore bast sandals, burlap around their legs, and long yellow sheepskin coats. I had them hang these in the hall. Their odor, when wet, lives with one for a long time.

"You are surprised to see us?" Guryi began. "We are friends now, yes,—since about a month."

Vladimir patted his brother on the back to prove it.

"—Two weeks ago Serge ordered the village Soviet to '*dekulakize*' the village. Every *kulak* was told to leave. Serge said that as long as they were in the village they would try to use their influence to destroy the *kolkhoz.*"

"I was too busy trying to get enough to last through the winter to think of politics," said Vladimir bitterly. "Even the peasants in the *kolkhoz* are killing and eating their horses."

"Yes, and they say the government is going to send us only camel meat. Well, Vladimir was ordered to go. If he refused he would be sent to a prison camp in the north. Where could he go? He could have a piece of land only in our village—nowhere else. What could he do?"

"So, we came to Moscow—" Vladimir began.

"Yes, we came to Moscow, to see Michael Ivanovitch Kalenin himself. He receives peasants and hears our complaints. We are staying at the Peasants' Home here——"

"For forty kopecks a night," Vladimir interrupted.

"When I heard of this 'dekulakization' I felt that it wasn't right. I went to Vladimir and we used two months wages and sold the two bonds I owned to get money to come here. I will tell Michael Ivanovitch right out that I am a responsible worker on our *kolkhoz* and explain that my brother——"

"What fools we peasants are," Vladimir continued the complaint. "There's a proverb,—'God looks out for fools, children and drunken men.' That's why we peasants have managed to get along. But no longer—we are short of food in the village and even God can't give us that when the Communists take it away from us."

It was difficult to recover from the first surprise of seeing them. They looked curiously at the many foreign things in my room: a typewriter, a camera, a foreign overcoat.

"But tell me, Guryi Fomitch," I said, "why did you decide to help your brother?"

XVII

GAVRIL BORISOVITCH: THE VILLAGE JUDGE

"I AM the unhappiest man in Russia," he said as he sat drinking tea with my host, Semyon Pavlitch, the village postmaster, and myself on my second night in Zelyonopol. He looked sad as he spoke and sadness did not become him. He was a man of forty, weighing scarcely a hundred and ten pounds. His short stumpy body was topped by a round orange-red face with a halo of unmanageable yellow hair. He resembled nothing so much as a stunted sunflower and his face seemed like a background on which there could be only laughter.

"*Nu, nu,* Gavril Borisovitch," said the postmaster, as if to comfort him, "remember the proverb, 'Good luck and bad luck ride together on the same sled.' "

"Good luck doesn't come to me," he replied, and grief deepened his voice. "For seven years the same thing has happened. I can't keep a single harvest. I thought I escaped this year, but you saw how they burned me out last night. The 'red rooster'—" he laughed bitterly.

Then I understood the remark of my driver as he and I approached the village the night before. Riding in a shovel-shaped sled all day, we had passed the forty verst stone in mid afternoon. Zelyonopol lay ten versts away. Darkness had come early and the

353

evening wind carried flying snow from the woods beside the road. Our way led out into open fields and up
a slope. Here the wind blew harder and colder. There
was no warmth either in the straw, in the blankets, or
in my sheepskin coat.

Suddenly, at the top of the hill, the driver cried,
"Look, look." I came out from under the straw. There
was a menacing red glow in the sky on the distant
horizon. "Fire in Zelyonopol," said the driver. "The
whole place may go." He hurried his horses so that the
last five versts were the fastest of our whole journey.
As we came near we saw the glowing framework of a
little building. A hand-pumping engine stood near by
and a bonfire to melt snow for the engine. The driver
seemed relieved as he said, "It's only Gavril Borisovitch's barn. Some one has let the 'red rooster' loose
again!"

Now the little judge used the same phrase and
added, "I tell you, I am the most unhappy man in
Russia. For eleven years I have been judge in this
village——"

"Before the revolution Gavril Borisovitch was the
best jockey in Russia," my host explained. "Three
times he rode horses before the Tsar."

"Yes, I was a good jockey," Gavril continued simply.
"During the revolution I joined the Communist Party
and worked in the Cheka, the secret police, as head of
the Revolutionary Tribunal here. The number of men
I tried! And the number who had to be executed! *Nu*,
you saw the 'red rooster' last night—arson. The relatives of people I have judged remember me, and every

year they set fire to my harvest. But I don't know
whether it is revenge for people I tried long ago or
during these recent years."

"How many have you sentenced to death in the past
few years?" Semyon Pavlitch asked.

"Only four since 1924. Three for highway robbery
and most recently, Alexeev. Yet every year someone
has loosed the 'red rooster' against me. And we have
never caught them. It's bad enough to have six children and a wife to keep on eighty-two rubles a month
but when they burn your grain and potatoes in addition—! If only I could get away from here to some
other district! Whenever I ask my superiors they only
say, 'You know this region best. Stay here'!" He shook
his head discouraged. "I could leave my position as
judge if I wished. The State Horse Farm near Voronezh would give me a position supervising horse-
breeding."

"Why don't you leave?" Semyon asked, laughing.

"Well—" Gavril shrugged his shoulders.

"Precisely, because you now are a power in this village, an 'important bird.' What are you going to do
about your burned barn?"

"We shall investigate. It is curious that I have
never been able to find who are the rascals, considering how gossip travels through a village. Different
people have done it at different times—of that I am
sure."

"You can keep guns away from them but the peasant always has an infallible weapon of revenge in a
box of matches. And the power of the *kulaki* isn't

broken in the villages around here yet. You have a lot of enemies, Gavril, and especially since the Alexeev case. Alexeev," my host explained to me, "was the head of the Soviet in a village near here. He had been a power there before the revolution and it was quite natural that he should lead it afterwards. He was wealthy, with much more land than the others. But the county government here dismissed him when he showed himself too friendly to the other *kulaki* and the priests. A Communist was sent from here to be head of the Soviet. Six months later, when Alexeev was drunk, he fought with the Communist about his taxes and he cracked his successor's skull with a vodka bottle. He came to the court here for trial."

"And I sentenced him to death," Gavril interrupted. "The courts are as much a class weapon as the factories. Alexeev was an enemy of the peasants, even if *they* didn't know it. He hired men at low wages to work on his land and he rented out his machinery to poor peasants."

"The people in that village and other villages felt that your sentence was too severe," Semyon remarked.

"Too severe? What would they have us do with our enemies when we find them openly opposing Soviet power?"

"Yes, Gavril, but that Communist you sent out wasn't very popular. They thought him an outsider."

"Since that time we've had no trouble with that village," Gavril concluded triumphantly. "The poorer peasants are on the Soviet and they have even agreed to a voluntary tax to improve the roads. The Alexeev execution was a lesson. You know the proverb, 'If it doesn't thunder a peasant won't cross himself.' "

"You began an investigation into your fire to-day?"

"The GPU agent found nothing. The two police-men were no more successful. No one was seen hang-ing around or running away. But the day after to-morrow we'll visit the Alexeev family. I suspect some-one in that village," Gavril said decisively. "I shall send the GPU over there to-morrow morning." He changed the subject, asking, "Are you going to stay here until next Sunday? There will be horse races."

Semyon explained that I would stay in the village ten days to study the operation of village government and that I was studying Soviet law.

"Good, you must come to court to-morrow. There is going to be a most interesting case. And the day after to-morrow you can drive with me to the other village. I'd like to know something about your Western laws. I am just beginning to read Roman law but, the Devil, it is so difficult."

Zelyonopol is in southern Russia, thirty miles from the railroad. The districts of the Soviet Union are divided into "counties" and Zelyonopol is more than a village; it is the county town. In it are located the administrative organs for a district embracing several hundred square miles and perhaps forty villages. Yet it is a village along with the others. Its three thousand inhabitants work the fertile fields that lie around it. Its streets are mud in spring and autumn. All the buildings, except the stores, the hospitals, the churches, the school, the jail, and the court house, are one story log structures.

A crowd of peasant sleds stood in the square before the court house on the following morning. There is little work in the village in winter and a good trial is a great diversion. The air in the building smelled like that of public buildings the world over, plus heavy odors from sheepskin coats and damp leather boots. Whitewash was peeling from the walls of the long corridor. There were a few posters calling attention to a new state loan.

The court room was the largest room in the building. On a raised platform, at one end, stood a long narrow necked water carafe. On the wall behind hung a picture of Lenin, framed behind flyspotted glass. The remainder of the room was filled with rows of chairs, all occupied. Men, women, and children were talking at the same time, in great confusion. Rows of peasants in their yellow sheepskin coats lined the sides of the room.

As we stood in the doorway, looking vainly for a seat, Gavril Borisovitch passed us. "I'll get a place for you," he said, and he ordered an attendant to clear two chairs in the front row. Their former occupants grumbled at losing the reward for coming early but their protests were useless.

The trial began when Gavril Borisovitch came from a side door and walked to the platform. He wore a peasant blouse, boots, and gray trousers stuffed into them. A woman with a red 'kerchief around her head and a man in a blouse followed and sat with him. The room quieted without any call for silence.

A clerk read the charge: "The accusation against Marfousha Lopatova is that, on November 24th, having given birth to a male child, she purposely killed it by hindering its breathing."

A very plain peasant girl, about eighteen, was brought forward by a policeman. She wore bark sandals and rags bound round her legs. A piece of rope, intertwined from the knee down, kept them in place and held the sandals on. She was crying nervously but said feebly, as she sat down, "I am not guilty. My baby drowned in a basin of water."

"Who was the father of the child?" Gavril asked.

"That's no one's business—he's far away," she replied and then began her story.

She lived with her father, a step-mother, and a step-sister her own age in a village ten miles away. Life had been miserable since her father remarried. Hers was all the dirty work, hers were all the curses and kicks. Then she met a worker who came to help rebuild the bridge and she had gone with him. Secretly, of course. Her step-mother watched her so closely! She knew her step-sister had her suspicions for one night their door was smeared with tar—a village way of casting aspersions on a girl's reputation—and she knew her step-sister had done it. Step-mother and daughter constantly demanded that the father drive her out. After the worker had gone away she learned that she was pregnant.

Expecting a child, her shame increased. She told no one. When it began to be apparent that she was with child, having no corset she got rags to bind herself tightly. She thought her deception was successful.

One night Marfousha left the house. Her step-sister saw her go into their grain storage house, a half mile away. She ran back for the mother who went with her to the outhouse. As they later testified, they saw Marfousha lying on the floor holding a new born baby by the throat. They ran home shouting to the father, "Come quick, Marfousha has had a baby and is trying to choke it." When they returned, the baby was dead.

Marfousha denied their story. She had given birth to the child alone in the darkness of the barn. Near by stood a basin and a pail of water to wash the baby. Suddenly she lost consciousness and, when she came to, she saw that the baby had fallen into the water and drowned. She accused the step-mother and sister of purposely falsifying the story in order to get her into jail and out of the house.

Gavril frequently interrupted the testimony of the various principals to ask some questions. Several times he asked the frightened girl, "Won't you tell us the name of the man? He is as much responsible as you are." Every time she refused. He did most of the cross-examining, in the absence of lawyers or attorneys. Sometimes his two assistants helped. The step-mother and her daughter were self-confident until Gavril asked three questions: "Did you know she was going to have a child?" "Did you suspect that she might kill it?" "Why didn't you do everything possible to help her have the baby in comfort?"

The village interne testified that the child did not die from drowning nor were there any marks on his throat. "Of course," Gavril interrupted. "Just leaving the baby out of doors for ten minutes on a November night might kill him."

The trial closed late in the afternoon. Everybody rushed for the samovar set up in one corner of the corridor. The verdict would be announced the next day.

Gavril came to the postmaster's that evening. He said very simply, "My assistants and myself came to a conclusion about that case in half an hour."

"And what did you decide, little Solomon?" Semyon asked.

"It's very simple. Marfousha killed the child. She will be sentenced to seven years but, since she did it because of the harsh surroundings in which she lived and because of the cruelty of relatives, the sentence will be commuted to six months. And she has already served four months while waiting for trial."

"That's fair enough," said Semyon.

"Yes, and there is a law that says a family must look out for the health of a child in it. We are going to try Marfousha's step-mother and step-sister for breaking that law. They'll get a couple of years each. The peasants must learn that the revolution removed all shame from the birth of any child. Why should a woman be punished by her family for having a baby? It's like serving mustard after dinner. But I wish I could get that man—I'd give him ten years!"

He settled down for an evening of talk and tea and asked me, "What would your American courts do with a case like that? What difference did you find between our court to-day and your American courts?"

I told him of the part that lawyers play in our system and he laughed. "We don't need them here except in important cases. There is a College of Defense in the district town whose members are assigned to defend cases. But why have lawyers here? They only complicate things and make them worse. Being a lawyer is a poor profession in Russia after the revolution. We don't use precedents and forms. There are a lot of Tsarist law books in my office. One of my assistants wanted to sell them to the grocery store so that they could make bags out of the pages. In most of my cases I hear the evidence, ask questions, and give a decision. If you know the customs of a place and the people in it you can always give a fair decision. Our People's courts work rapidly and honestly."

"Before the revolution there was a saying. 'The man with the most money is always the innocent one,' " said Semyon.

"Do I look as if I were taking bribes? I've not had a new pair of boots for five years and my shirts are passed right down the line of my seven children. Now and then some peasant remembers Tsarist days and tries to offer me a pound of butter or some eggs but they try it only once."

"I wish they'd try bribing the postmaster now and then," Semyon commented.

"The peasants are slowly learning that a government with new aims is in power. Our courts play an important part in showing them the aims of Soviet

government. Some of our new laws they know well—
every woman, whether literate or illiterate, knows that
she can get alimony from the father of her child.
Nearly half of my cases concern family affairs and the
women are not bashful in bringing suit."

"No group in Russia has progressed since the
revolution like the village women," Semyon added.

"Their progress is not apparent to the eye. They are
not better dressed or cleaner. But they are acquiring
a new psychology. 'If he doesn't beat you, he doesn't
love you' was the old saying. Now I have a case a
week in which some woman drags her husband to
court because he was showing his love in the old fashioned way."

"The old and the new are mixed in everything in
the village," Semyon commented as he called to the
servant to set another samovar.

"Yes, there was a case—you know those fancy religious posters that the peasants hang on their walls
showing the Resurrection or some view of heaven?
One woman went to the house of a friend and noticed
such a poster hanging there. 'Do you believe in that?'
she asked. 'Rot—after death we are only a handful of
mud.' Saying which, she tore the poster down. The
other woman attacked her and they had a frightful
hairpulling. The police brought them to court. What
could I do? I fined them each a *pood* of wheat and
told one to stop believing in superstitions and the
other to be more careful in her private anti-religious
campaigning. The new in the old, the old in the new,
—you find them intermingled everywhere."

"As in that Shipova case," Semyon reminded him.

"There was a case for your American courts! Alou-shya Shipova was very religious. She had a baby boy who caught diphtheria just before Christmas a year ago. She insisted on going to church Christmas eve although her husband was away and there was no one to leave the baby with. She took it with her—a three verst walk on that cold winter night. A neighbor pass-ing her on the road asked her if she had gone out of her mind, to take a sick child out on such a night. 'Of course not,' she replied. 'God wants us to go to church on this night and will He kill my baby for obeying his wishes?' The baby died and the husband demanded that she be brought to trial for murder. The baby was his first son. I let her go. She had another baby two months ago and I've sent the government midwife around to tell her how to treat a small child."

"You are as much an educator as the school teacher, Gavril," said Semyon.

"We Communists must use every instrument in the land for educating the people," he replied. "We try to show them that crime, except counter-revolution, is the result of environment or of ignorance. We have abolished the death penalty except for highway rob-bery, counter-revolution, or particularly brutal mur-der. Murderers usually get seven or eight years, and no one gets a jail sentence of more than ten years. There was a brutal murder two years ago in a village near here. A policeman got drunk and, wanting to show his power, he shot three men. A former Red Army soldier remonstrated with him. 'What?' the fool

shouted. 'You argue with me? I—I am the government here.' He shot the soldier. We shot him."

"What are your most frequent offenses?" I asked.

"Home-brewing and robbery. Home-brewing—!
We confiscate the apparatus and fine the owner. It's
an endless job, for every samovar can be made into a
still and a mash of sour wheat or potatoes produces a
fierier and cheaper vodka than the government produces. Robbery, too, goes on incessantly. Most of it
is petty but murder often accompanies it. The worst
form is horse stealing, for the horse is the most valuable thing a peasant has. I've had to break up two
gangs since I've been here. I'll give the death penalty
any time to a man who steals a horse. . . .

"Village Soviets give me a lot of work. These organs
of local government are often composed of peasants
who know little beyond what happens in their own
stables. They pass local orders and the population
comes running to me for help. Without any warning a
couple of villages descended on the court house one
morning. From the noise they made I thought they
came to hang me. The Soviet in the village where
they hold their weekly bazaar had passed an order
fining anyone who came to that village from other
places on the days before big church holidays. And
those days were the biggest bazaar days. The Soviet
meant well—they were trying to stop foolish religious
customs. But they were interfering with liberty. Of
course I made them rescind the order."

"Village government is very weak," added Semyon.
"It must constantly be controlled from the Centre.

Yet the Centre doesn't always co-operate intelligently. The peasants from Vlakhernsk came to court a month ago. Some Communist there had persuaded them to subscribe enough money for books for a reading room. They ordered three hundred rubles worth of books from Moscow and the Centre shipped them books on 'Advanced Economics,' 'Historical Empiricism,' 'The Development of Metallurgy.' 'What we wanted,' their spokesman said, 'were books on pig raising and planting. We are a dark people and don't want to know how to raise empiricism or economics.' "

"The central government is not popular in the village," Semyon remarked. "They still believe that a government only takes from the people, either money for taxes or men for the army."

"That is the part our courts play—to teach the peasants that we are interested in their life and liberty, in deciding their problems rightly. They need not fear the Centre any longer. Two years ago a census taker was murdered by a mob in Shremetovka, near here. They thought he had come to spy out new things to tax. The slogan of Tsarism is always in their minds—'Exploit the peasants.' They have learned to expect only exploitation. Our courts must teach them that from Soviet government comes only justice."

Gavril called for me next morning. He was driving a fine black horse hitched to a light box-sled. "A swift horse this," he said proudly as we started down the road. "If anyone ever harms him I'll execute the villain personally. It took four years of horse-trading and all the money I could gather to work up to owning this beauty. Wait till you see him race on Sunday!"

"Where are we bound for, Gavril Borisovitch?" I asked.

"To Kilasovsk. Alexeev, whom I ordered shot last year, lived there. His son still lives there. When Alexeev was sentenced all his property was confiscated by the State: land, machinery, everything. The son has his own house and land but he feels bitter toward me for reducing him to the poor peasant class."

"Your classification of peasants always puzzles me," I said. "You divide them into *kulaki*—the rich peasants; the middle peasants; and the poor peasants. They all look pretty poor to me."

"We Communists divide them thus to know who are our friends and who are our enemies. The *kulaki* are wealthy only relatively speaking. They are the group who would be rich if we gave them a chance. And getting rich is their only ambition——"

"Are they the most ambitious peasants?"

He dodged the question and continued, "They are out of sympathy with Communism. They do not understand that the village population must rise not as individuals but as a unit to a higher level. As soon as we permit private enterprise to flourish unchecked they become powerful, exploit their poorer neighbors, and offer every kind of opposition to Soviet power in the village. We must crush them at every opportunity. The factory workers cannot rule in the cities if the villages are controlled by groups hostile to Communism."

"Do the peasants themselves recognize the danger of permitting the *kulaki* to prosper?"

"Not always. Sometimes they believe the *kulaki* are their friends. The rich peasants are very clever and very sly. They offer bribes in order to get elected to the village Soviet or to control the village meeting. Then they arrange taxes and exemptions to suit themselves. Officially we state that the *kulaki* include that group which has some surplus grain to sell, over and above what they need to feed themselves. The middle peasantry are those with enough to last them the year round but with no saleable surplus. The poor peasants can't even grow enough to last them from harvest to harvest. But it is often hard to make Ivan Ivanovitch, poor peasant, realize that Andrei Andreitch, who lends him five *poods* of grain, is really his enemy."

"How do you check the power of the wealthier peasants in this district?"

"They are taxed more heavily. Where schools are crowded their children are not allowed to attend——"

"Is it fair to make the children pay for the political and economic sins of their parents?" I asked.

He shrugged his shoulders—"It is the class war in the village. We Communists cannot run Russia on sentimentalism. We must use every weapon, bar them from government stores, seize their grain. Remember, there are few Communists in the villages. Our power is in the cities and we rule in the villages partly because the peasants are unable to unite. At the same time we must show the great mass of peasantry, the poor and middle groups, that we are their

allies, that we side with them to stop exploitation and
to crush the *kulak*. There are all sorts of cases——"

We were moving swiftly and the black horse kicked
up the fine snow behind him. Only dim sled tracks
marked the location of the road across the broad flat
fields. We slowed down as we approached a little village. A couple of children in bark sandals, rag "stockings" and torn sheepskins opened a swinging gate that
hung across the road. We dashed down the deserted
village street and followed again the tracks that led
over the white fields.

"There was a case of a man in the village we just
passed," Gavril continued. "He had a cow and heard
of a rich peasant who had a fine bull. He agreed for
the bull's services but too late. His cow gave birth
to a stumpy little heifer. He asked the owner of the
bull to return the wheat he had paid. The *kulak* refused. They came to my court.

" 'I'm not to blame for the kind of heifer that was
born,' said the *kulak*. 'I had nothing to do with it.'
I agreed and asked how much he had charged for the
bull. 'Ten *poods* of grain, comrade,' he replied. Ten
poods! Double what he should have charged! Taking
advantage of a poor peasant! I made him return the
ten and ten more."

"Another *kulak* came to court. He had lent a poor
peasant fifty rubles and the peasant had not returned
it. 'How much interest did you ask?' I inquired. He
hesitated but finally said, 'Thirty per cent.' The
wealthy peasants have always been usurers. I fined
him for charging so much interest and then I remem-

bered that he had refused to buy more than twenty rubles worth of State bonds during our last drive, saying he was without money. So I doubled his fine!"

He clucked to the seemingly tireless horse. "I've won the race each time for the last four years," he said proudly. "I am very eager for Sunday."

"There will be peasants from villages other than Zelyonopol?"

"They come from all the villages in the county," he replied. "Once, long ago, before the revolution, we drove *troika*, three horses abreast. Not now—" he sighed. "A man is lucky to have one good horse."

We sped on in silence. Then he continued: "Two things hinder the application of our government policies in the village. The first is the inertia of the great peasant mass most of whom, seventy years ago, were serfs and could be bought and sold with the estates like the orchards. We must use patience. Force is of no use, no matter how much you beat a bull you can't get milk from him. The second hindrance is active opposition from a small part of the population—the *kulaki*. Against these we use force.

"It is strange but the priests are always in league with them. We have many cases in which a *kulak* advises his fellow peasants not to sell their grain to the government and the priest always supports him. Or, if the priest leads, the *kulaki* uphold him. Some of these cases become serious. . . .

"In a court in the neighboring district there was a trial of two *kulaki* and a priest. The priest had a piano in his house, the only one in the village. The

Communist school teacher wanted it in the school but
the priest objected. His daughter needed it. One day
the Communist and a few of his friends moved it while
the priest was away. When he returned he raised a
great scandal, saying that the Communist wanted it
for his own daughter. The *kulaki* supported him and
they so aroused the population that a mob attacked
the Communist's house and killed him. Of course, all
three were executed. Justice must be done."

The newspapers had been reporting daily acts of
violence in the villages against Communists and their
agents. I asked whether there had been any in this
district, in addition to the 'red rooster.'

"No, but there have been plenty elsewhere," he
replied. "When the *kulaki* see in some person a threat
to their safety and power they plan to remove him.
They turn to open counter-revolution; sometimes
there are frightful murders. Sometimes it is the head
of the Soviet, a school teacher, an instructor sent out
from the city, or, more often, a *selkor,* a 'village correspondent,' who is attacked. You know, we have an
informal chain of correspondents connecting every village with a city newspaper. Young people usually.
They write to newspapers about counter-revolutionary
conditions or anti-Soviet acts in their village. Russia
is large and this group, of several hundred thousand,
is one of our best organs of surveillance. Little that is
evil escapes for any length of time. I have had many
trials in my court which started because a *selkor* wrote
me about the intolerable actions of some person in his
remote little village."

"Is arson, as in your case, one of the commonest weapons used in this agricultural warfare?"

"The 'red rooster' is the simplest weapon. But *selkori* have been tied to trees and burned, they have been shot in the back. Some have been found with their eyes gouged out. The class war goes on steadily in the village and it will continue until there is a completely new generation. In the meantime some of the old generation fight us. Fools! 'The ocean is only knee-deep to a drunken man'! There is no doubt who is winning and the court is always ready to enforce *proletarian* justice."

We were approaching a little village that lay ahead on the road like a patch of brown leaves which the wind had uncovered from the snow. Another sled with two men in it approached us. Gavril slowed his horse saying, "Here come the policeman and the GPU agent." They stopped and talked with Gavril for a few minutes. "Alexeev has been sick in bed for ten days," said one of them. "All the neighbors testify to it." "Well, we'll see," Gavril replied, and we drove into the village.

We stopped before a thatched hut and entered without knocking. One corner of the room, opposite the door, was filled by a clay brick stove six feet wide and five feet long. In front it reached to the ceiling, leaving a broad shelf. A frame iron bed stood against the opposite wall. In the front corner of the house, furthest from the door, there was a table. Over it were hung the ikons with a cluster of paper flowers and dried pussy willows, the "palms" of Palm Sunday,

stuck behind them. Their gilt frames reflected the
light of the little spirit lamp that burned in front of
them.

A woman lay on the bed with a sheepskin coat as
her only blanket. A basket hung by four ropes from
the ceiling. A rope ran from the basket under her
coverings, enabling her to swing the basket and the
baby therein by moving her foot. A man lay on the
flat top shelf of the stove. A small boy was playing on
the floor with the works of an old alarm clock. Two
chickens walked about the room. The double windows
were sealed tight and the combination of heat and
odors was almost unbearable.

"Feodor Ilyitch," the judge called to the man on the
stove. "I hear you have been sick."

"Comrade Gavril, I have been sick for ten days.
My neighbors can tell you. They have had to help for
my wife had a baby just a week ago. I know why you
sent the police but, before God, I had nothing to do
with your fire. I have trouble enough as it is. The
midwife can tell you I am sick. We have no doctor
here and she gave me medicine, too. God deliver us, I
am innocent. I have not been out of the house for ten
days."

The wife did not even raise her head from the pillow
to look at us. The small boy went to the lone window
and stared out at the horse and sled.

We did not stay long. There was an hour's drive
home and Gavril wanted to make other calls in the
village. Night, in winter, comes early, suddenly. On
our way back Gavril said, "I suspected that man. 'The

lid is like the pot,' says our proverb, and his father was a rascal. I suppose he is innocent although the peasants are such awful liars. Now I don't know where to look for the culprit. I have many enemies. They don't understand that I must act as the instrument of my class, of our government. Am I any richer than they that they should burn my winter's food supply?"

It had snowed several times before the Sunday races. Semyon and I drove down to the course on the far edge of the village. The flat meadow where the races were to be held was covered with eight inches of fresh snow and there was an ice coated layer beneath it. In summer it was hummocky swamp land. Five hundred people watched a dozen sleds move slowly around the impromptu oval track in order to harden the course. "There would be more people if the weather had been clear," said Semyon.

Each contestant would have two chances to travel the distance, about a mile and a half, and the fastest driver would win the prize, a steel toothed harrow, furnished by the Zelyonopol Soviet.

It was colder than ever, at least thirty below, and a fine snow was blowing. The races, scheduled for eleven, showed no signs of beginning at noon. Most of the drivers were using the shovel-shaped peasant sled. Gavril with his black horse and the light box-sled had an advantage. No one seemed to mind. The crowd was talking animatedly, laying a few bets, and trying to edge as close as possible to the large bonfire.

The first driver made the circuit at one o'clock. The

snow blew harder and the sled was almost invisible at
the bend at the far end. Gavril's turn came sixth. He
travelled the course rapidly and, as he came to the
finish, took off his cap and smiled. His yellow hair
waved in the stiffening wind. There were murmurs behind me: "Might as well stop now." "He's won."

The drivers began their second round. The snow
now blotted them out a hundred yards from the start
and until they were a hundred yards from the finish.
Gavril started off. The crowd waited for him to appear
at the finish. "He's doing it much slower this time,"
said the voices behind me. "The snow stops even his
horse." "He's two minutes behind." "I don't see him
yet—it's five minutes."

Suddenly a figure on foot came from out of the veil
of snow. "Come, come, Gavril is hurt," he cried. "His
sled upset." The crowd broke into files floundering
through the snow.

Semyon and I got there a trifle late. They had put
the little judge in another sled, for his was smashed,
and began to drive him back. "They say there's an arm
broken and perhaps his skull," Semyon said. "They
must hurry—the hospital is at the other end of the
village. And he was such an excellent horseman!"

That night Semyon looked very menacing as he
returned from Gavril's house. "The interne says he
will recover—it's only a broken arm. But his sled
runner was filed through so that it would break and
throw him. He has enemies—! This is what they call
the class war in the villages. Remember, *amerikanyetz,*
we in Soviet Russia are still at war—a war between

classes that is more devastating than a war between nations. There will be no peace in Russia until one class—or the other—conquers.

"Remember that—we are at war, fighting just now on the internal front. When we have won in Russia we shall carry the class war to the world. We shall fight with every weapon to gain our ends—until our class dominates! And we have no use for sentimentality. We are realists; don't let sentiment blind your judgment of us. There will be no peace in the world until the Proletariat conquers."

During the next seven months I had two letters from Zelyonopol. The first came from Semyon Pavlitch a few weeks after my visit. He wrote: "Two days after you went away an old woman testified that she saw Feodor Alexeev hanging around Gavril's stable the morning of the races. Another saw him walking toward Zelyonopol about midnight. He was arrested and confessed and he admitted further that he had sent his young eight-year-old son to set fire to Gavril's barn. He was sentenced to the highest measure of social defense and will be executed next week."

The other letter came at the close of the following summer. I had written to Gavril and this was part of the answer: "Last week someone loosed the 'red rooster' against me again and part of this year's harvest went up in smoke. I have no idea who did it. I am the unluckiest man in Russia!"